FAMOUS REGIMENTS

The Red Devils

Pegasus and Bellerophon (*Statuette*). (Courtesy Cyril Peckham, F.R.P.S.)

The emblem of Airborne Forces is Bellerophon mounted on the winged horse Pegasus. The first recorded instance of an airborne warrior, his exploits are recounted in Greek mythology, where he is chiefly famous for slaying the fire-breathing monster Chimaera. Mounted on Pegasus, with spear in hand, Bellerophon rode into the air, swooped down upon the monster and destroyed it.

This emblem was chosen for British Airborne Forces by the late Lieutenant-General Sir Frederick ("Boy") Browning, GCVO, KBE, CB, DSO, DL, when he was appointed to raise Airborne Forces in 1941. The sign was designed in May, 1942 by Major Edward Seago, to be worn on the arm by all airborne soldiers.

In 1946 the beautiful bronze statuette, pictured above, the work of the sculptress Mrs. A. R. Oxenford, was accepted by the Royal Academy. It was commissioned by the Trustees of the Airborne Forces Security Fund and presented by them to the Museum of Airborne Forces on 1st October, 1968.

FAMOUS REGIMENTS

Edited by

Lt–General Sir Brian Horrocks

The Red Devils
The Story of
The British Airborne Forces

by G. G. Norton

Leo Cooper Ltd., London

First published in Great Britain, 1971
by Leo Cooper Ltd,
196 Shaftesbury Avenue,
London W.C.2
Copyright © 1971 by G. G. Norton
Introduction Copyright © 1971 by
Lt-General Sir Brian Horrocks

ISBN 0 85052 045 2

2nd Impression 1971

Photoset and Printed in Great Britain by
BAS Printers Ltd in Hampshire

The Red Devils

INTRODUCTION

LT—GENERAL SIR BRIAN HORROCKS

A few years after the end of the last war a young major from a very distinguished regiment asked if he could come and see me. On arrival he said, 'If this country became involved in another major war, wouldn't you rather have my regiment under your command than any other in the British Army'. Sadly I replied, 'No—I should ask for the Red Devils—the parachute brigade whom I consider to be among the best troops in the world.' He was very upset and even angry, but if he will now read this book I hope he will understand what I meant. Conscription was still in existence at that time, yet the Parachute Brigades were composed entirely of volunteers (fifty per cent of whom failed to make the grade owing to the severity of their training).

I must congratulate the author, Major G. G. Norton, who is the founder and curator of the Airborne Forces Museum at Aldershot, on this comprehensive account of our Airborne troops during the thirty years of their life. Started at Ringway Airport, Manchester on 21 June, 1940, under the title of the 'Central Landing School', in two years it had grown to a force of two divisions and an Independent Brigade each with their own Airborne Headquarters.

The first airborne operation was carried out by seven officers and thirty-one other ranks against the Tragino aqueduct in southern Italy on 10 February, 1941, and was completely successful, though all those taking part were subsequently captured.

The three most famous airborne operations in Europe were obviously D-Day, Arnhem and the Rhine Crossing. These have been brilliantly described by the author, so I will refrain from commenting in any detail.

The 6th Airborne Division was given the task of protecting the left flank of our landings on the Normandy Beaches by seizing the bridges over the River Orne and the Caen Canal and destroying the Merville Battery, a seemingly impregnable fortress protected by deep mine fields and thick barbed-wire fences, with the guns themselves embedded in deep concrete shelters. This battery dominated the beaches on which the 3rd British Division was to land.

The whole operation was completely successful despite high winds which often scattered the parachutists and gliders all over the countryside. It was under these sort of conditions that their tough individual airborne training really bore fruit. Each man had received his own personal briefing before setting out and had been taught from the days of his recruit training to act on his own initiative.

To my mind, one of the bravest acts of the war was the attempt by three gliders to crash-land on top of the Merville Battery. Owing to the wind they were blown off-course but the fact that they had volunteered for this almost suicidal operation shows the spirit with which General Gale had inspired his whole Division.

The second major operation, Arnhem, involved some 30,000 British and U.S. Airborne troops and lasted from 17 to 25 September, 1945. So much has already been written and spoken about this battle that I propose to restrict my remarks to a few comments.

There were two main reasons why, in spite of the vast airborne operation, XXX corps (the leading corps of the 2nd Army) failed not only to reach the Zuyder Zee which was its ultimate objective but also to join up with the 1st British Airborne Division on the north bank of the Neder Rhine.

Firstly the presence, unknown to us, of the 2nd S.S. Panzer Corps which had been sent back from the front to refit at Zutphen, only twenty-six miles from Arnhem. The lightly-equipped Airborne Forces, gallantly as they fought, were no match for these heavily-armoured German troops. The German C-in-C, Gen. Model, a very experienced commander from the Russian front, was therefore able to concentrate the reinforcements which kept on pounding in from Germany on the Fuehrer's orders ('Holland over-shadows everything' he had screamed at a conference on the 20th) against our long narrow lines of communication which consisted of one road up which we had to bring 20,000 vehicles. Three times this vital artery was cut. It was like trying to box against a tough opponent with one arm tied behind one's back.

The second reason was that by halting in Brussels for administrative reasons and then having to spend at least seven days in the preparation of the complicated operation, we had given the Germans, who are first class soldiers, time to recover. The whole essence of Montgomery's narrow thrust across the Rhine was speed—never to give the Germans time to draw breath, and this had not happened. My Corps has been accused of being slow. I can assure you that there was more desperate urgency about our operations in this battle than in any I have ever fought.

I don't believe any troops in the world other than the 82nd U.S. Airborne Division would have succeeded in crossing the swift-running, 400 yard-wide River Waal in daylight, using British assault boats which they had never seen before. The north bank was strongly defended and their casualties were heavy, but they still got across, formed a bridgehead, and then cut off the railway bridge from the road.

The most agonising part of the whole battle, which eventually I simply could not bear to watch, was those gallant R.A.F. pilots in their daily attempts to drop supplies to the beleaguered airborne troops. They were forced to fly into a concentrated deadly barrage at a height of 1,000 feet, maintaining a straight and level course before releasing their supplies. Their casualties were appalling, yet they never hesitated and their bravery was beyond praise.

I would like to have described just one action carried out by the S.A.S. the brain-child of David Stirling in the Western Desert, but space will not permit. As the S.A.S. are trained to operate behind the enemy lines they have been involved in so many remarkable adventures both in war and in the so-called peace-keeping role that they deserve a book to themselves.

Every man is a volunteer and eighty per cent are rejected owing to the high standard of toughness and initiative demanded of them. They are probably the best all-round troops in the world, and the capture of the 10,000 foot high Mt. Akhdar in Muscat and Oman by two squadrons of the 22nd S.A.S. will always rank as an epic of initiative and endurance carried out by British troops. It is an example of the supremely high standards which the Airborne Forces and the S.A.S. in particular demand of themselves.

Acknowledgements

This book is intended to provide the interested reader with a reasonably comprehensive background to the formation, development and achievements of British Airborne Forces in both peace and war. Whilst it is not intended as a treatise for the serious student of military history it will, I trust, serve as an introduction and background for further study. I have made no attempt to analyse or draw conclusions from the operations or campaigns described, leaving this to those who are more qualified than I to do so. Nor do I claim that this story covers all aspects of Airborne history. The contents are, I believe, in so far as I have been able to cross-reference them from private and official records, accurate. They are based primarily on the highlights of a short but but not uneventful period.

The completion of this history became for me a challenge, and I offer the finished result as a tribute to all soldiers who have, in war and peace gone into action by air, to the airmen who flew them and to those who, often at great sacrifice, supplied them from the air.

Space does not permit the mention of all those who have assisted me in this task. I would, however, like to acknowledge the assistance of Lieutenant-Colonel M. A. J. Tugwell, The Parachute Regiment, Lieutenant-Colonel D. Cardle, Royal Corps of Transport, Group Captain J. A. Moody, R. A. F., Mr. S. Veale of '*Esso Air World*', Mr. Hugh Popham and my wife. I am also indebted to The Imperial War Museum, the Royal Air Force Photographic Library and the Commandant General, Royal Marines for permission to reproduce photographs in this book. To all those whose names do not appear I offer my sincere thanks and my apologies for the demands I have made upon them.

Contents

Chapter

I

Formation, Development and Early Raids

'We ought to have a Corps of at least 5,000 parachute troops'
Winston Churchill, June 1940

T HERE IS something characteristically British about the origins of Airborne Forces — except, perhaps, for the fact that it was not we who first thought of the idea. That honour is shared equally by the Russians and the Germans, both of whom were developing this type of warfare as early as 1936; but even though General Wavell himself saw the former drop 1,500 men, with machine guns and light artillery, during the summer manoeuvres that year, and reported that 'if he had not witnessed it, he would not have believed such an operation possible', his testimony roused no enthusiasm for similar units in Britain. And when, in May of 1940, the Germans employed parachute soldiers and glider-borne troops with such devastating effect during their *blitzkrieg* on Western Europe, and it seemed that there might be something of value for us in this type of warfare, all that happened was that, as a result of a conference at the Air Ministry, it was stated that 'it has been decided to establish a parachute training centre', and the War Office detailed Major J. F. Rock, RE, 'to take charge of the military organisation of British Airborne Forces'. That was about the extent of his brief. 'It was impossible', Major Rock confided, 'to get any information as to policy or task'.

From this indeterminate beginning, and largely through the pioneering work of Major Rock and his Air Force colleagues, Wing Commander L. A. Strange, Wing Commander Sir Nigel Norman and Squadron-Leader Maurice Newnham, Airborne Forces grew and thrived. They received a timely boost from Churchill's minute, quoted above. Its demand for a powerful offensive force — at a time when most people in Britain were concerned only with defence — was

Parachutists dropping from converted 'Whitley' bombers, August 1942. (Courtesy Imperial War Museum.)

a defiant and far-sighted move that was to justify itself many times over as the tides of war changed. As a result of these separate initiatives, the Central Landing School was set up at Ringway Airport, near Manchester, on June 21; and exactly a month later men of No. 2 Commando were dropped, for the first time, from converted Whitley bombers. Central Landing School, which in August 1940 became Central Landing Establishment (and later Airborne Forces Establishment), belonged to the RAF; and it was some time before the duties and responsibilities of the two services were worked out. In the outcome, the RAF was in charge of parachute training, and the Army of the military requirements of airborne warfare.

Even with Churchill's backing, the call for '5,000 parachute troops', with all that that entailed in the way of equipment, was not one that could be easily met in the troubled second half of 1940. For, at the worst possible moment, we were trying 'to cover in six months the ground the Germans had covered in six years'. We had neither the aircraft nor the parachutes: and perhaps more important still we were totally without first-hand knowledge or experience. Everything had to be designed, worked out and built from the beginning. Even such elementary matters as the best way to drop parachute soldiers from the aircraft—through a hole in the floor, which was quite likely to knock their teeth out, or through a door in the fuselage—were a

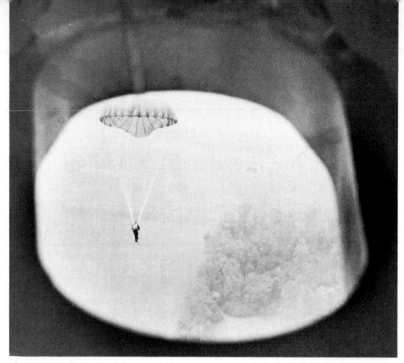

Early experiments in converting bomber aircraft to parachuting. This picture shows an RAF instructor having just jumped 'through the hole in the floor' of an Albermarle aircraft in 1940. (Courtesy Imperial War Museum.)

matter of trial and error. No. 2 Commando was transferred to parachute duties to become No. 11 SAS Battalion, and gradually the novel and difficult techniques of parachute warfare were perfected.

One small example was the elimination of all the bulky padded clothing (copied from the Germans) of the early experiments, and its replacement by normal fighting uniform together with the parachutist's smock. Another was the development of the 'X' Type 'statichute' which opened automatically and offered, within limits, a degree of control in flight; and the dropping of men in sticks of ten. Simultaneously, the amount of equipment that a parachustist could carry with him on a drop was being worked out empirically, and was steadily increased.

And so, at a time when the Germans were preparing for their most dramatic airborne stroke — the capture of Crete in May 1941 — the British were mounting their first small experimental operation. At this time, as for many years to come, parachute units were made up of volunteers from infantry regiments; and it was reported that by February 1941, these men were growing tired of training and inaction

4

Typical German Airborne soldiers (Fallschirmjäger). These were part of the group which rescued Mussolini, after his arrest by the Italians, in September 1943. (Courtesy Imperial War Museum.)

and were applying to go back to their own regiments. Then the rumour of impending action got around; there were no more applications; and when volunteers were called for, every officer and man of the 500 in the battalion stepped forward. But for that first, tentative employment of British airborne forces, only seven officers and 31 other ranks were needed.

Their objective was the Tragino aqueduct in southern Italy. The supply ports of the Italian Armies campaigning in North Africa and

Tragino Aqueduct. This picture, the only one which existed for planning purposes, was in fact taken in 1928 when the aqueduct was built. Some unfinished buildings, the workmen's huts and scaffolding can be seen. (Courtesy Imperial War Museum.)

Albania were Taranto, Brindisi and Bari, in the arid province of Apulia. They relied for their water on the 'Acquedetto Pugliese', an extensive pipeline from the River Sele through the Apennines, and it was believed that cutting the supply would cause serious dislocation in these ports. The vulnerable points in the pipeline lay inland, and since a seaborne raid was impracticable, and bombing had proved ineffective, the newly-fledged parachute troops seemed to be the obvious, and indeed the only means. A force of 38 men from the 11th Special Air Service Battalion was picked, with Major T. A. G. Pritchard, RWF, in command, and Captain G. F. K. Daly, RE, to lead the demolition party. They were to drop just north of the aqueduct from six Whitley aircraft of No. 91 Squadron, as two more made a diversionary bombing raid on Foggia. HM Submarine *Triumph* was to rendezvous near the mouth of the River Sele on the night of February 15–16 to bring them home.

After intensive training with mock-ups and models, the party assembled in Malta. The aircraft took off at dusk on February 10,

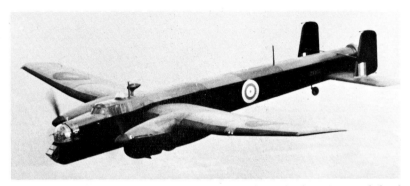

The Armstrong Whitworth 'Whitley'. This pre-war heavy bomber was soon declared obsolescent and adapted for parachute duties. Though difficult to use—the narrow fuselage was very cramped—and could only carry a 'stick' of ten men it performed yeoman service in the early days. Aircraft of this type carried troops on the first two British airborne operations of the war—Tragino Aqueduct and Bruneval. (Courtesy Imperial War Museum.)

arriving over the target three hours later. In the full moon dropping casualties were light, but, due to technical faults, two aircraft failed to drop their containers of arms and explosives. A third, carrying the main demolition party with Captain Daly, dropped two miles away in the next valley. Night navigation to these fine limits was still something novel; so the drop, over 400 miles from base, was remarkably accurate.

The force was short of arms, explosives, its senior RE Officer and five sappers. Second Lieutenant A. Paterson, RE, assumed command of the demolition and sufficient explosives were found to destroy a main Aqueduct pier and a bridge over the nearby River Ginestra. By 3 am on February 11, the waterway was effectively breached, and the force split into three groups to rendezvous separately with the submarine. After various adventures, all of them were captured by the next day—a misfortune that might have been mitigated for them had they known that the submarine had been unable to keep the rendezvous.

The raid was a success, but the damage was soon repaired, and its military effect was negligible. Nevertheless, it was all useful experience, both for the development of parachute equipment and aircraft, and for future operations. But it was just over a year before the second of these early raids took place.

In the interval much had happened. One of the most significant was the evolution of the military glider. No such flying machine existed in England prior to the autumn of 1940 when the first 400 Hotspurs were ordered by the Ministry for Aircraft Production; the Hotspur was a prototype which led, in time, to the great Horsas and Hamilcars of later years. Why were gliders needed at all? For two separate but interconnected reasons. First, in this early stage of air-borne development, the weapons and equipment which could be dropped by parachute were very limited; and therefore gliders were required to supply such essential items as jeeps, light tanks, Bren gun carriers and artillery. Secondly, the glider was a quick and economical means of flying in reinforcements to support the initial parachute landings. Their production was a slow business, for every factory

The Hotspur glider. The first British military glider, it carried a section of 8 men. Though superseded by the larger Horsa Glider and never used on operations, all the early air-landing training and experimental glider towing was carried out in these aircraft. Many of the Glider Pilots also received their flying training on this aircraft and over a 1000 were produced. (Courtesy Imperial War Museum.)

capable of building aircraft was flat out making fighters and bombers; and although a prototype Hotspur was towed past Winston Churchill as a demonstration during a combined airborne exercise on April 26, 1941, the first did not come into service until the end of the year. The Hotspur could carry eight men, but not a jeep, nor an anti-tank gun, nor heavy loads. The Mark I was a glider in the true sense, being capable of soaring. The second version had a much shortened wingspan, and was designed to glide direct to its target once released by the towing aircraft. The later, and larger, Horsas and Hamilcars, designed for cargo as well as personnel carriers, had hinged nose sections, which made for much easier and faster discharging. Even with large flaps, their landing speed was something in the order of 70 mph.

In December 1941, the Glider Pilot Regiment of the Army Air Corps was formed to fly them, though the RAF continued to be responsible for parachute training and despatching the troops from the aircraft. It is of interest that the glider pilots — all of whom were officers or NCOs — were trained infantrymen, and normally formed the Divisional Commander's reserve after landing. The glider, like the parachute, was a means to an end. In September 1941, the 1st Parachute Brigade was formed under Brigadier Richard Gale, to be followed by the 2nd and 3rd, a month or two later. And on October 10, 31 Independent Brigade Group, just back from India and mountain warfare trained, became 1st Air-landing Brigade Group. These were the troops who would man the gliders and support the parachute soldiers; a hazardous enough task, one would have thought; and yet it was decided that, unlike their air-dropped comrades, they needed little specialised training, and the work did not require volunteers. The main limiting factor lay in the shortage of gliders and pilots.

From their very beginnings, British Airborne Forces were a heterogeneous arm, volunteers drawn from two services. Thus, 38 Wing, RAF, who were responsible for parachute-dropping and glider-towing, and who kept in training by innumerable operations on the side, from bombing to dropping supplies to Europe's underground, are very much a part of Airborne history; and the man who was to become known as 'the father of Airborne Forces', Brigadier F. A. M.

Major-General Browning talking to the Prime Minister, Mr Winston Churchill, in 1943. (Courtesy Imperial War Museum.)

Browning, DSO, MC, was commanding a Brigade of Guards when he was appointed GOC, Paratroops and Airborne Troops. The choice of Major-General Browning, who had had no direct experience of airborne work, seems to have been fortuitous, but could not have been bettered. It was he who established the priorities and secured the equipment in the face of rivalry from the other arms and services; and from the date of his appointment, says the Official

Account, 'despite a multitude of difficulties and disappointments, there was no looking back. Airborne Forces were now an integral part of the British Army, and presently wore on their heads the maroon-coloured berets soon to become famous, and on their shoulders Bellerophon astride winged Pegasus'. Airborne Forces have always been something of a *corps d'élite*; and it is a fact that now, as for much of the 30 years of their existence, no more than half of those who apply to join survive the rigorous process of trial and selection.

Early in 1942 the chance of a further action arose. During the previous year the Germans had established a chain of radar stations along the French Channel coast; and since the increasing interception and destruction of British bomber aircraft was attributed to these installations, the need for accurate information about them became urgent. They were heavily defended against attack from the sea, and so, once again, the only practical solution appeared to be an airborne assault.

In January 1942, Admiral Lord Mountbatten, Chief of Combined Operations, proposed such a raid against the Bruneval station near Le Havre. Major-General Browning, realising that success would establish the newly-formed airborne forces, accepted. The recently formed 'C' Company, 2nd Parachute Battalion under Major J. D. Frost was selected for the operation. No. 51 Squadron (Whitleys), under Wing Commander P. C. Pickard, provided the aircraft, and the naval force to evacuate them was commanded by Commander F. N. Cook, RAN. A further 32 officers and men of the Royal Fusiliers and South Wales Borderers travelling with the naval force were to cover the final withdrawal to the landing craft.

Tide and moon dictated late February for the raid, and since many of 'C' Company had yet to complete parachute training this left little time for practice in combined operations. Planning and equipping proceeded rapidly; excellent intelligence provided air photographs and detailed scale models of the target; and local Frenchmen supplied accurate information on enemy defences.

The radar installation stood at the edge of the cliffs, in front of an isolated villa housing the technicians. Four hundred yards to the

BRUNEVAL. An oblique aerial photograph taken for the raid of the isolated house housing the radar technicians with the radar apparatus clearly shown. 'La Presbytère' is the clump of trees to the left rear. (Courtesy Imperial War Museum.)

north, in an enclosure called 'La Presbytère', were about 100 enemy soldiers. To the south, clustered round the steep ravine leading to the beach, lay the village of Bruneval containing an enemy platoon responsible for shore defence. The area was patrolled by night.

The plan provided for three groups, each forty strong, and named after famous sailors. 'Nelson' group under Lieutenant E. R. C. Charteris, dropping first, would take the shore defences and Bruneval. 'Drake' group, under Lieutenant P. A. Young, included Major Frost and an expert radio mechanic, Flight Sergeant C. W. H. Cox, RAF, and would take the radar station. 'Rodney' group under Lieutenant V. Timothy, arriving last, would contain the enemy in 'La Presbytère' and act as reserve. As soon as the radar was dismantled, the whole force would withdraw to the beach and be picked up.

THE RAID ON BRUNEVAL

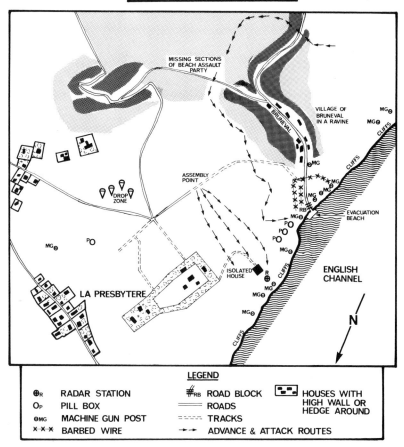

MISSING SECTIONS
OF BEACH ASSAULT
PARTY

VILLAGE OF
BRUNEVAL
IN A RAVINE

ASSEMBLY
POINT

DROP
ZONE

EVACUATION
BEACH

ISOLATED
HOUSE

ENGLISH
CHANNEL

LA PRESBYTERE

N

LEGEND

⊕R RADAR STATION	⚏RB ROAD BLOCK	HOUSES WITH HIGH WALL OR HEDGE AROUND	
OP PILL BOX	ROADS		
⊖MG MACHINE GUN POST	TRACKS		
X-X-X BARBED WIRE	→→ ADVANCE & ATTACK ROUTES		

The weather on February 27 was perfect. The naval force sailed in the afternoon, and was followed by the airborne troops, 119 strong, that evening. Enemy aircraft were drawn off by a diversionary attack from Fighter Command. The flight was uneventful, though there was snow on the French coast, which was to complicate matters later. The drop went as planned, apart from half 'Nelson' group, who landed two miles short. The rest assembled at the edge of the DZ and moved off.

'Drake' group achieved complete surprise, capturing the villa and radar station without difficulty. Enemy reaction from 'La Presbytère' was slow, and the radar was almost dismantled before effective fire was returned. But as this group withdrew their troubles began. The beach defences, not yet cleared, caught them by surprise and inflicted several casualties with heavy automatic fire. Control and movement were hampered by deep snow drifts, and by radio failure, which also prevented contact with the naval force.

The raiders return from Bruneval in the Naval M.G.B's. Major Frost, the force commander, can be seen second from the left on the bridge. (Courtesy Imperial War Museum.)

At this critical stage 'Nelson' group arrived. Lieutenant Charteris attacked with great dash and quickly subdued the enemy strong-points. By 0215 the whole force was concentrated on the shore, alerting the flotilla—which had been narrowly missed by a German destroyer and two L-boats—by emergency Very signal. Six landing craft, under intense supporting fire, then approached the beach. The noise was appalling, and was soon augmented by the explosion of enemy grenades and mortars. For a time, everything was in confusion; but the wounded, and the vital radar equipment, were stowed in one vessel, and the rest of the force—bar six who got left behind—scrambled aboard the others. All the boats reached the MGBs, and the flotilla withdrew safely.

At a cost of three killed, seven wounded and six missing, the raid had secured most of the German radar set and two experts to go with it.

Bruneval gave the Parachute Regiment its first Battle Honour; and the hard-pressed British a small, exciting taste of success at a time when successes were few and far between. Winston Churchill was delighted, and, at a special meeting of the War Cabinet, re-affirmed his belief in the future of Airborne Forces; but it was nine months before their next chance came.

The operation was called 'Freshman', and it demanded great daring, which was readily available, and technical skills and equipment, which were not. Quite early in the war, the Germans were known to be working towards the production of an atomic bomb; it was thought they had made considerable progress, particularly in the production of one essential component—heavy water. In order to delay production for as long as possible, attacks were planned in 1942 on these German research establishments, and specifically on the Norsk Hydro plant at Vermork in Norway, a village two miles west of Rjukan, sixty miles due west of Oslo and some eighty miles from the coast. For various reasons, attacks by bombers, troops landed by seaplane, and saboteurs, were ruled out, and a raid by glider-borne troops was decided upon.

From every aspect it was a most difficult and dangerous adventure. Rjukan was an isolated town, situated in a very deep valley whose thickly forested sides rose almost vertically for 3,000 feet from the river bed, and overlooked by the Gaustal Fjell, 5,400 feet high. The heavy water plant was built on a rock shelf 1,000 feet above the river with a steep and perilous climb above — an almost impossible terrain for gliders or parachutists. However, a landing zone of sorts was found some five hours' marching distance away, and it was arranged for this to be marked out by Norwegian agents.

The operation required a force of 12 to 16 men, all skilled engineers; and they were to be flown in by glider. Because of the hazardous nature of the task, and its importance, the party was duplicated. The soldiers were selected from volunteer parachutists of the 9th Field

The Horsa glider. Designed by Air-speed Ltd and the Royal Aircraft Establishment this was the maid of all work in World War II. Built by furniture manufacturers throughout England it took part in all the major airborne operations in the Middle East and Europe. It could carry 29 fully equipped soldiers, or a jeep and 6 pounder anti-tank gun and its crew or a variety of similar heavy loads. The Mark II was fitted with a hinged pilot's compartment which facilitated easy and direct loading of vehicles, or guns. A 'cordtex' explosive ring charge was also fitted to the fuselage so that in the event of damage on landing the occupants could blow the fuselage apart and so deplane rapidly. (Courtesy Imperial War Museum.)

Company (Airborne) RE, and 261st Field Park Company (Airborne) RE, and were commanded by Lieutenant A. C. Allen, RE, and Lieutenant D. A. Methuen, RE. Three Halifaxes—the only aeroplane then capable of towing a Horsa glider 400 miles and returning to base—were provided, under the command of Group Captain T. B. Cooper of 38 Wing, RAF.

Troop training was comprehensive and strenuous, both technically and physically, for not only had they to destroy the plant; they had to get to it first. Then, with the task completed, they had to make their way over the mountains to Sweden. Norwegian agents were to act as guides throughout. The radio location device 'Rebecca-Eureka' (air-to-ground) was to be used to locate the landing zone, and was smuggled into Norway beforehand by HQ Combined Operations. Security measures were strict and successful.

On November 17, 1942, two days before the operation was scheduled, the force moved to an airfield at Skitten, in Scotland. The meteorological forecast for the night of the 19th was reasonable, though not ideal.

Operating independently, the two aircraft and their gliders took off at 1750 and 1810. For the next five-and-a-half hours nothing was heard of either of them; then, at 2341, a faint signal was picked up from the second aircraft, asking for a course home. A bearing intersection established this as originating over the North Sea. At 2355 a signal was received from the first aircraft, saying 'glider released in the sea', though intersection proved this to have originated over the mountains of southern Norway. Only one aircraft returned: of the fate of the other, and of the two gliders and their occupants, nothing was known until after the war.*

The first party made an accurate landfall through patchy clouds; only to discover that the 'Rebecca' was unserviceable, and they had to navigate their way through the mountains by map reading. This, to their credit, they succeeded in doing, and on the first run-in they actually passed over the zone and the waiting Norwegian agents; but, as they turned for a second run, they flew into thick snow cloud. They

* See Chapter 10.

were unable to climb out of it, and ice formed on the aircraft, and on the tow rope, which broke. Unable to do more, the Halifax returned to base.

The glider crashed on to the mountainside. Of the 17 men in it, eight were killed at once and four were injured. The other five were captured, and, on January 18, 1943, were shot by the Gestapo. The four injured were poisoned by a German doctor on orders from the same source.

The second party also made a successful landfall; but, for reasons that are still unknown, the glider crash-landed in the mountains near Helleland; and the aircraft, after just clearing the mountain there, crashed into the next range, killing the crew. In the glider three men were killed immediately and the remainder were captured and shot within a few hours under the terms of a general order issued by Hitler. The Norsk Hydro-Electric plant was put out of action later by Norwegian saboteurs.

Though Operation 'Freshman' failed—largely through the breakdown of the vital homing beacon—this first British glider operation demonstrated the range and flexibility, and suggested the potentialities, of airborne forces. The soldiers and airmen who died in the Norwegian mountains that November night had taken part in one of the most daring and gallant small operations of the war.

Chapter

2

Middle East, 1942–3
The Classic Role

T RAGINO, Bruneval and Operation 'Freshman' were all daring and unorthodox examples of the use of airborne troops, and only Bruneval was wholly successful; but they gave the new arm something to sharpen its claws on. It was already growing larger and more formidable than even Churchill had envisioned in 1940.

It had —unofficially, at first—a Depot at Hardwick, in Derbyshire, which was established in April, and recognized by the War Office in December, 1942; and in June of the same year an Air Directorate was created at the War Office, headed by Brigadier Gale. In the following month the 2nd Parachute Brigade was formed; and on August 1 the Parachute Regiment came into being as part of the Army Air Corps and the parent unit of the parachute battalions. This was a tremendous moment in the history of Airborne Forces. In just over two years it had grown from little more than an idea —'without policy or task' —into a regular formation of enthusiastic men, trained to battle-pitch, and with a number of spectacular, well-planned actions to their credit. The slogging, patient groundwork had been done. Policy was defined and the task prescribed. Dakotas —by no means the perfect vehicle for parachutists, but an improvement on the old Whitleys, and an aircraft from which it was possible to leave 'like gentlemen' via a door —were being flown direct from the States in increasing numbers; and the 2nd Battalion, in particular, had the benefit of close liaison with 502nd Parachute Infantry, US Army, who were stationed at Hungerford and were thoroughly acquainted with the Dakota and its ways. The parachutists now wore their blue 'wings', and the emblem of Airborne Forces, the famous winged horse and rider, designed by Edward Seago, Camouflage Officer of Southern Command, had been accepted and was worn by all ranks.

The Corps was still growing. In November the 3rd and 4th Parachute Brigades were formed, the latter in the Middle East; and in the same month came the first opportunity for airborne forces to act

A Douglas C-47 or 'Dakota' dropping parachutists. This was 'the' airborne aircraft of World War II. Designed as a passenger aircraft it was easily adapted to parachuting and its side door exit eased many of the earlier difficulties experienced in using converted bombers. It took part in all major airborne operations of the War and is regarded with great affection throughout British Airborne Forces. (Courtesy Imperial War Museum.)

in their classic role, landing ahead of, and co-operating with, ground forces. For, on November 8, the Allies launched their much-debated assault upon the North African coast, known as operation 'Torch'. Its immediate strategic objective was Northern Tunisia, and it was intended to cut the Axis line of retreat from the advancing British 8th Army in the Western Desert. With Axis power destroyed along the southern shores of the Mediterranean, the way would be open to invade Europe through Sicily and Italy.

20

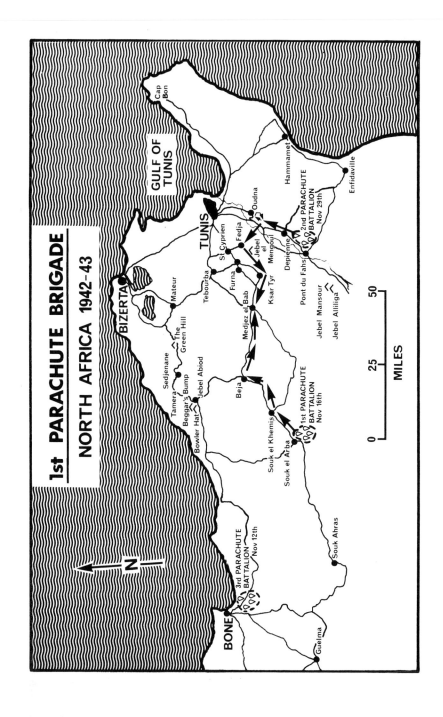

Lt.-Col. J. D. Frost, DSO, MC, Commanding Officer of the 2nd Battalion meets General Eisenhower after being decorated with the DSO by General Anderson at a special ceremony in the field, for his exploits in North Africa. (Courtesy Imperial War Museum.)

The 1st Army, which included the 1st Parachute Brigade (from 1st Airborne Division) landed east of Algiers, with orders to capture Bizerta and Tunis, 500 miles away to the east. The Germans, under General von Arnim, quickly recovered from their initial surprise, and regrouped to oppose them. The 3rd Parachute Battalion jumped on to and seized the vital airfield at Bône, between Algiers and Tunis, their arrival only just anticipating that of a number of Ju52s loaded with German parachutists with the same idea, which they then abandoned. The 1st Battalion, dropping near the airfield at Souk el Arba, occupied a key road junction at Beja only 90 miles from Tunis. Both operations were successful, and the airborne troops were quickly

relieved by the advancing main force. The 2nd Battalion, under Lieutenant-Colonel Frost, fared less well. Held initially in reserve, they
were dropped on November 29 at Depienne to destroy enemy aircraft
on the ground at Oudna. However, the airfield had been abandoned,
and the 1st Army thrust was halted by unexpected opposition; as a
result, the Battalion found itself far behind the enemy lines, almost
surrounded, and faced with an arduous withdrawal fifty miles back
to the nearest Allied positions. This retreat has the true, epic flavour
of so many of the Parachute Regiment's exploits, from Bruneval to
Arnhem. Lightly equipped, continuously attacked, desperately short
of ammunition, and spurred on by Frost's hunting horn, they arrived
at Medjez el Bab two days later, having lost 16 officers and 250 men.

The campaign now altered. The 1st Army, vigorously opposed by
an enemy reinforced from Europe and Rommel's retreating Afrika
Corps, was short of men. As winter weather prevented airborne
operations, 1st Parachute Brigade were required to fight in the normal
infantry role, and on February 8, 1943, they took up a position on the
right of the Allied line in the Bou Arada sector, where the enemy were
probing for a weak spot. It is an indication of their reputation that one
parachute battalion was warned that they might have to face ten

Soldiers of the 1st Parachute Brigade in action in North Africa. (Courtesy Imperial War
Museum.)

enemy battalions and a hundred tanks. It did not quite come to these odds; but despite superior forces, every enemy attempt to break through suffered heavy losses. Relieved on March 5 by American troops, the Brigade moved to the Tamera valley in the north. Here an enemy thrust threatened to break out along the coast road, and the Brigade plugged the gap. Though forced to withdraw by a series of desperate attacks from an enemy in divisional strength, and under constant artillery and aerial bombardment, they succeeded in holding the line. All this in conditions which one officer described as 'Mud, mud, mud, everywhere . . . rain and howling wind. Sunny Africa!'

The campaign now entered its last stages. The 1st and 8th Armies were about to join hands; Rommel was back in Germany; and von Arnim, with 300,000 men, had been ordered by Hitler to hold Tunisia at any cost. In the final Allied offensive, 1st Parachute Brigade opened the main coast road with an attack on March 28–29. Three weeks later, relieved by the 9th American Division, they returned to Bou Farik to refit in preparation for further airborne operations.

Airborne gunners manning their 75 mm pack howitzers in North Africa. (Courtesy Imperial War Museum.)

During the campaign the Brigade had undertaken three airborne assaults, the first major airborne operations of the war by British parachutists, and had fought for five months as infantry. They had taken part in more battles than any other formation in 1st Army, captured 3,500 prisoners and inflicted over 5,000 casualties for a loss of 1,700 to themselves. This had been achieved against a brave and resourceful enemy, in the bitterest of weather and over some pretty grim terrain. These fighting exploits earned 1st Parachute Brigade the name of 'The Red Devils'* from their German opponents. Accepted as a compliment, the name has remained to this day the unofficial title for British Airborne Forces.

Men of 1st Air-landing Brigade waiting to emplane in Hadrian gliders for the Sicily Operation. (Courtesy Imperial War Museum.)

During the final stage of the North African campaign preparations began for the invasion of Southern Italy using Sicily as a stepping stone. The depleted 1st Parachute Brigade was joined in June 1943 by the 2nd and 4th Parachute Brigades and the glider-borne 1st Air-landing Brigade from the UK. Together they comprised the operational strength of 1st Airborne Division.

* The authority came via a signal from Major-General Browning, dated January 15, 1943, to 'All Para Units'. It read: 'General Alexander directs that I Para Brigade be info that (they) have been given name by Germans of "Red Devils". General Alexander congratulates the Brigade on achieving this high distinction . . .'

Sicily. Air photograph showing the Ponte Grande Bridge over the Canal at Syracuse (top left) the objective of 1st Air-landing Brigade, July 9, 1943. The harbour area of the port itself is on the right. (Courtesy Imperial War Museum.)

The capture of Sicily was planned as a rapid pincer attack. The Americans were to advance across the island in a wide sweep from the west as the British 8th Army, under General Montgomery, moved up the east coast to block the enemy's escape route across the Straits of Messina. A rapid advance was required by 8th Army to prevent the Germans consolidating defences in the Catanian Plain and in the bottleneck between Mt. Etna and the sea. The airborne troops were therefore required to capture key bridges and ports ahead of the main force.

The seaborne assault was planned for dawn on July 10. To assist the initial landings, 1st Air-landing Brigade was to capture the Ponte Grande over the canal at the entrance to the port of Syracuse and

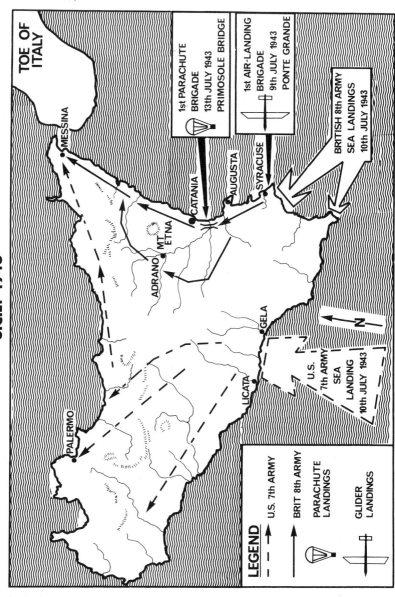

SICILY 1943

TOE OF ITALY

MESSINA

CATANIA

AUGUSTA

SYRACUSE

MT ETNA

ADRANO

GELA

LICATA

PALERMO

1st PARACHUTE BRIGADE
13th JULY 1943
PRIMOSOLE BRIDGE

1st AIR-LANDING BRIGADE
9th JULY 1943
PONTE GRANDE

BRITISH 8th ARMY
SEA LANDINGS
10th JULY 1943

U.S. 7th ARMY
SEA LANDING
10th JULY 1943

N

LEGEND

U.S. 7th ARMY

BRIT 8th ARMY

PARACHUTE LANDINGS

GLIDER LANDINGS

then the harbour itself. On the evening of July 9, 2,000 men in Hadrian and Horsa gliders towed by aircraft from 51 US Wing (Dakotas) and a small detachment of 38 Wing RAF, took off from North Africa. The weather was stormy—the invasion force had had to contend with gale-force winds—and the American aircrews were both inexperienced and suffered the serious disadvantage of only carrying a navigator in the leading aircraft of each section. When they were fired on—by friend as well as enemy—as they approached the coast, and several were shot down, disorder followed. Over half the gliders were released too early and landed in the sea; the rest were scattered for miles over that mountainous and unfriendly countryside. One officer remarked afterwards that he 'thanked God he went to battle by parachute and not by glider'.

The chances of success appeared slim, but the landing was a complete surprise. With great initiative, isolated parties took violent offensive action wherever they happened to be. This led the enemy to believe that a whole Airborne Corps had been dropped, and was of considerable assistance to the seaborne assault, which was practically unopposed. A platoon of one of the glider-borne battalions, the 2nd South Staffordshires, reached the Ponte Grande, captured it intact, and held it until they were driven off by a strong enemy counter-attack next morning. But they had gained valuable time; and the bridge was re-taken by the 2nd Battalion the Royal Scots Fusiliers, who arrived from the beaches that afternoon. At a cost of 300 men, most of them drowned, the route to Syracuse had been secured.

The 1st Air-landing Brigade's objectives included a coastal battery, and this they captured after daylight with a force of seven officers and ten soldiers from two Hadrian gliders, a party which, considering it consisted largely of senior officers—including the Deputy Brigade Commander and a padre—demonstrates the initiative and resource of all ranks in Airborne Forces. Six Italians were killed, six wounded and 40 taken prisoner, while the five field guns were destroyed and the ammunition blown up.

One Hadrian glider, loaded with men of the 2nd Battalion the South Staffordshire Regiment, landed 250 yards from the shore, one man being drowned and another killed by machine gun fire. The

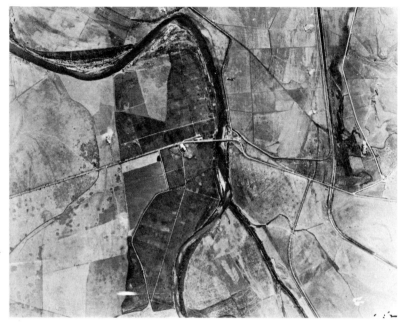

Sicily. Air photograph of the Primosole Bridge over the River Simeto near Catania—scene of the action by 1st Parachute Brigade on July 13, 1943. (Courtesy Imperial War Museum.)

remaining ten managed to swim ashore under fire; but only four officers and two soldiers were capable of moving off to their rendez-vous. This involved, initially, a crawl through 20 feet of barbed wire, covered by a pill box 100 yards away. Eventually, during the evening of July 10, after covering ten miles they succeeded in rejoining their battalion. By then they had captured two pill boxes, 21 Italians, three machine guns and an anti-tank gun.

Once ashore, 8th Army pressed on, through Augusta and across the coastal plain towards Catania. The town, surrounded by airfields, was a vital base for the final advance on Messina, and was expected to be heavily defended on the line of the Simeto River to the south. The 1st Parachute Brigade were therefore ordered to secure a bridge, where the main road crossed the river, called the Ponte di Primosole.

On July 13, 113 parachute aircraft and 16 gliders carrying 1,856 men, under Brigadier Lathbury, took off from North Africa. As the aircraft, flying in close formation, approached the coast that night, heavy anti-aircraft fire met them. Some were shot down, and again owing to 'green' air crews, many lost their way. Only 295 officers and men of the Brigade were dropped accurately enough to carry out the operation. The Primosole Bridge and the high ground to the south were captured by members of the 1st and 2nd Battalions, but the northern approach, 3rd Battalion's objective, could not be taken due to lack of numbers. At dawn the German 4th Parachute Brigade counter-attacked, first from the west, then from the north, the most vulnerable flank, but were held short of the bridge. Towards evening they crossed the river lower down and attacked again, from the east. Under pressure from three sides the small British force was compelled to abandon the bridge and withdraw slowly south where they took up a position for a last ditch stand. They were saved, however, by the arrival of the 8th Army vanguard an hour later. The handful of airborne troops had taken and held the bridge for longer than the original plan had stipulated; and it was finally recaptured by the 9th Battalion the Durham Light Infantry on July 16, after a fierce two-day battle.

But vital time had been lost and the Germans were able to build up their strength more rapidly than the British. The main drive was therefore switched from the coastal plain to a thrust inland, around Mt. Etna. Messina was reached eventually on August 17, 1943, and the fighting in Sicily ended.

The main Allied objective of the Italian campaign was to draw in, and contain, as many enemy divisions as possible, thus weakening the German ability to reinforce the Russian front and, eventually, his opposition to the proposed invasion of Europe. The mountainous Italian peninsula was, however, ideally suited to defence, and the campaign developed into a long, weary slogging match.

It opened on September 3, 1943, with the British 8th Army landing in the 'toe' of Italy for an advance to the Adriatic coast, followed, a few days later, by American landings at Salerno. To enable the British build-up to progress without interruption and prevent the arrival of enemy reinforcements and their preparation of defensive positions, light troops were required to operate in advance of the main force. The 1st Airborne Division was therefore ordered to capture the port of Taranto by a seaborne assault and to exploit northwards. The 2nd and 4th Parachute Brigades sailed from Bizerta on September 8, the remainder of the division being held in reserve. During the voyage, the unconditional surrender of Italy was announced, and the landing at Taranto was unopposed; though when the transport ship HMS *Abdiel* was blown in half by a mine in the harbour, 58 men were killed and 154 injured. With the harbour secure, the Division advanced rapidly northwards, mopping up pockets of enemy resistance as it went. During this period the Divisional Commander, Major-General Hopkinson, was killed by an airburst shell whilst watching an attack on the town of Castellaneta. Supplies, however, soon lagged behind, and the division was forced to improvise from local resources and captured enemy equipment, until, on reaching Foggia, their lines of communication were finally stretched to the limit and they were forced to halt. Here they were relieved and withdrawn to Taranto to re-organise.

Meanwhile, the Americans on the west coast had broken out of the Salerno bridgehead, captured Naples, and advanced to the line of the Volturno and Calore rivers. The Germans were in retreat along the whole front and the fall of Rome appeared imminent; but in October they stood fast on a series of intricate defences based on the shoulders of the Abruzzi Mountains — the 'Winter Line' — and it was to be many months before the capital was reached. The 1st Airborne Division played only a small part in this struggle, for in November all but the 2nd Parachute Brigade returned to England to prepare for the invasion of Western Europe.

The 2nd Brigade, under the command of Brigadier C. H. V. Pritchard, and composed of the 4th, 5th and 6th Battalions, was enlarged and renamed the 2nd Independent Parachute Brigade Group. As had happened before, and would happen again, soldiers of this quality were too valuable to be kept idle; and until they were needed for airborne operations, they joined the 2nd New Zealand Division under General Freyberg, and fought as infantry.

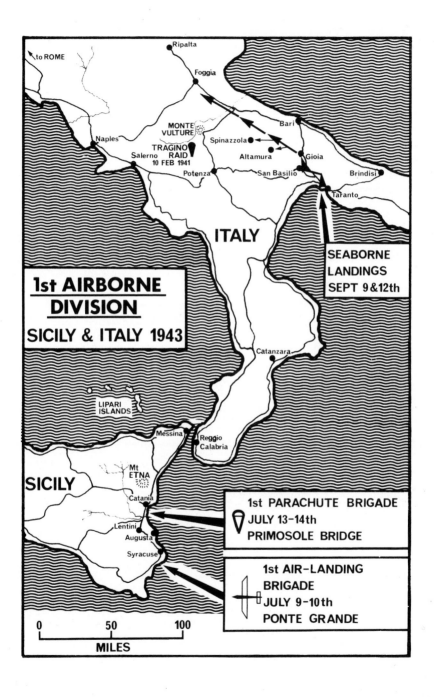

to ROME

Ripalta

Foggia

MONTE VULTURE

Naples

TRAGINO RAID
10 FEB 1941

Salerno

Spinazzola

Bari

Altamura

Gioia

Potenza

San Basilio

Brindisi

Taranto

ITALY

SEABORNE LANDINGS SEPT 9&12th

1st AIRBORNE DIVISION

SICILY & ITALY 1943

Catanzara

LIPARI ISLANDS

Messina

Reggio Calabria

SICILY

Mt ETNA

Catania

Lentini

Augusta

Syracuse

1st PARACHUTE BRIGADE
JULY 13-14th
PRIMOSOLE BRIDGE

1st AIR-LANDING BRIGADE
JULY 9-10th
PONTE GRANDE

0   50   100

MILES

When the Brigade returned to action at the end of November, the 8th Army was drawn up along the River Sangro and the American 5th Army faced a string of mountain forts at the entrance to the Liri Valley, the most formidable of which was Monte Cassino. In appalling weather, the Allies now began an assault on the main defences of the Winter Line. The 8th Army crossed the turbulent Sangro and advanced towards Orsogna with the 2nd Parachute Brigade protecting the left flank. Adverse weather and stiff enemy opposition brought them to a halt on the outskirts of the town. Here, on an exposed ridge between Orsogna and Guariagrele, the three battalions each spent a rugged and testing four months. Their positions were overlooked, and frequently pin-pointed, by the enemy—one Company HQ received 17 direct hits during a single day—but this did not stop them patrolling with ingenuity and aggression. Draped in sheets when there was snow on the ground, they would creep up on the Germans in their lairs, snatch a prisoner or two, or an entire section, and slip away again—though not always with impunity. 'It was tricky and dangerous work', wrote one officer, 'with mud, snow and mines to contend with', and, inevitably, there were casualties.

At the same time, the American 5th Army had been held up at Monte Cassino; and at the end of March the 2nd Parachute Brigade was transferred to the Cassino front. Despite its ferocious reputation, and apart from the prevalence of mines, it proved in many ways less unpleasant than their previous sector. 'Weird' is how the 5th Battalion history chooses to describe it, 'dominated by the monastery which would be suddenly illuminated by a star shell at night, or obliterated . . . with smoke by day'. But, as at Orsogna, they were dependent on the unpredictable mule for food and ammunition; and 'curiously enough', records the 6th Battalion history, 'it was always the mule with the "attractive" stores—rum, sugar or NAAFI goods—' that got blown up or fled. It is of interest that the average age of the Brigade HQ Mess at this time was 24; the Brigadier, Pritchard, was a greybeard of 37 and ten years older than the oldest of his officers.

As spring approached it was decided to by-pass Cassino and drive straight for Rome up the Liri Valley. The 2nd Parachute Brigade stepped up its patrolling activities around Cassino, to give the impression that a fresh assault was pending in that sector. When the attack began, on May 11, 1944, the German right flank collapsed and the 5th Army raced for Rome.

With the fall of the Winter Line, the Germans retreated to another prepared position, the 'Gothic Line', stretching across the peninsula between Pisa and Rimini. As they withdrew they destroyed bridges and installations of possible value to the Allies, and here, at last, was an opportunity for the parachutists to do the work they had volunteered and been trained for. General Sir Oliver Leese, 8th Army Commander, decided to drop airborne troops along the route from Sara to Avenzzano to forestall these demolitions. Brigadier Pritchard allotted a force of 60 men from the 6th Parachute Battalion, commanded by Captain L. A. Fitzroy-Smith, for the operation.

They were dropped near Torricella by three Dakotas of US Troop Carrier Command, in daylight, in wild country, with absolute precision, together with a number of dummies to exaggerate the size of the force. In three groups they raided the road successfully for a week, and kept one entire German division away from the front at a time when its presence might have been invaluable. Inevitably there were casualties; and of the survivors, half were captured as they tried to return to the Allied lines.

This was the last action by the 1st Airborne Division in the Italian campaign. Winter weather once again delayed the offensive; and, while the Allies prepared to assault the Pisa–Rimini line, the 2nd Parachute Brigade was withdrawn for an airborne attack on Southern France to coincide with the Normandy invasion. The German armies in Italy finally capitulated on May 2, 1945.

Chapter

3

Special Air Service

THROUGHOUT 1942 and '43 the Corps continued to grow, as regiment after regiment—the Somerset LI, the Royal Warwicks, the Green Howards, the South Lancashires, to name just a few—contributed battalions. The 6th Airborne Division was raised in April '43, with D-Day in mind; and in July, the 1st Canadian Parachute Battalion arrived in the UK to join the Division and add to the growing number of parachute battalions. In December the rank of the commander of the airborne forces was raised to Lieutenant-General.

In two years the force had grown from nothing to two divisions and an independent brigade, with its own headquarters, its development watched over and encouraged, as it had been from the start, by Churchill. When one remembers his continuing passion for irregular units, and his unorthodox ideas, from the Naval armoured cars of World War I to the monstrous novelty of the Mulberry harbours, one need not be surprised that he should have taken airborne forces to his heart.

In the meantime, in the Western Desert, a separate kind of offensive action, more akin to, though different in scope and detail from, the early airborne raids was being evolved.

In January 1941, a commando formation known as 'Lay-force' under Brigadier R. E. Laycock (later Major-General and Chief of Combined Operations) arrived in the Middle East. Among them was Lieutenant A. D. Stirling, who devoted considerable time and thought to the problem of raiding behind the enemy lines. He concluded that the key to a successful raid was surprise, and that several small groups attacking a number of targets simultaneously would be more effective than the commando technique of sending a relatively large force against a single objective.

Stirling's plan for a special force to undertake such operations was put to the Commander-in-Chief and pursued by Stirling personally with dedicated determination, infectious optimism and a bland disregard for red tape. Despite opposition at Staff level for such 'untried crack-brained schemes' he secured General Auchinleck's personal approval to raise an experimental force. 'L' Detachment, SAS Brigade, came into existence at the end of July 1941, consisting of seven officers and about 60 men, all trained parachutists.

A British 'Bombay' pre-World War II bomber. This was the type of aircraft adapted by David Stirling to train the first SAS volunteers for parachuting in Egypt. Six of these aircraft took the SAS on their first and only parachute operation in the Western Desert on November 17, 1941. Due to severe sandstorms the raiding party was dropped in the wrong place and the raid was unfortunately abortive. (Courtesy Imperial War Museum.)

The first SAS operation preceded General Auchinleck's offensive against the Germans on the night of November 17, 1941. The plan was to attack five main forward fighter and bomber airfields at Timini and Gazala. Unfortunately, due to severe sandstorms, the airborne parties were dropped in the wrong area; the operation was a complete failure; and the SAS launched no more parachute attacks in the Middle East. Instead, they relied on the Long Range Desert Group for their transport, and between December 1941 and March 1942 made about 20 raids behind the enemy lines, destroying 115 aircraft and numerous vehicles.

By April 1942, 'L' Detachment was beginning to expand and had under its command a number of Allied units, including the Free French Parachutists. For the next year the force developed its own specialized type of warfare: with jeeps as machine-gun carriers, their

The 'Jeep' machine gun carrier as developed by the SAS for their raiding operations in the Western Desert. (Courtesy Imperial War Museum.)

sallies grew more daring and their scope wider. The need to overcome Staff reluctance to approve recruiting for more ambitious plans became acute. Stirling put his requirements to Monty in person. Recalling this many years later, Field-Marshal Montgomery described the incident as follows: 'Saucy young feller. Came barging up to my caravan and asked me if he could go round 8th Army selecting volunteers. "Not likely", I said; "I'm not having you pinching all my best chaps". And off he went and did it just the same.' So, on the highest authority — or rather, without it, the men were obtained. At first, forward enemy aerodromes were the main objectives; then, as a prelude to the battle of El Alamein, all efforts were directed against Rommel's lines of communications, and deep penetration, harrassing and reconnaissance were mounted to keep pace with the advance of the 8th Army. Early in 1943 the 1st SAS Regiment was formed from 'L' Detachment, and its eventual strength was about 1,100 men of many nationalities.

Lt.-Col. David Stirling, DSO, greets Lt. McDonald's SAS patrol returning after 3 months behind enemy lines in the Western Desert. (Courtesy Imperial War Museum.)

As the war in North Africa drew to a close the nature of the SAS tasks changed, and the 1st SAS Regiment was split into a Special Raiding Squadron and a Special Boat Squadron. In May 1943, it was joined by the 2nd SAS Regiment, and together they took part in raids on Crete, Sardinia, the Dodecanese, the Greek Islands, and the invasions of Sicily and Italy with the 1st Airborne Division.

These early exploits of the SAS and the Long Range Desert Group, and similar operations by Major-General Orde Wingate in Burma, had demonstrated the value of small forces operating behind the enemy's lines. What was wanted now was a completely 'guerilla' force for the eventual operations in Western Europe. At the end of 1943, SAS forces were returned to the UK to form the nucleus of a Special Air Service Brigade under Lieutenant-General Browning's command. It consisted of the 1st and 2nd SAS Regiments, 3rd and 4th French Parachute Battalions, and a Belgian Independent Parachute Squadron, amounting in all to 2,000 men and commanded by Brigadier R. W. McLeod. Organization and equipment of the new brigade proceeded rapidly, and a concentrated parachute course was run at the Parachute Training School, Ringway. In the spring of 1944, training began in Ayrshire, Scotland.

The tasks of the SAS Brigade were twofold: strategically—to harass the enemy in the rear and assist local resistance movements: tactically—to delay the deployment of enemy reinforcements to the beaches; and to launch diversionary raids. They were always to operate in uniform and would expect to be treated as normal prisoners of war, if captured, and not as spies or saboteurs. During the invasion of France the SAS planned to operate in the rear of the coastal belt behind the German front lines. Special bases would be established in conjunction with the Resistance, where SAS parties could be concentrated and concealed, re-supplied, and re-organized as necessary for further operations in the locality. This system was successfully adopted throughout the campaigns in France, Belgium and Holland.

From June 6 to October 31, 1944, the SAS Brigade carried out 43 operations, delivered and supplied by Nos. 38 and 46 Groups of the RAF. At first their activities were confined to Brittany, and the establishment of a ring of bases from which attacks could be carried out on communications leading to the Normandy Bridgehead. Then, as the Allies began to break out, they were switched to harassing the retreating enemy. This pattern was repeated throughout the various stages of the Allied advance across North-West Europe—in Central and Southern France, Belgium and Holland.

Late in 1944 the main battle front along the west bank of the River Rhine became virtually static, there was little hope of a major Allied advance during the winter; and the scope for SAS activities accordingly diminished. The 3rd Squadron, 2nd SAS Regiment was sent to Italy under command of Major R. A. Farran to work in close co-operation with the Italian Resistance—large, enthusiastic, but uncoordinated.

Conditions in Italy differed from those in Northern Europe. Greater Allied air superiority made possible more regular air supply, but the mountainous country restricted operations to a few vital and well-guarded roads and railways. For the first time, heavier weapons were carried and used to good effect. The Squadron remained in Italy until the German surrender, during which time they launched two major operations, and, in a final flourish, attempted to block the

Brenner Pass to the retreating Germans by causing a landslide.

In the spring of 1945 the Allies at last broke out across the Rhine. In this, the final drive to victory in the West, the SAS was called upon to save key bridges and airfields in Holland from demolition as the Germans pulled out.

In North Africa and Europe the SAS established its techniques for the future, and demonstrated the benefits to be gained by infiltration behind the enemy lines, especially when the front stabilized to form a 'crust' of enemy troops about 30 miles deep. The area behind this crust was relatively empty and became their happy hunting ground. Their activities caused the enemy to deploy large forces on guard and lines-of-communication duties, and spread alarm and confusion in rear areas out of all proportion to their numbers. They provided reliable intelligence, including target acquisition* for the RAF bombers; disrupted road and rail communications, and inflicted heavy losses on the enemy. Finally, by their presence in enemy-occupied territory they encouraged, trained and co-ordinated the activities of local Resistance groups to assist the operations of the Allied armies.

Formed originally in the teeth of strong opposition from those accustomed to more conventional units, they fully justified their existence as a specialized force with a particular and valuable application; and the work they achieved was out of all proportion to their size. Their contribution to victory in Europe was considerable. The tradition they established is kept alive today by both regular and volunteer SAS Regiments.

---

* i.e. discovering suitable targets.

D

Chapter
4
The Far East
I

'Granted the power to maintain forces by air and direct them by wireless it is possible to operate regular ground forces for indefinite periods in the heart of enemy-occupied territory to the peril of his war machine. This is because the value of such forces is disproportionate to their cost, one fighting man at the heart of the enemy's military machine being worth many hundreds in the forward battle areas.'

Major-General Orde Wingate, 1943

WINGATE occupies a somewhat paradoxical position in a history of Airborne Forces. Neither he himself, nor the units under his command, were members of the Parachute Regiment or its allied formations, and for this reason his ground campaigns lie outside the scope of this book. At the same time, because of the military imagination of the man, the originality of his strategic and tactical ideas, and the nature of the country in which he was fighting, his two campaigns, of 1943 and '44, produced a whole battery of innovations which have deeply affected the manner of airborne operations since.

Wavell summoned him to the Far East in 1942. Wingate had just recovered from the effects of his legendary four-month march from the Ethiopian border to Addis Ababa with the Emperor Haile Selassie; in that astonishing campaign, as in his use of night-squads to defeat Arab terrorism in Palestine earlier, he had shown that he possessed, as Wavell himself said, 'a genius for novel and unorthodox methods of warfare'.

The retreat in Burma was already in progress when Wingate arrived; but he just had time to visit the front and form his own opinions of the country and the enemy. From his observations he came to three conclusions. The first was that Long Range Penetration Groups, operating far behind the Japanese lines, would be effective in spreading havoc and confusion: the other two, which followed, were to exploit to the full the two comparatively new tools of military science, the aeroplane and the radio. In effect, in these three ideas, he was thinking like an airborne soldier, and this is the key to his importance in airborne history, for Wingate, for all his crankiness, was, as Wavell said of him, 'a man of unquestioned military genius', and the methods to which he applied his genius in Burma happened to be airborne methods.

His first expedition in 1943 was his justification; and although the tactical effects were small, the moral effect was enormous. As a direct result, the Japanese High Command changed their plan of sealing the Burma Road and extinguishing the air lift from Assam across the 'Hump' to China, because attacks by Long Range Penetration Groups clearly jeopardized their entire system of communications.

That first operation proved that the power of supply and control was limited only by the number of aircraft and trained crews available; and Wingate was told to go ahead and develop all forms of air supply and transportation, including that of mules, horses and guns, using Dakota aircraft and gliders. Much of this was breaking entirely new ground. The calculated risks involved have often been unwittingly referred to as mistakes: they were not, and it is of the utmost importance that this should be realized.

Wingate's objective in 1944 was to capture and dominate all the Indaw-Kaha area down to the 24th Parallel, which he would hold until relieved by the joining up of the Chinese under Stilwell, the Yoke Force then facing the Japanese 56 Division on the Salween River, and the 14th Army. This area would then be the springboard for the autumn offensive as soon as the monsoon ended. His requirements were six Long Range Penetration Brigades plus certain ancillaries, amounting to six brigades, Indian, British and West African, which became known by the code-name of '3rd Indian Division'; and he accepted gratefully the support of the American No. 1 Air Commando, under the joint command of Colonels Philip Cochran and John Alison, USAAF. This included bombers, fighters, transports and gliders, as well as a large number of L1 and L5 light aircraft for evacuating casualties. One of the worst aspects of the 1943 campaign had been the inevitability of leaving the severely wounded behind.

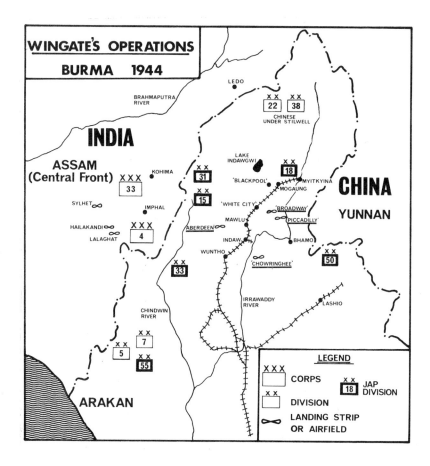

WINGATE'S OPERATIONS
BURMA 1944

LEDO

BRAHMAPUTRA
RIVER

X X 22   X X 38

CHINESE
UNDER STILWELL

INDIA

**ASSAM
(Central Front)** X X X 33

KOHIMA

X X 31

LAKE
INDAWGWI

'BLACKPOOL'

X X 18

MYITKYINA

MOGAUNG

CHINA

SYLHET

IMPHAL

X X 15

'WHITE CITY'

'BROADWAY'

YUNNAN

HAILAKANDI
LALAGHAT

X X X 4

ABERDEEN

MAWLU

PICCADILLY

INDAW

BHAMO

WUNTHO

X X 33

'CHOWRINGHEE'

X X 50

IRRAWADDY
RIVER

LASHIO

CHINDWIN
RIVER

X X 7

X X 5

X X 55

LEGEND

X X X

CORPS

X X 18 JAP
DIVISION

X X

DIVISION

LANDING STRIP
OR AIRFIELD

ARAKAN

Wingate's plans were ready by the end of January 1944. His intention was to compel the enemy to withdraw from the whole of Burma north of the 24th Parallel. This was the objective he had pledged himself to attain when the proposition was first discussed at Quebec, and which he pursued up to his death.

For its fulfilment, it required a determined advance by General Stilwell from the north, an attack by the Chinese Yoke Force across the Salween from the east, and a follow-up division from the 14th

Army to take over Indaw. In the event, none of these took place.

The penetration of the 3rd Indian Division into Burma may be divided into three phases:

Phase 1. The approach march of the 16th Infantry Brigade under Brigadier Fergusson.

Phase 2. The fly-in of the 77th Indian Infantry Brigade under Brigadier Calvert, and 111th Indian Infantry Brigade under Brigadier Lentaigne, to the three landing strips of 'Broadway', 'Piccadilly' and 'Chowringhee'.

Phase 3. The follow-up air lift of the 14th Infantry Brigade under Brigadier Brodie and 3rd West African Brigade under Brigadier Gilmore.

1. On February 5, just a month before the airborne operation was due, Brigadier Fergusson and his brigade left the road-head at Hamtung and moved across some of the most difficult country it is possible to imagine. Hacking steps up and down hillsides and revetting each step to enable men and animals to follow, they made their way via Hkalak Ga to Kanglai, on the banks of the Chindwin, where they were met, on February 29, by Wingate himself. Accompanied by Fergusson's second-in-command, who was in charge of the air base, he landed without incident on a sandbank in the Chindwin in an American UC64 aircraft. Shortly afterwards, four gliders, loaded with river-crossing equipment, also landed safely. The material was swiftly assembled; and the brigade, after a short rest, completed the crossing by March 5.

A couple of days before the 16th Brigade arrived, two gliders had landed on sandbanks south of the crossing place, carrying patrols of the Black Watch, who blocked and booby-trapped the approaches from which Japanese reinforcements might be expected to appear and interfere with the river crossing. These gliders all went in single-tow, there being no necessity to use double-tow. Valuable supply-dropping experience had been gained during Brigadier Fergusson's approach march by 231 Squadron USAAF, which had had no previous experience of these techniques in bad country. The dropping zones were invariably of knife-edge width and often only about 60 yards long, and anything which missed the zone was lost. The first badly bungled drop to the 16th Brigade gave the USAAF a sharp lesson, and after it they came into line with the drill which had been evolved by the RAF with Special Force during training. By the time the Chindwin was crossed, their efficiency had increased tremendously.

2. For the second phase, the fly-in of the 77th and 111th Brigades, it was arranged that the aircraft should operate from three airfields, Hailekandi and Lalaghat in Assam, and Tulihal in the Imphal plain, while the gliders were all concentrated at the second. The minimum safe altitude to clear the mountains was 8,000 feet on the way in, and 9,000 feet on the way out. Fifty RAF fighters were massed by the 3rd Tactical Air Force to counter any air attack that might develop on the bases. Colonel Philip Cochran, USAAF, Commander No. 1 Air Commando USAAF, was in charge of the operations on D-Day, as the entire lift on that day was to be made by the WACO gliders of his force. As the double-tow procedure was to be used, and his pilots alone had had experience in this, it was arranged that each of his 26 Dakota pilots should act as first pilot and that Troop Carrier Command should provide 26 pilots to act as second pilots for the occasion.

The maximum strength of the tug aircraft was thus limited to 26. The plan therefore consisted of two stages; 26 gliders to each airstrip in the first, and 14 to each in the second. March 5, 1944, was the chosen date, to allow the maximum moonlight. Flights into 'Chowringhee' were not to begin until D + 3.

At 1630 hours on D-Day, half-an-hour before the first glider was due to take off, one of Cochran's L1 aircraft landed, and the pilot was brought in a jeep to where Wingate and Colonel Cochran were standing at the head of the line of gliders. He unrolled a blown-up air photo of 'Piccadilly' which revealed the fact that the entire landing zone had been blocked by the enemy with large felled trees.

Plans were quickly revised, the number of gliders was reduced from 80 to 60, and the first pair took off at 1812, only an hour late. Eventually 51 were airborne.

Because of the threat of immediate ground attack when the first gliders touched down — subsequently proved to be baseless but at the time eminently possible — the initial number of gliders was reduced

A Dakota 'tug' takes off with two Hadrian gliders in tow. Others can be seen above ·
(Courtesy Imperial War Museum.)

to eight. These contained engineer stores, communications, strip lighting and control parties, with a small specially selected ground protection party headed by Lieutenant-Colonel Scott, Commanding Officer of the King's Regiment, who were the spearhead of the attack.

The Pathfinding Team, consisting of Colonel Alison, USAAF, his control staff and the covering troops of the King's Regiment, landed at 'Broadway' after an uneventful flight of two and a half hours. This party was followed 15 minutes later by Brigadier Calvert and Advance Headquarters, 77th Indian Infantry Brigade. The strip lighting (oil-burning duck lamps) was set up by pacing along compass bearings from a central light. This was completed just before the arrival of the main body.

The method of approach was for the tug aircraft to fly low along the line of lights and the gliders to 'cut' at a pilot light half a mile short of the landing zone. This method was adopted because it was believed that the landing was likely to be opposed and they would thus be vulnerable to small-arms fire for a shorter period. The first two gliders of the main body landed safely and rolled clear. The next three pairs fouled a drag ditch which knocked their wheels off and caused them to swing round and block the strip. Before the lights could be realigned one of the next pair crashed into the wreckage. Two men were killed and six seriously injured. The gliders which followed succeeded in avoiding this obstacle, two by taking off again and clearing it, the remainder by landing in the newly marked landing zone.

When the first flight of gliders was completed it was decided to accept no more that night, and the code word agreed for the cancellation of the operation was sent to Lalaghat. This message was not received until 0227 hours, by which time nine of the second wave, now flying at single tow, were already on their way. Eight were recalled and landed safely at base. The ninth, containing a bulldozer, was released over 'Broadway'. This one, landing at speed, overshot the strip, discharging its load into the jungle as it struck two trees. The co-pilots were lifted bodily as the nose raised to emit the bulldozer, and were unhurt, but the bulldozer was destroyed.

By first light the obstructions on the landing zones had been dragged clear. The five tracks leading into the 'Broadway' area were blocked by strong standing patrols and a mobile reserve was in position commanding the strip. Inner ring patrols were operating round the strip, and the airfield engineers were busy preparing for the Dakotas, assisted by a working party of 100 men from the covering troops using picks and shovels. By dawn on March 6 some 400 men were in 'Broadway'.

This was a classic example of a 'stronghold', according to Wingate's specification: remote from any motorable road; secret while it was being established — though not thereafter — suitable for an airstrip for transport aircraft, self-contained, and invulnerable. Floater columns were to operate outside it and attack the attackers to prevent them setting up a firm base. Once these conditions were fulfilled, a stronghold became a dagger wound in the enemy's back, through which an increasing quantity of his life's blood was to flow.

At midday, by which time a short strip had been cleared, 12 light aircraft flew in from Ledo under the command of Captain Rebori, USAAF, and removed the wounded. This was the first time these aircraft had operated over enemy territory. By dusk that evening a 1,600-yard strip had been completed; and at 2000 hours the first Dakota, piloted by General Donald Old, USAAF, and carrying a modified load of 4,500 lb, flew into 'Broadway'. To the consternation of ground control, it approached from the wrong end, but landed without difficulty. The strip was pronounced so good that the second wave of Dakotas from Hailekandi landed with the full load of 6,000 lb.

That same night, an advance party of the 111th Brigade and American engineers, in 12 gliders, landed, single-tow, on 'Chow-ringhee' at intervals of 12 minutes, the interval of five minutes, on 'Broadway', having proved too fast for ground control. One glider overshot, its crew of three were killed and the tractor it was carrying was damaged beyond repair. The tractor was replaced, also by glider, from 'Broadway', which by then had no further use for it; and some additional engineer stores were also sent across. The two strips were only some 40 miles apart.

Next day a tremendous effort was put in on the 'Chowringhee' strip, and at 2315 hours the codeword 'Roorkee' was received. This meant that it was ready for fully-loaded Dakotas, and 20 were promptly despatched. Movement Control were suspicious, however, and sent a signal to check that the strip was really long enough for the full loads. To their horror the answer came back that it was only 2,700 feet. All aircraft were promptly recalled to base; but seven of them, which did not receive the message, flew on and landed without incident. The remainder returned to base with their crews in a very bad temper!

On D+4 (March 9) Wingate, after a discussion at the morning planning conference, decided to land only four columns at 'Chow-ringhee' and to divert the rest of 111th Brigade to 'Broadway'. The 'Chowringhee' strip had served its purpose well, and had drawn

Glider 'snatch'. A Dakota practising the pick up of a Hadrian glider at Netheravon in 1943. The line between the two upright poles has been caught by the hook underneath the aircraft and the poles are about to collapse. This tricky operation under ideal conditions was doubly hazardous in the jungles of Burma. (Courtesy Imperial War Museum.)

attention away from 'Broadway', but it was only 15 miles from Katha airfield and near a good motor road, so that the Japanese were likely to react very quickly. The Brigadier General Staff flew in on the last plane to 'Chowringhee' that night and explained the Commander's change of plan to Brigadier Lentaigne, who made immediate arrangements to leave at dawn the following day. By 1100 hours 'Chowringhee' was empty except for some damaged gliders, and, two hours later, it was heavily bombed and strafed by Zeroes and light bombers, who repeated the attack the following morning. The evacuation had been well timed.

By D+6 (March 11) the first airborne landing was complete. Four gliders were landed that night on the banks of the Irrawaddy with equipment for Lentaigne's crossing. Two of these were snatched* safely and returned with four prisoners who were being interrogated at base within a few hours of their capture; the other two gliders were abandoned and destroyed.

* A system devised to recover gliders from clearings or landing zones too small for a powered aircraft to land or take off. Two light poles were erected with a nylon rope stretched between the tops. This was in turn attached, by a series of specially rigged loops to give elasticity, to the glider. The glider was offset from the poles clear of the flight path of the tug aircraft. The tug, with a metal hooked arm mounted below the fuselage, flew over the poles, hooking the cable between them. The poles collapsed as the tug put its engine to full boost and the glider was 'snatched' into the air. This tricky operation was successfully accomplished on many occasions.

Phases 1 and 2 of the plan were now complete. By mid-March, three Long Range Penetration Brigades were embedded behind the enemy's lines and more or less at the centre of four Japanese divisions. The stronghold at 'Broadway' was firmly established, and Brigadier Calvert was within two days' march of Henu where he was to impose a complete stranglehold for weeks on the main lines of communication leading to the 18th (Japanese) Division, which faced General Stilwell in the Hukawng. Morris Force (4/9th Gurkha Regiment) was well on its way to block the Bhamo–Myitkyina Road, and the 111th Brigade were crossing the River Irrawaddy to attack and destroy the Japanese supply dumps and to block the lines of communications to the 31st (Japanese) Division.

On March 17 a strong patrol, code name 'Bladet', under Major Blain, was landed in five gliders to operate against the Japanese lines of communication in the Kawlin–Wunthe area and to direct Allied bombers to worthwhile targets. These gliders were subsequently 'snatched' and returned to base.

3. The next air-landing operation — Phase 3 — involved the fly-in of the 14th British Infantry Brigade and 3rd West African Brigade to the Meza Valley, which Fergusson's 16th Brigade had now reached after their long march.

At this stage the 23rd Infantry Brigade was removed from the 3rd Indian Division and put under command of the 33rd Corps where it was to operate in a short range penetration role. Wingate, afraid that he might lose the rest of his force, now committed them earlier than he had intended. On March 21, he landed near Mahnton in a light aircraft, and met Brigadier Fergusson. He completed the reconnaissance of this new strip (code name 'Aberdeen') on a borrowed pony.

At first light on March 22, six gliders containing American engineers and their airfield construction machinery landed without difficulty, and by the following evening the strip was ready for Dakotas. This almost instantaneous creation of makeshift airfields in the depths of the Burmese jungle was another of Wingate's ideas, and almost miraculously successful. Much of the success of the Long Range Penetration Group resulted from it. It was originally planned to complete the Dakota lift in a series of 360 sorties over a period of six nights; but in the interval the Japanese offensive against the 4th Corps had developed alarmingly; worse, things were going badly for the 14th Army, who were beginning to realize the magnitude of the Japanese attack, and needed all available supply-dropping aircraft themselves. Consequently, only 15 Dakotas could be guaranteed by Troop Carrier Command for the build-up at 'Aberdeen', and not more than ten could be relied upon from No. 1 Air Commando. The air lift of these two brigades, though finally successful, dragged on over a period of 20 days. Bad weather, which put both home and target airstrips out of action for considerable periods, and the constant risk of interference from enemy fighters, which necessitated fighter cover by day, added to the difficulties. The strip at 'Aberdeen' could be approached only from one end, which made night landings extremely hazardous. The Japanese made several air attacks on 'Aberdeen', and on one occasion the last Japanese fighter going home was still over the strip when the first of 12 Dakotas came in view. Fortunately they did not meet.

On March 24, one of Cochran's Dakotas reported that it had seen an air crash near the village of Pabram, between Imphal and Silchar, during a thunderstorm. The following day it was learned that Wingate had left Imphal—which he had visited on his way back from 'Broadway'—the previous evening, to return to his headquarters at Lalaghat. On March 27 a ground reconnaissance party from Main Headquarters, 3rd Indian Division, which was sent out to investigate, found the wreckage of a B25, the type in which he had been travelling. The aircraft had exploded and there was no hope of identifying the bodies; but some papers and, most important of all, the Commander's characteristic Wolseley topee—unique in itself and known to every man in Special Force—had been thrown clear of the debris, and left no doubt that General Wingate had been killed. His death cast a deep gloom over the whole Force.

By the beginning of April, the 77th Indian Infantry Brigade had established a blockade—known as 'White City'—firmly astride the road and rail communications from Indaw to Mogaung and Myitkyina, and also the River Irrawaddy. This block had had precisely the effect which Wingate had expected. Considerable efforts had been

A Dakota drops supplies to Wingate's troops behind enemy lines in Burma 1944. (Courtesy Imperial War Museum.)

made to dislodge it, but they had all failed; and the enemy, whose losses had been heavy, were now faced, for the first time in the Burma theatre, with the problem of attacking well dug-in troops of high morale instead of trying their usual trick of infiltration. It was fully realized that the enemy would step up his attacks, for these lines of communications were absolutely vital to the Japanese 18th Division facing the comparatively inert Stilwell. General Lentaigne—who had assumed command of the 3rd Indian Division—therefore decided to close down 'Aberdeen' as a stronghold and to reinforce 'White City', strengthening the garrison's defence with 25-pounders, Bofors, and 2-pounder anti-tank guns. This, of course, meant the construction of a Dakota strip, for the existing one was only fit for light aircraft; and so, on April 3, five single-tow gliders, with American engineers and their equipment, were landed at 'White City', and work immediately began. Six Japanese aircraft watched them with interest, but, strangely, made no effort to interfere.

On April 4, Cochran made an inspired raid on Aungban airfield, destroying 25 aircraft on the ground and one in the air and damaging many others, without loss to his air commando.

On the night of April 5, a storm broke over 'White City' and the new strip became waterlogged. The Japanese were strong in the vicinity, and a major attack was expected at any moment; yet, controlled only by Aldis lamp, 26 aircraft landed that night, carrying between them 250 men, four 25-pounder guns, six Bofors and two 2-pounder anti-tank guns. The Japanese striking force was actually on the spot at the time, and must have observed the whole proceedings; but they made no effort to interfere, a fact which they came to regret bitterly afterwards. This was a typical example of the extraordinary lack of initiative which frequently afflicted the Japanese. They would fight to the death, and at the same time allow a dangerous situation to build up under their very noses.

The following day, they launched a heavy attack on the stronghold, but definite news of the situation did not reach Headquarters, 3rd Indian Division, until three of the night's sorties were airborne. Fortunately it was possible to divert both them, and those that took off later, to 'Aberdeen'. The reinforcement of 'White City' had been timed to a nicety, thanks, not least, to the inertia of the enemy.

The attacks by tanks, artillery and heavy mortars continued until April 15. On this day, the Japanese put in a final effort, but like the others, and at great loss, it failed. From that time, until 'White City' was voluntarily evacuated, no further serious effort was made to dislodge the garrison. Between 1,500 and 2,000 of the enemy had immolated themselves against the most efficient Japanese-killer of the whole Burma campaign. The Direct Air Support was superb throughout, and is discussed in more detail in the summing-up later.

Phase 3, the follow-up, ended on April 27 and, with it, all hopes of realizing General Wingate's strategical objective. His tactical objectives, on the other hand, had been fulfilled, for the country in a 40-mile radius of Indaw was dominated by Long Range Penetration Brigades; and since March 19, a clamp had effectively been placed on all main road and rail-borne communications with the 18th Japanese Division facing Stilwell. The lines of communication between

Bhamo and Myitkyina, although not as firmly closed, were neverthe-less dominated by Morris Force, which had destroyed bridges and roads, and constantly ambushed enemy movement along that route. A small force was planted in the Kachin country to the east of the Irrawaddy, prepared to lead a Kachin revolt as soon as Yoke Force showed any signs of life; and, finally, the Japanese 31st Division's base supply dumps had been destroyed, and the lines of communica-tion through Banmauk to Humalin had been cut.

The US WACO CG-4A or 'Hadrian' glider as it was known in airborne forces. Similar to the Horsa though with a slightly less load capacity it was the standard U.S. glider of WW II. It was used extensively by British airborne units on the general 'lease lend' that operated throughout the war between British and American airborne forces. It was used in airborne operations in the Far East and particularly by General Wingate's Special Force in Burma. This one is seen in its RAF markings. The pilot's compartment was hinged to raise upwards to discharge its cargo. When 'Jeeps' were carried a system of pulleys attached to the back of the vehicle automatically raised the nose as it drove out. (Courtesy Imperial War Museum.)

To counterbalance these gains, however, there were a number of less favourable developments. Stilwell had not yet put in a serious attack, and consequently the 18th Japanese Division had had no need to call on their 3rd Line ammunition and supplies, as they could live on their hump; Yoke Force was totally immobile; and the 14th Army, far from being in a position to exploit the successful situation by putting in a division to take over from the 3rd Indian Division, had at an early stage been forced to take away the 23rd Infantry Brigade, the only remaining reserve brigade to Special Force, in order to protect the railway running from India to Assam.

This, in fact, proved unnecessary; and the 23rd Brigade were able to sweep round in a short-range penetration movement, cutting the Japanese supply lines one after the other. This action began the disintegration of the 31st Japanese Division, and started to tip the scales in the Allies' favour. Being trained to move and fight without the use of roads, their value was above price to the 33rd Corps, as their Corps Commander testified.

It was clear that, at this stage, Special Force was an embarrassment to the 14th Army, since the latter was unable to exploit the situation. The troops surrounded in Imphal needed every available Dakota, and more. At a conference which was held at General Stilwell's Headquarters on May 1, which was attended by the 14th Army Commander and General Lentaigne, it was arranged that the 3rd Indian Division was to act in future entirely in support of the Chinese Army and would come directly under their command at a later date. The tactics practised in the ensuing period bear little or no relation to the principles laid down by General Wingate for Long Range Penetration operations.

Briefly, the plan now was, first, to evacuate the 16th Brigade which had been operating for more than three months and was exhausted; secondly, to give up all existing strongholds and road blocks; and, lastly, for the 11th Brigade to establish a new block, code name 'Blackpool', between Pinbaw and Hopin in the Mogaung Valley, and nearer to Stilwell's army. The 77th and 14th Brigades were to act as floating brigades to protect this new block from attacks from the east and west.

This plan was contrary to Long Range Penetration principles and in fact never succeeded in blocking communications to any appreciable extent. It annoyed the Japanese, however, and fresh enemy troops were attacking it from the very first day that advance elements of the 11th Brigade started to invest the area; and a swift enemy build-up was subsequently made. Thus, no surprise was achieved and there was no opportunity to fortify and strengthen the perimeter in advance of this build-up. In addition, the monsoon had by now begun in earnest, and night supply was too hazardous. The Japanese quickly realized this, and brought up anti-aircraft guns in addition to the ground artillery already there, which made day supply equally risky. On the last attempt, every aircraft which took part was hit and severely damaged, and only a very small percentage of their supplies fell inside the perimeter. Direct air support from Hailekandi and Lalaghat was impossible under monsoon conditions; and, in any case, No. 1 Air Commando was due for a refit. On May 20 it ceased support of the 3rd Indian Division; and on May 25 'Blackpool', running low on ammunition and supplies, was evacuated after heavy fighting. The evacuation took place at 0550 hours, and all wounded were taken out over the hills and down to Lake Indawgwi where they were evacuated by two Sunderland flying boats. The route was blocked and booby-trapped, and the Japanese did not follow. Without air support or air supply, Long Range Penetration operations could not succeed; and localized blocks on main arteries would have been suicidal under such conditions.

The final operations, carried out by the 14th, 77th and 3rd West African Brigades, culminated in the capture of Mogaung, taken by the 77th Brigade, and the belated linking-up of these brigades with Stilwell's force. A series of land-battles of great ferocity followed, during which three VCs were won. Direct air support continued when weather permitted. This was carried out by American squadrons with whom no training had taken place: its success showed that the methods which had been evolved were foolproof. Many sick and wounded in the area of Lake Indawgwi were rescued by the two available flying-boats, and two separate parties of parachutists were dropped; one to reinforce the 77th Brigade with flame-throwing equipment — which was used at the capture of Mogaung — and the other, consisting of a party from an Airborne Brigade Field Ambulance, RAMC, to organize a field hospital.

The main lesson which emerged from these operations was that Wingate's theories on Long Range Penetration, and his assessment of the probable Japanese reaction to such tactics, had been sound. He had forced the Japanese to attack on ground chosen by himself. Special Force had gnawed a hole in the entrails of three Japanese divisions, and this had weakened them to such an extent that their eventual collapse was assured.

E

Other points were that, if a ground reconnaissance of the target air strip was impossible, it should be undertaken by a parachute reconnaissance party—at the last possible moment, in order not to jeopardize surprise; and the supreme value to morale of light aircraft in direct support for casualty evacuation. In this context, the work of the pilots of No. 1 Air Commando cannot be too highly praised.

A YR4 two-seat helicopter was used with success, and to some extent reduced the importance of glider-snatching. This was the first time that helicopters were used operationally, and the YR4 flew a total of 23 sorties.

It was found that bombers and fighter-bombers, acting in close support, could be readily controlled from the ground by R/T; and employed with great accuracy when comparatively small land forces, i.e. up to two brigades, were involved. RAF officers, equipped with ground to air radio in the forward areas were used to 'talk' the aircraft onto their targets. The methods used were simple and foolproof.

Finally, as a result of Wingate's first operation, the myth, current in India in 1943, that Japanese soldiers were superior to those of the Allies, was exploded once and for all. Brave they certainly were; but they were also exceedingly stupid.

Chapter
5
The Far East
II

A LTHOUGH there were no airborne operations in the Far East
(except Wingate's) on anything approaching the scale of those
in Europe, there were several that varied in size from brigade
groups downwards, some by parachute and others by glider. In addition, there were a number of large-scale air-transported operations,
for South East Asia Command used air transport for strategical
moves of troops and equipment on a far greater scale than did the
armies in Europe.

Of the minor actions, operation 'Dracula', the securing of Elephant
Point is an admirable example of economical and effective use of
airborne forces. Before an amphibious assault could be launched
against Rangoon, the 24 miles of the Rangoon River, which had been
heavily mined by both Japanese and Allied aircraft, had to be cleared.
And before minesweepers or landing craft could begin, the coastal
defences on the west bank, especially those at Elephant Point, had to
be eliminated. They could not be dealt with by gun-fire, because of
the hazards at the river mouth, and the success of a seaborne landing
on the point itself was problematic at that time of year. By far the best
solution was to seize Elephant Point by an airborne operation.

Unfortunately, time was short; and the 50th Indian Parachute
Brigade was in a far from operational condition. The old 152nd
Indian Parachute Battalion had been split to form the new 1st and
4th Indian Parachute Battalions; half of the 2nd Gurkha Parachute
Battalion was on leave; half of the 3rd was just moving to join the 77th
Indian Parachute Brigade, and the other half was also on leave. The
best that could be mustered was an improvized Battalion made up
from the 2nd and 3rd Gurkhas, under the command of Major G. E. C.
Newland. That the result was beyond expectations is clear from the
despatch by Lieutenant-General Sir Oliver Leese, Commander-in-
Chief, Allied Forces South East Asia: 'It was very much to the credit
of the Indian Airborne Division that this was efficiently organized

Indian parachute soldiers in fine fettle after the capture of Elephant Point near Rangoon in May 1945.

and carried out up to time'. There was one other problem — aircraft; but this, too, was solved, by borrowing two American Air Commandos from 4 Corps.

The battalion concentrated at Chaklala, India, where it was expanded to a battalion group and joined by a field ambulance and various detachments of Indian engineers, pathfinders, signals, and an intelligence section. Three air exercises were carried out; and on April 14, 1945, the force moved to Midnapore, where it arrived on April 18. Here it spent ten days, collecting equipment, and carrying out a rehearsal. On April 29, it was flown to Akyab for final briefing, where it was joined by a reserve party 200 strong, drawn from the 1st Indian Parachute Battalion, 2nd Gurkha and 3rd Gurkha Parachute Battalions.

The battalion group was to be carried in 40 aircraft from the 1st and 2nd US Air Commandos; but the crews had never before dropped parachute troops. The crew chiefs were therefore given a short course, and jumpmasters with experience of handling Indian and Gurkha troops were found from the 435 and 436 Squadrons, RCAF. Finally, parachute racks, modified for British containers, had to be fitted to the aircraft.

The force was to be dropped in two lifts five miles due west of Elephant Point. The first, consisting of two aircraft, were to take off 30 minutes before 'H' Hour carrying Pathfinders, Visual Control Posts, Force 136 agents, members of the press and a protective platoon. The second consisted of eight aircraft with the reserves organized as a company group. According to last-minute information it was believed that the Point had been evacuated, so opposition was considered unlikely.

The first lift of two aircraft took off at 0310 hours on May 1, in rain. The flight lasted four hours, and the drop was made on time and in the right place. Intelligence had been right: there was no opposition, and assembly was completed quickly. As a result the first two-and-a-half miles of the advance were covered ahead of schedule, and there was a long wait while the Strategical Air Force bombed targets on Elephant Point. The troops were more than 3,000 yards from the target, yet one company was bombed and machine-gunned by Allied aircraft and suffered over 40 casualties.

The second lift also dropped successfully, at 1530 hours. The fact that there were no container failures in either lift was a triumph for the Air Force armourers, who had put in 48 hours of hard work.

The leading company reached the Point at 1600 hours and was fired on from the north by enemy in a bunker, and by some small ships. Aircraft were called for and the ships were set on fire; but the bunker proved more obstinate, so a company attack was put in with flame throwers, and it, too, was eventually set on fire. At 1600 hours there was a successful pre-arranged supply drop; and at 2000 hours the rain started. It continued remorselessly for the next three days. That night there were abnormally high spring tides, and the whole battalion area was covered with three feet of water.

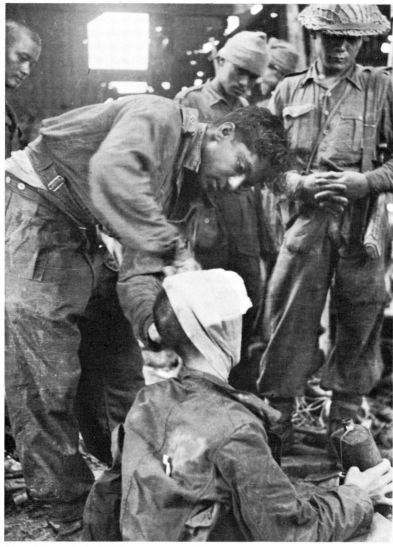

Capt. Rangaraj, the RMO, treats a wounded Japanese prisoner at Elephant Point while Gurkha parachutists look on—May 1945.

The force spent the following day watching the seaborne convoys go past, and searching bunkers and shipwrecks. On May 3, leaving a detachment at Elephant Point, the battalion group moved to Sadhaingmut, half-way up the west bank of the river. The march there, over flooded paddy fields intersected by flooded ditches, in pouring rain, took them eleven hours. Three days later they were moved by sea to Rangoon, where they were engaged on anti-looting patrols; and on May 17 they embarked once more for India.

During their stay in Burma, the battalion had killed 43 Japanese and taken one wounded prisoner. Apart from losses in the bombing incident, their casualties were one British officer killed and one wounded, and two Gurkha other ranks killed, two wounded, and one drowned during the march from Elephant Point to Sadhaingmut.

Chapter
6

Normandy

P REPARATIONS for the invasion of Europe spanned three years
and every continent. Ships at sea, squadrons in North Africa,
battalions in Italy and the Middle East, found themselves
brought home at the appointed time and slotted into the increasingly
complex pattern. Units changed and grew, and new ones were
created as the plans took shape.

On May 18, 1943, a second British airborne division, the 6th, was
formed under the command of Major-General R. N. Gale from the
nucleus of Brigadier S. J. L. Hill's 3rd Parachute Brigade. The three
battalions were soon joined by a Canadian parachute battalion, commanded by Lieutenant-Colonel G. F: P. Bradbrooke; and in its final
form, the 6th Division consisted of the 3rd and 5th Parachute Brigades, and the 6th Air-landing Brigade.* The number '6' was chosen
in order to mislead the enemy: there was, at that time, only one other
British airborne division, the 1st, and Browning, promoted Lieutenant-General, was appointed GOC the two.

To begin with — and not for the first or last time — the 6th Division
were short of aircraft. The 38 Wing RAF, though allocated to support
the new division, were still deeply involved with the 1st in North
Africa; and it was not until January 1944, when both the 38 and 46
Groups, under the operational command of Air Vice-Marshal L. N.
Hollinghurst, were allotted to the role, that aircraft strength became
realistic. In the interim, the 9th US Troop Carrier Command lent
invaluable help with training.

At the same time, glider training was progressing steadily, and by
November, exercises with as many as 40 gliders were being successfully mounted. From January to April, 1944, the 38 Wing (soon
expanded to a Group), in conjunction with the 9th US Troop Carrier
Command, continued joint training. The climax came on April 24
when the entire 6th Division was lifted for an exercise. This, though

* For details, see Appendix A.

'*Horsa and Hamilcar gliders with their Halifax tugs wait to take off for Normandy on 'D' DAY.* (Courtesy Imperial War Museum.)

those taking part were not to know it, was a dress rehearsal for Normandy. 'What you get by stealth and guts', Gale told his officers in a message just before D-Day, 'you must hold with skill and determination'.

The airborne task in the initial stages of the invasion was to protect the flanks of the sea assault by seizing strategic points and communication centres, and so prevent the movement of enemy forces towards the beach-head. The responsibility for this was given to the US 82nd and 101st Airborne Divisions on the right flank dropping near Sainte Mere-Eglise, and to the British 6th on the left, in the area north-east of Caen.

This flank included the double obstacle of the River Orne, and the Caen Canal, and the higher ground that overlooked it further to the

Major-General Gale commanding 6th Airborne Division about to climb into his glider to take off for the Normandy invasion — picture taken at approximately midnight on the night of June 5/6, 1944. (Courtesy Airborne Forces Museum.)

NORMANDY — AIRBORNE OPERATIONS
D DAY 6th JUNE 1944

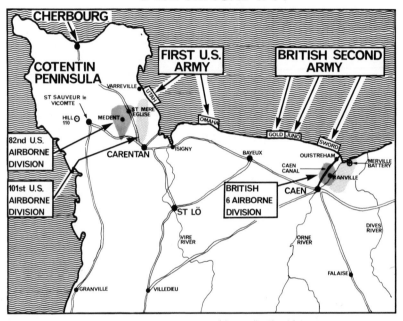

east. The seizure of this dominating ground, and the coastal defence battery at Merville, were vital; from the former the enemy could interfere with the actual landings over the beaches, and with the latter could rake the beaches themselves. Bridges over the canal and river had to be secured since they carried the main coast road by which the enemy could advance against the Allied flank, and, conversely, they would link the Division with the seaborne force. The 1st Special Service Brigade (Commandos) was to come under command of the 6th Division after landing by sea.

The combined aircraft of the 38 and 46 Groups RAF were insufficient to lift the entire division at one time; but as the Germans had erected poles and other obstacles to gliders on all likely landing zones, it was necessary for parachute troops to arrive first and clear selected sites. Consequently, most of the 6th Air-landing Brigade was destined to arrive by the second lift. Certain of the divisional tasks — notably the silencing of the Merville Battery — had to be completed before dawn on June 6, and this and other factors dictated that the first lift be by night. This helped to achieve surprise, and provided some protection, but involved a risk of units being dropped wide or being scattered. The pathfinders were to take with them the Eureka beacons for the aircraft to home on.

Normandy. The 'Pathfinders' set their watches before take off on June 5, 1944 — their tasks; to mark the drop zone for the main body of the parachute force dropping on 'D' DAY in Normandy. They are (L to R) Lieutenants Robert de Latour; Donald Wells; John Vischer; Robert Medwood. Lt. de Latour is thought to be the first Allied soldier to land in France on this day. (Courtesy Imperial War Museum.)

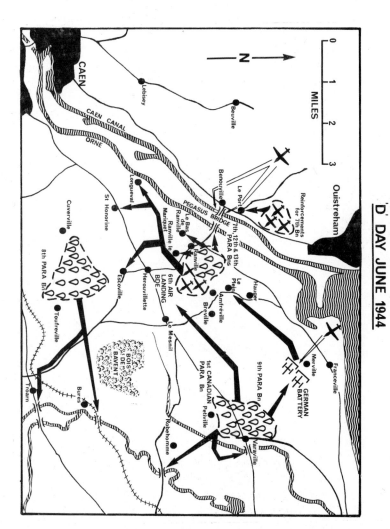

6 AIRBORNE DIVISION
'D' DAY JUNE 1944

The night of June 5–6 was moonless with visibility of only three miles. Clouds scudded across the sky, and the wind at ground level was blowing between 10 and 20 mph. Not ideal conditions, by any means; but by June 5 the decision to proceed with the invasion had been irrevocably made, and the fleets and convoys were converging on the coast of France. Soon after midnight that night, the first parachutes opened above the dark land, as the pathfinders of the 22nd Independent Parachute Company went down to mark the dropping zones; and the gliders of the *coup de main* party whose objectives were the Orne and Caen Canal bridges came swooping out of the night sky. Thirty minutes later, the main bodies of the two Parachute Brigades started their drop, to be followed, during the hours before dawn, by Divisional HQ, and the 4th Anti-Tank Battery of the Royal Artillery in their gliders.

The darkness and the strong breeze blew many of these tidy schemes awry. Troops were dropped over the wrong dropping zones and were scattered like leaves in autumn; yet enough landed as planned, or reached the rendezvous on foot, to carry on. Many a man, as he set off through that hostile countryside to try and find his unit, must have remembered Brigadier Hill's wise and prophetic words before they left: 'Gentlemen, in spite of your excellent training and orders, do not be daunted if chaos reigns. It undoubtedly will'.

Before we follow the fortunes of the main bodies, it will be convenient to describe the two magnificent actions which were the prologue, so to speak, of the 6th Airborne's achievements in Normandy — the capture of the two bridges, and the destruction of the Merville Battery.

The former was the task of the 5th Parachute Brigade. A reinforced company of six platoons drawn from the 2nd Battalion the Oxfordshire and Buckinghamshire Light Infantry ('D' Coy) commanded by Major R. J. Howard, the 6th Air-landing Brigade and a detachment of Royal Engineers, were carried in six gliders, leaving base a little before midnight. Of the six, five landed exactly on time, four with great accuracy right alongside the bridges; one half-a-mile away, and the sixth beside a different bridge over a different river, eight miles away. This was the first British unit to land on French soil.

'*Pegasus' Bridge over the Caen Canal. The* coup de main *gliders can clearly be seen on the far bank. Their proximity to the bridge after being released at 10,000 ft over the Channel to glide in darkness to the target speaks highly for the skill of the Glider Pilots.* (Courtesy Imperial War Museum.)

Surprise was so complete, and the assault was delivered with such speed and precision, that the enemy's defences were overrun after a brief, brisk action. Both bridges were captured intact and a close bridgehead was established on the western bank.

The Orne Bridge. *Taken on 'D' DAY—one of the gliders can be seen close to the bridge. The other is in the extreme right top of the picture.* (Courtesy Imperial War Museum.)

The drop, half-an-hour later, of the 7th Parachute Battalion who were to reinforce them, was scattered; but after a couple of hours nearly half the battalion had reached the bridges, and more men continued to come in throughout the day. On arrival, the battalion assumed responsibility for the position, and enlarged the bridgehead on the western bank to a depth of 800 yards. Enemy counter-measures, consisting of isolated and unco-ordinated attacks by tanks, armoured cars and infantry, began at dawn and continued with increasing intensity all day long. It was while holding these bridges that the 7th Battalion had a 'naval battle' with two German coastal craft, which had retired from Ouistreham, and were on their way up the canal to Caen. The first inkling they had that the bridges had changed hands was when they were fired upon; one promptly ran aground, and the other fled. During the day the Germans made an unsuccessful air attack; one 1,000 lb bomb actually hit the canal bridge, but bounced off without exploding.

That evening, after beating off all attacks, the force was relieved by the 3rd British Infantry Division, commanded by Major-General T. G. Rennie, which had landed on the beaches that morning, and had rushed to support the Airborne Brigade and make sure the bridge remained in the proper hands.

Meanwhile, the 9th Battalion, Parachute Regiment (3rd Parachute Brigade) under Lieutenant-Colonel Otway, were engaged in the difficult and delicate task of dealing with the Merville Battery at Franceville Plage. This battery was sited in such a way that it directly menaced the beaches on which the 3rd British Infantry Division was to land, from the flank, and could sweep the whole length of them. It was thought to consist of four 150 mm guns, established in concrete emplacements 12 feet high and 5 feet deep, with concrete walls 6 feet 6 inches thick, and the roof covered with 13 feet of earth. All doors for access were of steel and the battery was protected by 20 mm dual-purpose guns and machine-guns. The position, some 400 yards square, was surrounded by a cattle fence, enclosing a minefield 100 yards in depth and bordered on its inner side by a barbed wire fence 15 feet thick and 5 feet high. To the seaward side was an anti-tank ditch 15 feet wide and 10 feet deep. Additional minefields had been

The Merville Battery. An air photograph showing the battery under construction. The incomplete casements show the concrete housing clearly. On the left, the dark line of the excavation for the anti tank ditch to protect the front of the battery can be seen. (Courtesy Imperial War Museum.)

laid on all open approaches to the battery with machine-guns sited to cover them. These defences were manned by between 180 and 200 men. This virtually impregnable fortress had to be silenced 30 minutes before the first assault vessel came within its range.

The planning and preliminary training had been meticulous in detail and painstaking in execution. An area similar to Merville was found near Newbury, permission to use it was obtained from seven different Ministries in 48 hours — which must be a record of some kind — and it was sealed off. Bulldozers and excavators worked night and day to prepare the landscape and a complete full-scale model was constructed from air photographs and maps. On this, the 35 officers

THE ATTACK ON THE MERVILLE BTY

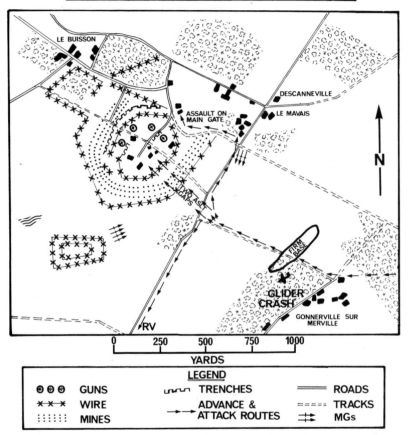

and 600 soldiers of the 9th Battalion practised continuously for several weeks, till they knew their own tasks precisely. Five day and four night rehearsals were held with live ammunition to give an exact idea of conditions and enemy strength. These were followed by a final and special briefing lasting five days, after which each man was required to produce a sketch from memory of the part he was to play. Security measures were tight; and to test them, a number of attractive and specially trained young women were employed to try and extract information from the troops by means which have not been disclosed. Despite the fact that Brigadier Hill had deliberately given the plan to all the officers and men, withholding only the actual place and time of the attack, they learnt nothing.

The plan was for two special parties to be dropped in advance, one to organize the rendezvous, the other to reconnoitre the battery. A third party, under the Second-in-Command, was to establish a firm base, while others would snipe the defenders and create a diversion against any other German troops in the neighbourhood. The main body of the battalion, with a Royal Engineer party, would form the breaching and assault forces. Among the special equipment carried in five gliders, were anti-tank guns, jeeps, scaling ladders for crossing the anti-tank ditch, and explosives. Three gaps were to be blown in the defences by demolition parties, whereupon the battalion would enter, kill or capture the enemy defenders, and destroy the guns. Three gliders manned by volunteers were to land, not near, but on top of the battery. The pilots would crash land on the positions, dis-

Having unloaded their crashed glider on 'D' DAY men of the 6th Airborne Division race off to their objectives in Normandy. (Courtesy Imperial War Museum.)

gorging three officers and 47 soldiers among the defenders as the main assault from the ground was mounted. Ten minutes before the battalion arrived a hundred Lancaster bombers were to bomb the battery. So much for the well-laid plans of men. Things turned out rather differently on the night.

The fly-in was uneventful, except that the aircraft ran into moderate flak over the French coast. But, again, the wind took a hand, and the 46 Group's Dakotas dropped the troops over a very wide area, some many miles away, when their navigators mistook the River Dives for the River Orne. The CO and his batman, for example, landed on a German HQ, but managed to avoid capture, and later rejoined the battalion. The battalion report puts the situation succinctly:

'By 0250 hours the battalion had grown to 150 strong with twenty lengths of Bangalore Torpedo.* Each company was approximately 30 strong. Enough signals to carry on — no three inch mortars — one machine-gun — one half of one sniping party — no six-pounder guns — no jeeps or trailers or any glider stores — no sappers — no field ambulance but six medical orderlies — no mine detectors — one company commander missing. *The Commanding Officer decided to advance immediately.*'

Almost at once they were attacked by a herd of cows, maddened by the aerial bombardment from the Lancasters, which had completely missed the battery but almost annihilated the reconnaissance parties. However, the latter had cut gaps in the outer fence, penetrated the minefield and fixed the exact location of sentries and posts. The white tape to mark the gaps was missing but the lanes were marked by heel scuffs in the dust.

No sooner had they reached their base position than the battalion came under fire from artillery and six machine-guns. The battalion's solitary machine-gunner was despatched to deal with the MGs, and silenced three of them; the other three were dealt with by the main

---

* A pole charge designed by a Royal Engineer officer in Bangalore, India, whose purpose is to blow a gap in enemy minefields and wire entanglements. The 'Torpedo' is a hollow metal pole, 6 ft long, 2 ins in diameter, filled with high explosive. Any number, to give the required length, can be joined together to push across the ground. When detonated it blows a 'safe' lane 2 ft 6 ins wide exploding the mines beneath and cutting the wire above the lane. An assault party may then advance through the gap.

gate diversion party. As the battalion moved into the outer defences two of the gliders which were meant to crash land on top of the battery appeared overhead — the third failed to arrive, having broken its tow-rope on the way across; but as there were no mortars, the signal flares could not be fired, and there was no way of contacting them. One, mistaking the village for the battery, landed half-a-mile away; the second crashed into an orchard 50 yards from the perimeter. This was lucky, for as the troops left the glider they encountered a German platoon hurrying to reinforce the battery and stopped them dead. They continued to hold the orchard for four hours, and prevented reinforcements getting through.

The depleted battalion now hurled itself upon the fortress regardless of the consequences. Two gaps were blown in the wire with the Bangalore Torpedos, and the attackers streamed through. The German gunners resisted stoutly enough; but then they emerged from their bunkers to attack their attackers, not realizing that they had elected to fight at close quarters men specifically and thoroughly trained for just such work. They offered a stout resistance, 20 finally surrendering the rest having been killed or wounded. The guns — 75, not 150 mm, as it turned out — were spiked with Gammon bombs*.

Exactly half-an-hour before HMS *Arethusa* was due to begin her bombardment — the insurance against failure — the signal for success was fired; and if it had cost the battalion five officers and 65 soldiers killed or wounded, there is no computing how many lives it saved among the troops who, at that very moment, were heading shoreward.

The battalion was now reduced to a mere 80; but their night's work had only begun. They moved off at once to secure their second objective, the high ground near Le Plein. Warned by a Frenchman that the village of Hauger was held by the enemy, they attacked immediately. However, they were faced with 200 determined men in a fortified

---

* Gammon bomb — designed by Captain R. J. Gammon, MC, (original 1st Parachute Battalion) to provide a ready-made explosive charge light and easy to handle. Plastic explosive was placed in an elasticated stockinette bag which contained a detonator mechanism in a screw cap at the neck. The explosive, being malleable, was easily 'squashed' into a pocket or pouch, and the amount could be varied to suit the task. It could be used as a demolition, to destroy vehicles or as a concussion anti-personnel grenade, and was a favourite weapon of the early airborne soldiers.

chateau — not, in fact, Germans, but pressed Russians who had been told that the British would shoot them — and were unable to capture it. Instead, they had to content themselves with investing it until they were reinforced in the afternoon by the 1st Special Service Brigade.

While these two separate and brilliant actions were in train, the bulk of the 3rd and 5th Brigades had crossed the coast and joined their comrades upon the continent of Europe.

The 3rd landed all over the place, Brigadier Hill and several sticks of Canadians being dropped near the River Dives, and Hill himself and many others being wounded before they reached their objectives. Despite these misfortunes, the 1st Canadian Battalion succeeded in blowing up the bridges at Varaville and Robehomme in the face of a surprised enemy, and took up their defensive positions in the Le Mesnil area. The 8th Battalion, also widely scattered, assembled and set off to destroy two bridges at Bures and one east of Troarn. Its sapper detachments, wrongly dropped on the 5th Brigade's DZ, sensibly made straight for the bridges, and met up with the battalion on the way. The Bures bridges were destroyed; but at Troarn fierce opposition was encountered. However, the sapper detachment, mounted on a jeep, rushed through the battle, the town and a road-block, reached the bridge, and demolished it. The 8th Battalion then moved north and consolidated its bridgehead.

Gliders and parachutes litter the British drop zones in Normandy on 'D' DAY. The fuse-lages of the gliders are not broken but have been 'blown' off by a special ring charge operated by the passengers inside to facilitate easy unloading. (Courtesy Imperial War Museum.)

Gliders landing in Normandy on 'D' DAY in the American sector. The Dakota tugs can clearly be seen 'peeling' off having released their gliders to land in the fields below. (Courtesy Imperial War Museum.)

A similar dispersal afflicted the 5th Brigade, and the 12th and 13th Battalions succeeded in mustering only two-thirds of their strength; but they seized the area round Benouville, Ranville and Le Bas de Ranville and held it against powerful and repeated counter-attacks. Fortunately, at a critical moment, they were reinforced by a Commando force from the 1st Special Service Brigade, under Brigadier The Lord Lovat, which came marching up with pipes playing.

During the evening of D-Day, as planned, the main body of the 6th Air-landing Brigade arrived on the DZ cleared by the 5th Brigade's sappers, and linked up with those who had landed during the first lift. They, together with the Commandos, made the bridgehead secure.

Recounted like this, it all sounds neat and tidy and according to plan. In fact, of course, it was far different. The Division suffered 800 casualties in the first 48 hours; and, because the drops were widely scattered, 1,000 men and more found themselves separated from their units and adrift in a hostile land. This was the moment when the Airborne practice of detailed individual briefing for every single officer and man paid a handsome dividend. Combined with the trained habit of instant initiative — 'the parachutist' wrote one, 'fights a lonely battle . . . he has no real front or rear, and gets the feeling he is fighting the war all by himself' — it ensured that every isolated man or group of men knew where to make for, and was ready and eager to take on as many Germans as possible on the way. 'By stealth and guts' a good many Germans were kept usefully diverted during those important few days; while the strays struggled through river and marsh to rejoin their units. Theirs is all part of the saga of the 6th Airborne's invasion, a footnote, like the little drawings along the bottom of the Bayeux tapestry.

More important, in spite of all the difficulties caused by the scattered drop, the operations were a complete success; indeed, the widely-spread landings confused the enemy and made it difficult for him to identify their real objectives and react accordingly. It had been hoped to relieve the 6th Airborne Division once the beach-head was firm, but for various reasons this was impossible. The Division was therefore committed to a defensive role against heavy and mounting

American air-landing troops deplane from a British Horsa glider in Normandy. Throughout the war British and American parachute forces freely interchanged ideas and equipment — a close liaison forged in battle has continued since the War. (Courtesy Imperial War Museum.)

pressure, culminating in the battle for Breville; and there were none too many of them for the scale of counter-attack they had to meet.

The enemy had managed to hold on to this village, situated between the 3rd Parachute Brigade and the 1st Special Service Brigade, overlooking the Ranville area. A successful enemy attack through this gap would split the Division in half and threaten the beaches. The Germans attempted this with increasing intensity between June 8 and 12, and over and over again the situation had to be restored with local counter-attacks by the airborne units. By the 12th, the position was critical; the 3rd Parachute Brigade was severely depleted and reserves were minimal. It was obvious that Breville must be captured and held if the bridgehead was to remain secure.

American parachute soldiers in St. Mere Eglise on 'D' DAY. This village was the scene of a tragic error when some of the aircraft dropping the US 82nd Division during the night of June 5/6 overshot the DZ. As a result the troops were dropped into the heavily defended village square. St. Mere Eglise is now a place of pilgrimage for the US parachute veterans of 'D' DAY and possesses a museum devoted to the fierce battles fought in and around it. (Courtesy Imperial War Museum.)

General Gale decided on a calculated risk: at the end of a hard day's fighting, the Division would attack once more, and hope to catch the Germans unprepared. And so, at 2230 hours on June 12, the 12th Battalion the Parachute Regiment, now very weak, and the only divisional reserve, with one company of the 12th Devons, one squadron of tanks and the 22nd Independent Parachute Company — the Pathfinders — flung themselves into a last desperate assault. Though they lost their Commanding Officer and 133 all ranks in the process, they routed the enemy and finally cleared the town.

This battle was the deciding factor on this front, and henceforth enemy attacks posed no serious threat. For the next two months, the Division continued to hold the left flank, consolidating their positions, and engaging in minor attacks and aggressive patrolling. This static warfare, though much against the grain of troops trained to the offensive, and bad in principle, since they were masters of certain valuable special skills, was vital for the protection of the Allied build-up for the final break-out, and therefore unavoidable. The same thing had happened in North Africa, and would happen again during the coming winter; for the parachutist is, first and foremost, a superlative fighting-man.

On August 17, orders for a general advance were received, and the Division, with the Royal Netherlands Brigade 'Princess Irene' and the Belgian Brigade under command, were given the task of maintaining pressure on the enemy right flank along the coast, and of securing the crossings at the mouth of the Seine. The Division was not expected to do more than follow up a withdrawing enemy, as there were not enough vehicles to make it mobile. General Gale, however, had other ideas. Moving his brigades in a series of leap-frogs, and commandeering all available transport, he pushed ahead so rapidly, and maintained such pressure, that the enemy were never given time to rest or recoup and their withdrawal became a retreat. Attacks were delivered by day and night unceasingly, and the troops, tired as they were, responded magnificently. By August 26 they had advanced fighting, largely on foot, 45 miles in nine days, had taken over 1,000 prisoners, liberated 400 square miles of France and driven the enemy across the Seine.

Lieutenant-General Crerar, Commander-in-Chief, 1st Canadian Army, showed no doubt whatever of the value he put on the Division's role at this time, in a signal to the Corps Commander:

'Desire you inform Gale of my appreciation of immense contribution 6 Airborne Division and Allied contingents under command have made during the recent fighting advance. The determination and speed with which his troops have pressed on in spite of all enemy efforts to the contrary have been impressive and of greatest assistance to the Army as a whole.'

It was a fitting summary of the 6th Airborne's share in the invasion.

Chapter
7

The South of France : Greece

WHILE the main invasion of Europe took place on the beaches of Normandy, a secondary assault, two months later, was launched on Southern France, between Frejus and St Raphael. Its purpose was to advance rapidly up the Rhône Valley and take the enemy in the rear, and it coincided almost exactly with the start of the break-out from Normandy. Like that other, greater operation, it consisted of a combined sea and airborne attack: it is with the latter, and specifically with the activities of the British 2nd Independent Parachute Brigade Group, that we are concerned here. The Brigade formed, with five US parachute battalions and one US air-landing brigade—for this was largely an American show—1st Airborne Task Force, which was commanded by Major-General R. T. Frederick, US Army.

The task of the British brigade was to seize the area between La Motte and Le Muy, destroy the enemy there, and prevent him reaching the coast. The flight, from five airfields near Rome, was in the hands of the 51 US Troop Carrier Wing for the parachute drop, with 61 Hadrian and Horsa gliders for the guns to follow. Because the land behind the coast is hilly and steep, and the DZs therefore difficult and rough, parachute troops were to be dropped and gliders released exceptionally high, at 1,500–2,000 feet.

D-Day was August 15, 1944. By 0323 hours the pathfinders, 1st Independent Parachute Platoon, had landed unopposed and set up the Eureka wireless beacon to guide in the main force, which was due an hour-and-a-half later. Unfortunately, before they arrived, cloud and mist closed in and reduced visibility to less than half a mile, and their troubles began. The beacons were not entirely reliable, nor was the equipment in the aircraft—the crew chief in the leading machine which was to give the dropping signal, spent most of the flight trying to mend the electrics with a screwdriver—and of the 125 aircraft involved, only 73 dropped their troops accurately. The remaining 52

Landing in the South of France. This aerial view of the landing zones shows the difficult nature of the drop amongst the hills and valleys of the area. Gliders can be seen scattered about on the fields. (Courtesy Imperial War Museum.)

strayed as far as Cannes and Fayence, 20 miles or more away. All pilots had been ordered not to return with troops on board, and they did as they were told. Luckily there was little opposition.

On assembly, Brigade HQ was found to be complete, but the 4th, 5th and 6th Parachute Battalions were all at half strength or less. But the initial objectives were quickly secured, and one of the two small enemy garrisons surrendered to the 6th (Royal Welch) Battalion. The next task was to clear the glider landing zones of obstacles; and at 0920 hours the 64th Light Battery RA, in Hadrians, landed safely. The Horsas, with the 300th Air-landing Anti-Tank Battery RA, were forced back to Rome by the bad visibility but returned to land successfully later in the day.

By 1015 hours the brigade had accomplished all its first tasks, and was in radio contact with the seaborne force. The only fighting had resulted in the 4th Battalion killing 16 and capturing 29 Germans for a loss to themselves of seven killed and nine wounded. Many of the

The drop in gale force winds at Megara, Greece, October 1944. (Courtesy Imperial War Museum.)

troops who had been dropped wide rejoined during the day, fighting several small actions en route. There was no sign of a major enemy counter-attack; and by nightfall they were firmly established across all three of the main roads he might have used.

And that was that. Apart from one or two minor actions, the brigade's work in southern France was over; on the 17th they linked up with the seaborne force, which passed through three days later. On the 26th the brigade returned to Italy to prepare for further operations in the Eastern Mediterranean.

The triumphal entry, on commandeered transport, of 2nd Parachute Brigade into Athens in October 1944. This joyful welcome was soon marred by the outbreak of fighting between rival political factions. (Courtesy Imperial War Museum.)

By August, 1944, the Allied offensive on German-occupied Europe was gathering momentum, and under pressure from east and west, German forces began to contract and concentrate in central Europe. The Russian drive in the Balkans would, at any moment, force them to evacuate Greece; and the Allies were well aware that the Communists were waiting to fill the vacuum which they would leave behind. It was, therefore, desirable to establish a regime in Athens which would be favourable to Western Europe.

The 2nd Independent Parachute Brigade Group, having completed its task in southern France, returned to the airborne base near Rome and prepared for operations in Greece. On September 8 the brigade moved to a camp near San Pancrazio, 20 miles east of Taranto. The Germans finally evacuated Athens in October, and at midday on the 12th one company group of the 4th Battalion dropped on Megara airfield. A wind of 20 mph is normally considered the maximum for safe jumping. At Megara that day it was blowing a gale, and half the force was injured on landing; but the risk had been assessed in relation to the urgency, and the rest quickly took the airfield. Two days later the remainder of the brigade followed. The Germans had blown up the road to Athens, but every form of local transport was commandeered, and the brigade entered the city on October 15. There they were joined later by the 23rd Armoured Brigade.

For the next three months the brigade was busy, following up retreating Germans, establishing and maintaining law and order, and helping the Greeks to reorganize their country. Their activities ranged from Thrace to Salonika and the Bulgarian border. But the most important task was in Athens itself, where continuous riots and battles flared up between the rival Greek political parties. At the end of November the brigade was joined by the 4th Indian Division, and throughout December, British troops were involved in serious warfare against the Greek rebels. These wore no uniform, and were not afflicted with the scruples of ordinary men: one of their less endearing practices was to advance driving a screen of women and children before them. To add to the difficulties, 20,000 Greek civilians had at one period to be fed daily. During the final battle in Athens, 240 rebels were either killed or wounded and another 520 taken prisoner. They were finally driven out of the city in early January, 1945.

This thankless and bloody business cost the 5th Battalion more than a hundred casualties, and the 6th all its Company Commanders killed or wounded, and was all the more disheartening for being widely misunderstood by both press and public opinion at home. The Russians were still our allies; and the true nature of international communism, with its blatant imperialism, was not generally

Men of the 6th (Royal Welch) Parachute Battalion, supported by tanks, attack E.L.A.S. strong points in Evripidou Street, Athens. This picture clearly reveals the ferocity of the bitter fighting in the city at this time. (Courtesy Imperial War Museum.)

British parachutists on duty in the streets of Athens await the next outburst of firing. (Courtesy Imperial War Museum.)

Sir Walter Citrine heading a Trades Union Delegation interviews men of the 2nd Parachute Brigade about conditions in Athens at the height of the troubles, January, 1945. (Courtesy Imperial War Museum.)

appreciated. But the British soldiers in Greece, confronted daily with the atrocities perpetrated by the communists against their own countrymen, had all the evidence they needed.

So acute was the discrepancy that a Trades Union Congress delegation, led by Sir Walter Citrine, visited Athens to investigate. They interviewed no less than 400 soldiers; and as a result, on their return to England, 'made a very bold press announcement, upholding all that the brigade had done and was doing in Greece', and the criticism ceased. Athens is a battle honour borne upon the Parachute Regiment's Colours.

By January 1945, the brigade's work was done; they were relieved by other units, and in February they returned to Italy. Here they spent an intensive period of training and planning for airborne operations which, in the event, did not materialize. Between March 6 and May 4, 1945, no fewer than 32 were initiated and then cancelled. With the surrender of all the remaining German forces in Italy in May, the brigade was no longer needed in the Mediterranean, and in June it returned to England.

Chapter
8

Arnhem

'There has been no single performance by any unit that has more greatly inspired me or more excited my admiration than the nine-day action by the 1st British Parachute Division between 17th and 25th September.'

Dwight Eisenhower, General US Army
Allied Commander Europe

IN August 1944, General Montgomery proposed an Allied offensive based on one powerful thrust through Holland and across the Rhine, to isolate and occupy the Ruhr, thus depriving Germany of more than half her industrial potential. The plan required many divisions and virtually all the logistic support available to the Allies in Europe. Partly because he did not wish to halt all the other Armies, which were going well, particularly in the south, partly because he regarded such an advance as risky, Eisenhower rejected the proposal. But he did agree to a modified scheme, whereby the 21st Army Group would attempt the narrow thrust to and beyond the Rhine, largely supported from its own resources.

The plan was to lay an 'airborne carpet' along the Eindhoven–Arnhem road, across which the British 2nd Army could advance quickly to and beyond the Rhine, the last great natural barrier to the Reich, and turn the Siegfried Line. The essential task of the airborne operation was to seize intact the bridges over the canals and rivers en route, notably those at Grave, over the River Maas, the crossing of the Maas–Waal Canal, the great steel bridge over the Waal at Nijmegen and the road bridge over the Rhine at Arnhem.

Three airborne divisions—the US 82nd and 101st and the British 1st, together forming the 1st Airborne Corps of the newly formed 1st Allied Airborne Army under Lieutenant-General Lewis H. Brereton, USAAF—were assigned to the operation. Dropping simultaneously, the Americans were to open the corridor from Eindhoven

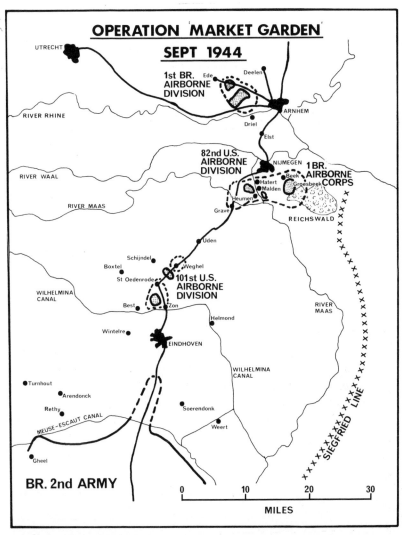

OPERATION 'MARKET GARDEN'

SEPT 1944

to Nijmegen and the British to seize the bridge at Arnhem. The Airborne Corps was to operate for 48 hours unsupported, though the 2nd Army was expected to link up by the end of that time. Such was the plan.

Dutch villagers of Valkenswaad near Eindhoven watch the 1st Division on their way to Arnhem. (Courtesy Imperial War Museum.)

An airborne action relies for success on the element of surprise, enabling the lightly-armed soldiers to seize their objectives before the defenders can bring superior forces and fire-power to bear. This limitation puts them at an overwhelming disadvantage if the enemy can quickly bring against them self-propelled guns and tanks. Three factors combined to deprive the 1st Airborne Division of this advantage in the battle of Arnhem.

First, and, as it proved, most critical, there were insufficient aircraft available to lift the whole division on the first day. Only the 1st Parachute Brigade, 1st Air-landing Brigade, plus Divisional HQ and some supporting arms, could be carried in the initial lift. The 4th Parachute Brigade and 1st Polish Parachute Brigade, the latter under the command of the 1st Division for the operation, would drop on D + 1 and D + 2 respectively. Thus only half the division could benefit from surprise at all, and of this, most of the Air-landing Brigade was detailed to protect the dropping zones for the subsequent lifts. So far as the battle for the bridge was concerned, only the 1st Parachute Brigade was available on the first day.

Secondly, the open areas south and south-east of the bridge were waterlogged and crossed by eight foot-wide irrigation ditches. These made them unsuitable for massed glider landings and less than ideal for parachuting. Furthermore, anti-aircraft defences in the area of Arnhem were believed to be strong. Major-GeneralUrquhart, GOC 1st Airborne Division, finally selected dropping and landing zones to the west, the furthest eight miles away.

Thirdly, Allied intelligence was misleading. Although the division was warned that counter-attacks by Germans at Brigade strength, supported by tanks and self-propelled guns, were possible, it was not known that the 9th and 10th Divisions of the 2nd SS Panzer Corps were refitting east and north-east of Arnhem: or, more accurately, information to this effect reached the 2nd Army HQ from the Dutch Resistance, but was discounted. As a result, instead of being faced with a brigade group, the 1st Airborne Division was to be met by a Panzer Corps.

The plan assumed that the Airborne Reconnaissance Squadron, followed by the 1st Parachute Brigade, would reach the bridge

The landings at Arnhem. This excellent action shot shows parachutists in the air as others land amongst the gliders, while overhead the Dakotas start their turn for home. (Courtesy Imperial War Museum.)

quickly. The remainder of the division were to take up blocking positions on the approaches the next day, and the Poles to relieve the 1st Brigade on D+2, to create a reserve. In view of the scale of the opposition which actually materialized, this plan could work only if everything went smoothly — which, after a deceptively propitious start, it did not.

The first lift arrived on time on September 17, there was little flak, and a very high percentage of the parachute and glider troops reached their RVs as planned.* But amongst the 38 gliders (out of 320) that

---

* With them went no fewer than 15 Army Chaplains, of whom two were killed, ten taken prisoner, and three crossed the river during the final withdrawal. An account of their work and adventures is given in Chapter IX.

Gliders at Arnhem. The landing tracks of the gliders can be clearly seen, as can the vehicle tracks from the Hamilcar glider in the centre to the woods at the top. (Courtesy Imperial War Museum.)

failed to arrive were some of the armoured jeeps of the Reconnaissance Squadron. The weather, too, important for the timely arrival of later lifts for re-supply, and for fighter-bomber support, clamped down. In the light of what has been said above regarding the extended lift, the irony of this needs no emphasis. Nevertheless, provided that the 2nd Army could keep to their planned timetable, success was still possible.

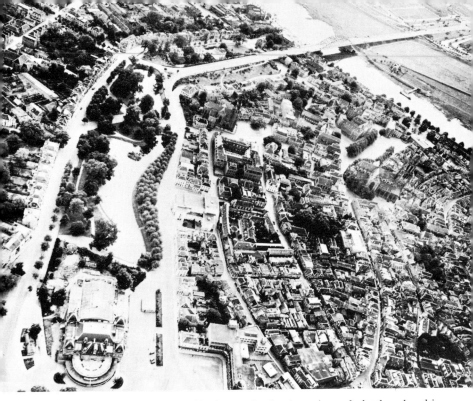

Arnhem—the town and bridge. Air photograph taken just prior to the battle and used in planning the attack. (Courtesy Imperial War Museum.)

The 1st Brigade set off on foot for the objective. The 2nd Battalion, under the command of Lieutenant-Colonel J. D. Frost, the veteran of Bruneval, the retreat from Oudna, and Sicily, advanced to Heelsum and then on by the southern road running close to the north bank of the river. At the same time, the 3rd Battalion advanced on the main Heelsum–Arnhem road to approach the bridge from the north. The 1st Battalion initially remained with Brigade HQ, in reserve.

In Heelsum, the 2nd Battalion ambushed some German vehicles and took 20 prisoners. Members of the Dutch Resistance passed information that there were few Germans in Arnhem itself, and the battalion pressed on towards the bridge, which was still six miles away. They arrived at the railway bridge too late to prevent its destruction, met and overcame opposition in Doorwerthsche Wood, but were held up by enemy occupying the high wooded ground called Den Brink. 'B' Company was sent to capture it while Frost with 'A' Company hurried on into the town in the fading dusk, killing or capturing small scattered parties of enemy on the way.

Between 2030 and 2100 hours, they reached the road bridge: it was still intact. Swiftly and silently they secured the northern end; and Frost ordered Lieutenant J. H. Grayburn to lead his platoon across. The Germans were solidly established, with an armoured car's machine guns and two 20 mms firing straight along the bridge. There was no cover, and Grayburn was hit almost at once; yet he pressed on until ordered to retire, and thus initiated 48 hours of resourceful leadership and unassailable courage that led, eventually, to his death and the award of the VC—one of five won during the next nine days at Arnhem. In an attempt to cross lower down and so outflank the Germans, Frost sent a platoon to the pontoon bridge, but it too had gone, and there were no barges.

That night, therefore, the road bridge was still in one piece but far from secure. All Frost could do was commandeer and fortify the nearby houses at the northern end, and try and gather in the missing members of his battalion. By morning his force had grown to between 300 and 400 men.

Meanwhile, the 3rd Battalion had run into infantry, supported by armoured cars, at a road junction west of Oosterbeek. The armoured cars were eventually destroyed by PIAT* fire; but the infantry continued to hold them up. 'C' Company, ordered to find an alternative route to the bridge, became split up, the platoons fighting individual actions until, much reduced in numbers, they met at the railway station in Arnhem. After another skirmish in the town, what was left of the company finally reached the bridge and joined the 2nd Battalion. The rest of the 3rd Battalion advanced from the crossroads before dawn on the 18th, and fought their way to the railway station. Here they were halted by concentrated fire from 88 mm guns. Throughout the day they continued to battle against increasing enemy pressure from infantry, supported by self-propelled guns and intense mortar fire, and suffered heavy casualties. A final attempt to continue at 1600 hours made no progress; and the battalion, now split into two groups, found itself surrounded. At dawn on the 19th all that were left reached the river bank and seized a large house called

* Projector Infantry Anti-tank. The rifleman's anti-tank weapon firing an HE Bomb effective against armoured vehicles up to a range of about 120 yards.

A German tank in action against the parachute soldiers amongst the shattered buildings of Arnhem (German official photograph). (Courtesy Imperial War Museum.)

the Pavilion; but could advance no further. Here they were joined eventually by the remnants of the 1st Battalion.

The 1st Battalion had enjoyed no better fortune. Advancing along the railway, they were soon engaged in confused and desperate fighting with an enemy, reinforced with tanks and armoured half-tracks, who had moved in behind the other two battalions. Fierce and sporadic clashes continued throughout the night of September 17–18, and the battalion's casualties were heavy. It was impossible to make headway. At dawn on the 18th, the battalion attempted to disengage and bypass the enemy to the south, moving through back gardens and houses and continuously sniped at. The battalion history notes that the enemy defences had been thoroughly prepared, and there were few gaps in the fire plan.

Men of the 1st Battalion use a shell hole for cover at Arnhem. (Courtesy Imperial War Museum.)

Attacks and counter-attacks continued throughout the day; and that evening, after 24 hours fighting, while Frost and the 2nd Battalion were desperately clinging on to the northern end of the bridge and praying for the arrival either of reinforcements from the 1st and 3rd, or of XXX Corps from the south, the 1st Battalion had been brought to a standstill in the north-western suburbs, and the 3rd was similarly held up near the St Elizabeth Hospital. From here they established radio contact with the 2nd Battalion at the bridge who were calling urgently for reinforcement. But the 1st Battalion, reduced by this time to barely 100 men, could do no more.

The Bridge at Arnhem at 5 pm on the second day. This photograph was taken as the battle raged below—the knocked out enemy vehicles can clearly be seen as can the buildings on either side of the road at this point—the scene of the epic stand of the 2nd Battalion. (Courtesy Imperial War Museum.)

General Urquhart himself became embroiled in the confused and bitter fighting. When visiting his units after landing on the 17th, he found Brigadier Lathbury with the 3rd Battalion. Together they were forced to remain with the battalion; and when they were eventually able to proceed, they were immediately involved in fighting the enemy at close quarters. Lathbury was wounded, and General Urquhart personally despatched one enemy soldier with his pistol. 'It is seldom in modern war that the commander of a division has an opportunity to fight the enemy at such close quarters', Urquhart wrote; and the author of *Red Beret* comments: 'But this division was airborne, and every man in it, from its commander to the most junior private, was trained to arms and expected to use them at any moment'. One remembers the exploits of the glider full of staff officers at large in Sicily.

At the bridge at dawn on the 18th, Colonel Frost found himself in command of a mixed force that had grown to some 600–700 men, with a few six-pounder anti-tank guns. At 1130 hours the bridge was rushed from the south by five armoured cars and six half-tracks. The armoured cars were knocked out by the six-pounders; the half-tracks by the Sappers from a building overlooking the bridge, and their crews killed. 'When we dealt with them', Frost wrote, 'they smoked and burned in front of us almost to the end of the battle'; and they effectively blocked the bridge to further traffic.

That morning the second lift was due. Owing to fog in England, it did not take off until after midday; and although this drop was as near-perfect as the first, these battalions, too, were soon in trouble, pinned down here and there in their attempts to reach the bridge, for the Germans had effectively sealed off the centre of Arnhem. The 10th Battalion ran into guns and tanks on the Utrecht road and had to dig in; and it was here that Captain L. E. Queripel of the 10th Battalion distinguished himself repeatedly through a long and fire-swept day. Wounded in the face and both arms, he was last seen covering the withdrawal of his men with the handful of grenades they had left. He also won a posthumous VC.

By the second day, therefore, all the forces that had dropped to reinforce Frost and his men at the bridge were themselves on the defensive; and the day's ill fortune was still incomplete. The re-supply drop that afternoon went astray and fell, complete, into enemy hands; and the arrival of the Polish Parachute Brigade by glider provoked a furious German retaliation, which fell most severely on the 4th Parachute Brigade, who found themselves marooned in the suburbs of Oosterbeek. It was at this point that General Urquhart was forced to admit that nothing they could do would enable his forces to reach the bridge, and he formed a defensive perimeter where he was, in the hope that the 2nd Army would arrive before it was too late. During this contraction, the three battalions, the 10th, 11th and 156th, were all virtually wiped out. In this sector on the following day, the 20th, the third VC of the battle was won, by Lance/Sergeant J. D. Baskeyfield who, first with his section and later single-handed, accounted for two tanks and two self-propelled guns. He, too, was

6 pounder anti-tank gun in action at Arnhem. This gun was actually firing at a German self-propelled gun only some 75 yards away as this photo was taken. (Courtesy Imperial War Museum.)

killed. Arnhem was like that. By sheer guts and fighting ability, the men of the 1st Airborne Division maintained a moral superiority over the enemy to the last, exemplified by Grayburn, Queripel, Baskeyfield, and, not least, by Major R. H. Cain of the 2nd Battalion, South Staffordshire Regiment, who stopped tanks, self-propelled guns, flame-throwers and infantry alike with PIAT-fire and finally with a 2-inch mortar. Unlike the others, however, he lived to tell the tale.

Meanwhile, at the bridge, mortar and shell fire continued all through the 18th, and steadily demolished the buildings in which the force was holding out. On the evening of the 18th, although a further attack was beaten off, and the enemy lost two tanks and many troops, four of the defenders' houses were set alight and had to be evacuated. At sunset, a spirited bayonet charge, accompanied by the battle cry of 'Whoa Mohammed!'* dispersed more German infantry who were forming up for yet another attack.

Sporadic fighting continued during that night, though, in a lull some time after midnight, Frost was able to sleep briefly for the first time in two days. All next day heavy shelling and mortar fire continued, interspersed with attacks by tanks firing into the houses, and infantry assaults. But in spite of mounting casualties, and a growing shortage of ammunition, the defenders held on, sustained a little by rumours that relief was on the way. By midnight on the 19th, the key house commanding the northern end of the bridge had been burned down and the force, now dangerously weakened, were under constant small-arms fire.

September 20 brought no relief; yet, hounded from house to house, they were still able to deny the Germans the bridge—or even the satisfaction of blowing it up. Grayburn saw to that. Colonel Frost was badly wounded, though he continued to take major decisions, water was short, and all the radios were out of action. By an ironic domestic touch, however, Frost was still able to talk to Divisional HQ by telephone, thanks to the operators of the Dutch Resistance, whom, for their temerity, the Germans subsequently murdered.

---

* This improbable exhortation derived from the 2nd Battalion's time in Tunisia in early 1943. One of the native donkey-drivers thus addressed his charges, and it became the battle-cry of the 1st Brigade.

H

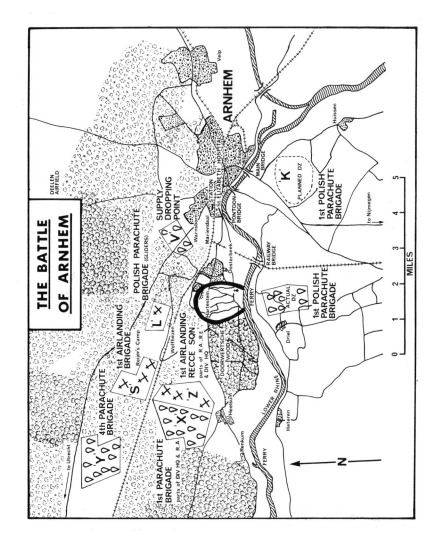

THE BATTLE
OF ARNHEM

ARNHEM

Velp

Huissen

DEELEN
AIRFIELD

SUPPLY
DROPPING
POINT

STATION
ST ELIZABETH HOSPITAL

Warnsborn

Mariendaal

PONTOON
BRIDGE

MAIN
BRIDGE

K
PLANNED DZ

POLISH PARACHUTE
BRIGADE (GLIDERS)

1st POLISH PARACHUTE
BRIGADE

to Nijmegen

Oosterbeek

RAILWAY
BRIDGE

L

FERRY

1st AIRLANDING
BRIGADE

Reijer's Camp

Hartestein

ACTUAL
DZ

Wolfhezen

1st POLISH PARACHUTE
BRIGADE

4th PARACHUTE
BRIGADE

S

1st AIRLANDING
RECCE SQN

Driel

parts of R.A., R.E.
& DIV HQ

Z

DOORWERTSCHE
WOOD

Heelsum

to Utrecht

LOWER RHINE

Heteren

Y

parts of DIV HQ & R.A.

Renkum

FERRY

1st PARACHUTE
BRIGADE

N

0   1   2   3   4   5
MILES

News that the 2nd Army would attack the southern end of the bridge that afternoon sent hopes high. But no help came, or could come; and during the day they were forced out of the shells of their battered, burning houses until they were fighting in the ruins close to, or beneath, the bridge. Enemy aircraft strafed the positions. The six-pounders were out of action and PIAT ammunition was exhausted. Tanks could advance almost with impunity. Finally, only a school in which the wounded had been gathered remained; and that evening it was set on fire. Under a flag of truce, they, with Frost among them, were taken away by the Germans.

Now only a handful remained, 120 officers and men, commanded by Major C. H. F. Gough of the Reconnaissance Squadron; and at dawn on September 21 they made a final attempt to regain the houses from which they had been prised. The attack failed, and with that failure, the operation. The bridge was back in German hands; and the surviving remnant, a mere 50 or so, melted away, to try and reach the perimeter, or cross the Rhine. A few, a very few, succeeded in doing this.

It is worth recapping. According to the plan, the bridge was to have been taken, and held for not more than 48 hours, by the entire 1st Airborne Division. By then, XXX Corps, storming up from the south, should have relieved them. As things turned out, the bridge was held for three days and four nights — from the evening of the 17th to dawn on the 21st — by less than one complete battalion.

The bridge — the central purpose of the operation — had gone. The fragmented battalions within the perimeter, shrunk now into the western edge of Oosterbeek with a foothold on the river bank, held on for four days more. Hungry, thirsty, tired to the bone, and with the casualties steadily mounting, they drove off attack after attack. Attempts to reinforce them from across the river were as doomed as those to supply them from the air. And the latter were haunted by a tragic irony. Time and time again the RAF pilots flew straight into the wall of flak; many of them continued their run with their aircraft on fire; but, as one officer on the ground described it, 'We thought that some would not face it and would jettison their cargoes, in which case we should get them, for they would fall short and therefore in

WELL NOW, THE FORM
IS, I HAVE WITHDRAWN
YOU FROM THE OPEN
GROUND BY THE RIVER. I
WANT YOU TO REST HERE
FOR 2 HRS. IN WHICH TIME
GET A MEAL FROM WHAT
YOU HAVE LEFT, GET YOUR
SELF CLEAN & BE PREPARED
TO MOVE UP TO A NEW
POSITION AROUND THE HOUSES
ON THE SOUTH SIDE OF THE
PERIMETER. ON THIS POSITION
WE MUST STAND OR FALL &
FIGHT TO THE LAST ROUND
THIS EDGE OF THE PERIMETER
IS BEING HELD BY A MIXED
BAG CONSISTING LONSDALES FORCE HQ AT THIS CHURCH
2ND ARMY POLISH BDGE
SO FAR WE HAVE HAD A GOOD
BATTLE AGAINST GOOD TROOPS, TROOPS
THAT ARE NOT UP TO OUR STANDARD
WE HAVE FOUGHT THEM IN N.A
SICILY & ITALY & AT TIMES
AGAINST ODDS. THEY WERE
NOT GOOD ENOUGH FOR US THEN
& I AM CERTAIN THEY ARE NOT
OUR MATCH NOW. TO GET
YOURSELVES DUG IN AND SHOOT
TO KILL. GOOD LUCK.

Major Londsdale's message, scratched on the door of the Church at Oosterbeek, during the final stages of the battle in the perimeter. The message typifies the spirit of the airborne soldiers after a week of continuous and bitter fighting. (Courtesy 'Soldier', The British Army Magazine.)

The rail and road bridges at Nijmegen, objectives of the American parachute landings on Operation 'Market Garden'. The bridge construction can clearly be seen by the shadows cast on the river. (Courtesy Imperial War Museum.)

our lines; but they all stuck to their course and went on . . .'* Herein lay the tragedy. The planned dropping zones had not been captured, but the message informing the RAF of the necessary changes had never got through. The troops on the ground did everything they knew to mark the new zones; but among the trees, their signals were virtually invisible from the air; and less than 8 per cent of the stores dropped were recovered. On the worst day, September 21, the RAF lost a fifth of their aircraft in these brave, forlorn sorties.

Meanwhile, the two US Divisions had dropped on September 17, and the 2nd Army operations to advance up the 'carpet' to Arnhem began successfully enough. Men of the 101st Division seized their objectives, though one bridge was found destroyed. The Guards Armoured Division built a replacement and pressed on towards the 82nd, holding Grave and the high ground south-east of Nijmegen.

* One of them was Flight Lieutenant D. S. A. Lord, DFC, of 271 Squadron, Transport Command, who circled for eight minutes and made two runs with his starboard wing blazing, and crashed with his aircraft. He was awarded a posthumous VC.

The 82nd Division, however, had been driven back from their final objective—the bridge over the River Waal north of Nijmegen. It was recaptured, intact, by the Guards Armoured Division and 504 US Parachute Regiment.

All this time, though, south of Grave, enemy counter-attacks delayed operations, and, combined with fierce resistance north of the Waal, blunted the point of the 2nd Army's advance. Far from being a rapid thrust against light opposition, it became a savage slogging match: far from relieving the 1st Airborne inside 48 hours, the 2nd Army was never able to reach them at all.

The 43rd Infantry Division finally took over the lead and succeeded in reaching the Polish Brigade. But enemy pressure on the 2nd Army's flanks prevented a full-scale link-up with the perimeter across the river. Some hardy members of the 4th Dorsets crossed the Rhine, but it was too little, and too late. During the night of 25th/26th the survivors of the 1st Airborne Division were ordered to withdraw south of the Rhine. Of the 10,095 all ranks, including glider pilots, who landed, fewer than 3,000 returned across the river.

The bid to end the war in 1944 had failed: the battle of Arnhem was over.

Chapter

9

Arnhem Aftermath

THE battle of Arnhem was a magnificent disaster. Less than one third of the 1st Airborne Division came back across the Rhine, and even fewer of the 15 chaplains who went with them. Their stories are as heroic as those of the fighting troops, and are told briefly here.

The Rev. R. Talbot Watkins, CF, Chaplain to the 1st Battalion, the Parachute Regiment, led a party of 50 wounded men from the Regimental Aid Post by Oosterbeek Church to the river, and across it by assault boat, on the night of September 25. Most of his charges were so badly injured that the journey was accomplished by sheer will-power—his as well as theirs. When they were safe, Watkins returned to the north bank to see if he could bring any more wounded across. He found no-one; but was then caught by the dawn and had to lie low to avoid German patrols. The next night he swam across the river and rejoined the Allied positions.

The Rev. W. R. Chignell, CF, Chaplain to No. 2 Wing, the Glider Pilot Regiment, also made the two mile journey with a party of 20 wounded men. He had to cross by boat as he could not swim.

The Rev. J. Rowell, CF, Chaplain to the 1st Battalion, the Border Regiment, brought 12 wounded from the Hartenstein Hotel. Subsequently he conducted a service of Thanksgiving for their deliverance, and in memory of those who died, standing with General Browning on a kitchen table in the cellars of a Roman Catholic Missionary College at Nijmegen. Watkins, Chigwell and Rowell were the only chaplains to escape.

The Rev. H. J. Irwin, CF, Chaplain to the 11th Battalion, the Parachute Regiment, and Fr. Benson, Chaplain to the 181st Airlanding Field Ambulance, were both killed during the battle, and three others were taken prisoner; the Rev. R. F. Bowers, CF, Chaplain to the 10th Battalion, the Parachute Regiment, who broke an ankle on landing, and the Rev. A. C. V. Menzies, CF, Chaplain to the 156th Battalion, the Parachute Regiment, and Fr. B. M. Egan, SJ, CF, both of whom were wounded.

The other seven chaplains survived the battle, but chose to stay with the wounded when the withdrawal from Arnhem took place. Of these, the Rev. J. G. Morrison, CF, Chaplain to the 7th Battalion, the King's Own Scottish Borderers, and the Rev. E. L. Phillips, CF, Chaplain to the 3rd Battalion, the Parachute Regiment, were captured almost immediately.

The Rev. S. Thorne, CF, Chaplain to the 1st Air-landing Light Regiment, RA, spent the entire time with the Regimental Medical Officer of the Gunners, whose Aid Post was by the church at Oosterbeek. As it filled to overflowing with wounded men, the padre found himself increasingly busy, feeding and comforting the sick, burying the dead, and, when the doctor was wounded, doing his work as best

Men of the 1st AB Division being interrogated after the battle in Arnhem. (Courtesy Imperial War Museum.)

he could. Eventually the only way to move inside the house was by walking on stretcher handles over the casualties. On the final Monday the Aid Post was fired at by a Tiger tank, and Thorne, together with a Bombardier Medical Orderly went out and forced the tank to withdraw, armed only with a Red Cross flag.

That evening, an escape plan was announced, but Thorne said he was far too tired, and, indeed, fell into a deep sleep on a pile of tins in a corner of the kitchen. Early the next morning the Germans appeared, and he was taken, with the wounded, first to the St Elizabeth Hospital in Arnhem and then to a barracks converted into a hospital at Apeldoorn.

The Rev. G. A. Pare, CF, Chaplain to the 1st Wing, the Glider Pilot Regiment, also ended up at Apeldoorn. He spent most of the nine days of the battle either at Divisional HQ or at the Schoornord Hotel, which was used by the 181st Air-landing Field Ambulance. On the last night, weakened by hunger and exhaustion, he fell asleep during a heavy bombardment, and woke on the Tuesday morning to a strange silence. The RSM told him that the Division had gone, and Pare had the painful task of breaking the news to his patients.

Presently the Germans arrived with a fleet of ambulances to transport the wounded to Apeldoorn. The dead were buried in a common grave behind the hotel, in spite of Pare's protests, and in spite of German assurances that they would have a Christian burial in a cemetery.

The Rev. A. W. H. Harlow, DSO, CF, the Senior Chaplain of the 1st Airborne Division, was taken prisoner on Sunday, September 24, when a company of SS overran the Tefelberg Hotel. He went first to the St Elizabeth Hospital in Arnhem, and then to Apeldoorn. Here he helped convert the barracks into a hospital, and was particularly useful in establishing the prisoners' rights under the Geneva Convention, having been a PoW in Italy not long before. The hospital occupied three blocks of Kaserne Willem III Barracks; and Harlow had with him Pare, Thorne, and the Rev. A. A. Buchanan, CF, Chaplain to the 2nd Battalion, the South Staffordshire Regiment. He placed a chaplain in each of the blocks, and the 23 doctors and two dentists, who acted as anaesthetists, were similarly divided.

There were 1,200 wounded in the barracks, and the chaplains were kept busy going from bed to bed, comforting the dying, and encouraging the others. Pare collected a list of the dead and wounded Glider Pilots which he hoped to get back to England, and also acted as barber. A chapel and office were opened; ward communions were administered, and a service held each week in the dining hall.

Quite soon, men began to escape; and privileges were consequently withdrawn until eventually the local Dutch doctors were not allowed inside the hospital, and only the chaplains could go outside on parole. They thus became valuable sources of information and a link with the outside world.

As soon as the wounded were fit to travel they were moved to prison camps in Germany. The first two batches had an appalling journey in locked cattle trucks, but after a strong protest, a complete hospital train arrived to take 500. Harlow asked Thorne, a single man, and Pare to go on this train, and they boarded it with the patients and shared the work of settling them in. It was two days before an engine could be found, and when the train did leave it rambled along at 20 mph. Pare saw his chance. He had information and messages to take back, and little hope, in Germany, of being allowed to stay with his soldiers. He collected a few necessities in the pockets of his parachute smock, told the CO what he was doing, then jumped off the train and vanished into the evening mist.

The others reached Fallingbostel next morning, and were taken to the large, multi-national Stalag XIB. Thorne found himself in a hut with four other officers, under Major Peter Smith, RAMC, a surgeon. The French, who had been there the longest, ran the camp, and the new arrivals were soon caught up in the inevitable routine. The doctors were kept busy, and Thorne, with Gedge as the Senior Chaplain, visited the hospital, producing library books for the patients, and providing for their religious needs. On Sundays he would take services in the hospital, and then assist Gedge at a general service in the theatre.

At Christmas, 1944, Gedge and Thorne also held services at a neighbouring RAF PoW camp. They went to Père Chennais' Midnight Mass, and he and other chaplains reciprocated by attending their carol service. They then had a Christmas dinner with food that had been saved for weeks. The Allied armies reached Stalag XIB just after Easter, 1945, and all British prisoners were repatriated ten days later.

The Rev. Fr. D. McGowan, CF, Chaplain to the 16th Parachute Field Ambulance, had worked in the St Elizabeth Hospital in Arnhem, which was overrun by the Germans in the early stages of the battle. The British wounded had left their weapons in the care of the hospital as usual, and McGowan and Captain Lipmann Kessel, RAMC, evolved a daring scheme for getting some of them to the Dutch Resistance before they were confiscated. A burial was arranged. Lipmann Kessel and a corporal carried one stretcher, two orderlies another, and Fr. McGowan followed them, seemingly reading from his Missal. The two *corpses*, shrouded in blankets, actually were three Bren guns, a German light machine-gun, some grenades and several dozen magazines of ammunition. The procession moved with solemnity to two rather shallow graves. As the 'corpses' were lowered, the padre appeared to pronounce the correct words, and the bearers stood back smartly and saluted. Later, three Dutch railwaymen, led by Piet von Arnhem, exhumed the weapons and carried them away in the lidless box of a butcher's tricycle. The next day the rest of the arms were collected by the SS.

There still remained nearly 500 prisoners at Apeldoorn after Thorne and Pare's hospital train had left, and the Arnhem party, including McGowan, joined them on October 12. The total number of wounded was then 200, with a staff of 200. It was obvious that the Germans would not allow this state of affairs to continue, so Colonel Warrack obtained a few volunteers to remain with the wounded and the rest started planning to escape. A number got away after Sunday Service on October 15, and this caused such consternation among the guards that Fr. McGowan and Lieutenant-Colonel Herford, RAMC, decided to escape immediately before the whole camp was moved. That evening, they were helped out of the operating theatre window by Colonel Warrack and two other doctors. McGowan was a stoutish man, and it took some time to push him through. Outside, it was raining and windy, and they lay hidden in the shadow of the building

One that got away. Sgt. Bennet of the 1st Air-landing Brigade who swam across the river during the break out from Arnhem, September 25, 1944. Although he had to abandon all his uniform he still retains his Sten gun and helmet. (Courtesy Imperial War Museum.)

for what seemed like hours, while sentries passed within feet of them. McGowan could hear Herford's heart beating, as well as his own, as they waited for a chance to dash across the shining expanse of wet concrete between them and the compound fence.

All went well, however; and four days later they were almost at the river bank — and almost at the end of their tether from hunger and exhaustion. They had crossed the glider landing zones in broad daylight, wearing British gas-capes which they found lying there, and berets turned inside out. There were Germans all round them also wearing gas-capes, but they were not challenged. That night, though, they got separated, and while Herford reached the river and swam across to safety, McGowan found himself in the German front line. An enemy trench was close in front of him, and as he lay in the darkness wondering what on earth to do, a soldier came out of it, tripped over him, and jabbed at him with his bayonet. He was a prisoner again with the Rhine only yards away; and, this time, he was sent to a PoW camp in Germany.

Only Pare's adventures remain to be told. After jumping the train, dressed in a parachute smock, red beret and dog collar, he was free, and well behind enemy lines. He set off southwards, and soon made contact with the Dutch, who hid him in a shooting lodge deep in the woods. This was a thatched box eight feet square, raised on wooden posts ten feet high, with a ladder to a trap door in the floor. They assured him that the Germans would never search it, as it was on their own artillery ranges. He spent three days there, disturbed only by the whining of spent bullets and the tapping of woodpeckers; and then one morning the two Dutchmen who brought him food climbed in to hide with him, saying the SS were searching the area. That afternoon they heard troops in the woods, and the occasional shot. They listened as the hunt came closer, and at last the Dutchmen decided to bolt. They were caught, but Pare had persuaded them to lock him in before they left, and although the SS reached the hut and climbed the ladder, they did not bother to force the trapdoor. Pare lay with thumping heart until they went away.

But it was too dangerous to stay there, and that night he set off north-west through the artillery ranges. On the walk he kept hearing

German sentries, who had a peculiar habit of calling to one another while on duty. He was challenged once, out of range, and narrowly missed detection by a motor cyclist. In the early hours of the morning he knocked at a farm and got no answer, then at a cottage where a woman and her daughter let him in but were so terrified that he could not stay. In desperation, with dawn approaching, he went back to the farm and spent the day hiding on top of a haystack. When night came, he tried another farm, where he was luckier, and was given a meal and a hiding place under the floor of a shed in company with a German Jew.

The next day he was interviewed by the local pastor, and then began a life of continual movement from house to house. By March 1945, even the Dutch thought he was a deaf and dumb Dutch refugee. He did not get back to the Allied lines until British troops entered Holland in April, 1945.

After the war a cemetery for those who died was established at Oosterbeek where the 1st Airborne Division held its final perimeter in the closing stages of the battle. The Arnhem–Oosterbeek War Cemetery is administered by the Commonwealth War Graves Commission and contains the graves of 3,328 British and Commonwealth soldiers. It is annually a place of pilgrimage for the survivors and the relatives of those who died. At this pilgrimage Dutch children from the local schools parade and lay flowers on the graves of the fallen. It is of interest to note that Arnhem is historically associated with gallant sacrifice, for it was here, in the autumn of 1586, that Sir Philip Sidney died, nearly a month after the famous incident in which, although wounded and parched with thirst, he passed the draught of water offered him to a dying soldier. It is perhaps interesting to know that although no chaplains were involved there were, in the late autumn of 1944, two major crossings of the Rhine by Airborne soldiers who had remained in hiding after the battle. In the first, over 100 managed to cross the river to safety. The second party was, however, intercepted short of the river and the majority were captured, though some managed to escape. Thereafter, it was impossible to organize more mass crossings as the Germans took thorough precautions.

Chapter

10

Across the Rhine : Norway Again

D URING the winter of 1944–5, the 6th Airborne were rushed
across the Channel once more — but by ship — to help counter
the German Christmas offensive in the Ardennes; and in
January Field-Marshal Montgomery was appointed Colonel Commandant of the Parachute Regiment. By the beginning of March,
1945, advance elements of the Allied Armies had reached the Rhine,
and by the third week of the month were drawn up along its western
bank. The final barrier to the heart of Germany had been reached.
The Germans had suffered heavily in their last offensive, and during
their subsequent retreat to the Rhine. The gateway to the Reich,
though shut, was but insecurely bolted, and the Allies stood poised
to burst it open.

The crossing was to be on a front of two Armies, the US 9th on the
right, the British 2nd on the left. The British 6th and US 17th Airborne Divisions, forming XVIII US Airborne Corps under Major-
General M. B. Ridgway and his deputy Major-General R. N. Gale,
were placed under command of the 2nd Army with orders 'to disrupt
the hostile defence of the Rhine in the Wesel sector by the seizure of
key terrain . . . in order to deepen rapidly the bridgehead to be seized
in an assault river crossing by ground forces, and facilitate the further
offensive operations of the 2nd Army'.

After Arnhem, Brigadier Chatterton, the commander of the Glider
Pilot Regiment, developed the *coup de main* landing technique so that
an entire brigade could be landed in tactical groups close to battalion
or company objectives. In effect, this meant that the aircraft carrying
each platoon or section of a platoon, flew in one 'lane', and thus, all
members of a company landed together. As an added refinement, the
men with the heaviest loads landed nearest to their rendezvous. As
the Rhine crossing called for descents on to enemy-held positions,
the leading battalion of each parachute brigade also adopted tactical
landing, with soldiers making straight for their objectives.

The air armada. Tug aircraft and their gliders cross the Rhine between Rees and Wesel, March 24, 1945. (Courtesy Imperial War Museum.)

American Hadrian gliders of the 17th US Airborne Division landing at the Rhine Crossing. The pilot's cabin of this glider was raised to facilitate rapid unloading and can clearly be seen in the centre glider. (Courtesy Imperial War Museum.)

This time, the airborne divisions would benefit both from the hard-learned lessons of earlier operations, and also from the vast amounts of war material of every kind which were now available. The lean years of hard endeavour and short supply, along the road from North Africa to Arnhem, were over. Even so, the RAF were hard put to it to find sufficient aircrew; for this time, both divisions would land at full strength in one drop, in a full-scale, tactical airborne assault, timed to overwhelm the German defenders after the amphibious crossing of the Rhine had begun, and to link up immediately with the ground forces.

RHINE CROSSING - MARCH 1945

XVIII U.S. AIRBORNE CORPS

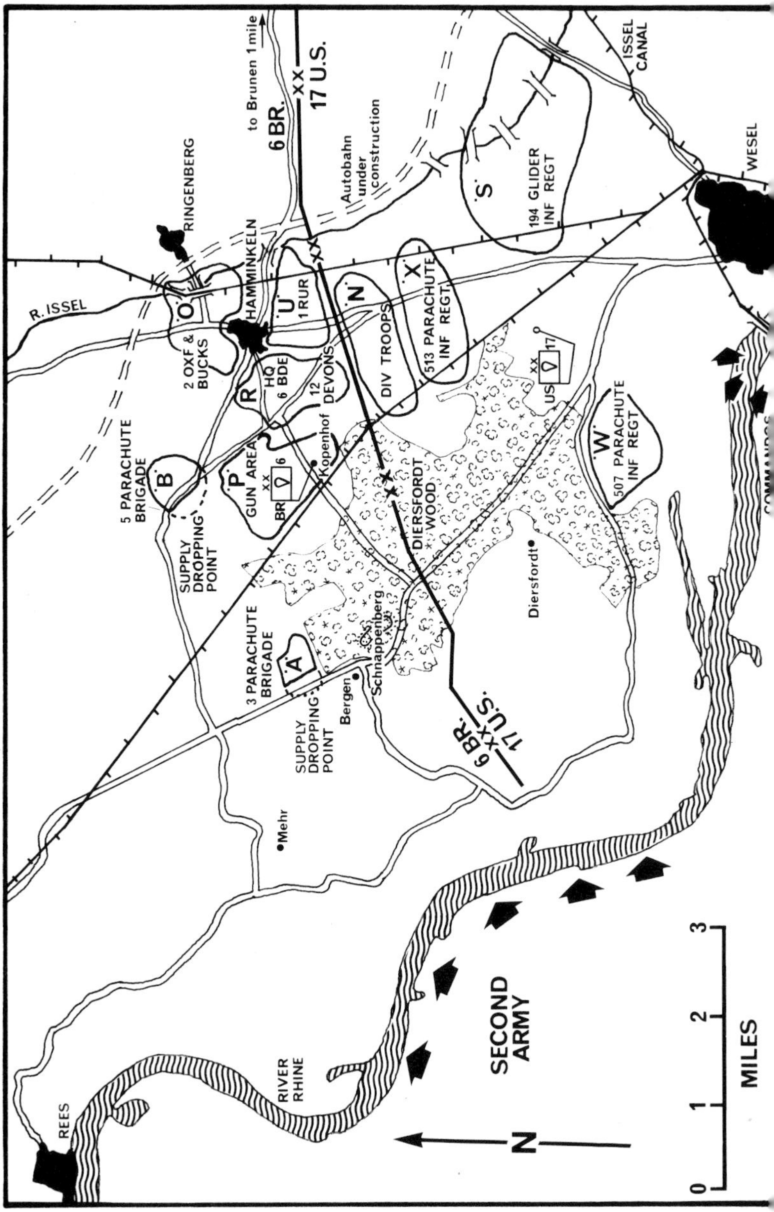

As to specific objectives, the 6th Airborne was to drop and seize the high ground east of Bergen, the village of Hamminkeln and the Issel bridges, and establish contact with the 17th US Airborne Division to the south. The parachute brigades — the 3rd under Brigadier Hill, the 5th under Brigadier J. H. N. Poett — were to drop first, followed closely by the gliders of the 6th Air-landing Brigade under Brigadier R. H. Bellamy.

Since the operation was to take place in full daylight, exceptional care was taken to suppress enemy flak and ensure the safety of the vast and vulnerable fleets of aircraft and gliders — over 1,100 for the 6th Division alone. A total of 544 guns — the entire armoury of the 12 Corps and the Airborne Corps artillery — was drawn up to support the drop, with officers of the Forward Observer Unit landing with the parachutists to control the fire; while the RAF sent fighters, fighter-bombers and heavies to pound airfields and flak positions, and

Gliders in the fields near Hamminkeln (which can be seen in the background) after landing east of the Rhine. (Courtesy Imperial War Museum.)

provided continuous fighter cover for the air armada. During this preliminary air assault, 52 German aircraft were destroyed in the air, and 115 on the ground. Despite all these precautions, and the fact that no enemy fighters appeared during the fly-in, of the 242 parachute aircraft carrying the 6th Airborne, 18 were shot down and 115 damaged by anti-aircraft fire.

The morning of March 24 was fine and clear, and the fly-in went according to plan. But, as they dropped, the parachutists were fired on by light anti-aircraft guns and small arms, and there were a good many casualties, especially among those who came down over the trees which bordered the DZ. Thirty-five gliders failed to reach the Rhine for various technical reasons. Many more were destroyed as they landed. In the south the Americans suffered similar casualties.

The 8th Battalion, Parachute Regiment, leading the 3rd Parachute Brigade, cleared the area of the brigade drop-zone rapidly, despite fierce resistance. The 9th Battalion and 1st Canadian Battalion then moved off to their objectives. By 1345 hours they had seized Schnappenberg, the wooded ridge which was vital to the German defence, and in mid-afternoon they linked up with the ground forces, though the 8th Battalion was isolated until the following day.

The 5th Parachute Brigade, not quite so accurately dropped, immediately came under heavy fire and suffered casualties from airburst and mortar fire as they rallied. Practically all the farms and houses were held by the enemy, but by 1530 hours the 7th, 12th, and 13th Battalions had cleared them and the whole objective had been captured. Contact with the 6th Air-landing Brigade was also established.

Arriving last, the 6th Air-landing Brigade had its task made more difficult by heavy flak and the 'fog of war' caused by haze and dust from the artillery bombardment. The German gunners had recovered from their surprise and from the preliminary bombardment, and, having zeroed in on the Dakotas, awaited the lumbering gliders and shot many of them down. Glider pilots had difficulty in selecting their landing points, and a number finished in the wrong place. However, the *coup de main* parties landed by their bridges, and enough of the remainder arrived accurately to overcome the enemy in the first

Soldiers of the 6th Air-landing Brigade climb on a jeep outside Hamminkeln in the Rhine Crossing operation. One of the first German prisoners taken can be seen with his hands on his head in the back of the vehicle. (Courtesy Imperial War Museum.)

rush. By 1100 hours the bridges over the River Issel were secured, and the town of Hamminkeln captured. The British were assisted by men from the 513th US Parachute Regiment who had been dropped in the wrong place but who, spiritedly disregarding this error, took on all enemy in sight. Presently, the only organized German defence left were some four or five tanks and a considerable force of infantry near Ringenberg. These were contained by four light 'Locust' tanks, glider-landed with the Armoured Reconnaissance Regiment, a platoon of the 12th Devons and some glider pilots, until they could be mopped up the following day.

Divisional HQ was established in Köpenhof Farm, Major-General Bols landing only 100 yards away. During the night of March 24–25, Major-General Ridgway was able to visit and issue orders for next day. On his way back he was involved in a brush with the enemy, and accounted for at least one personally.

Throughout that night activity continued. The Germans counter-attacked with infantry, and Tiger tanks—to which the lightly-armed airborne troops were at a particular disadvantage; but were beaten off, though the bridge immediately west of Ringenberg had to be blown up to prevent its recapture. On the 25th the link-up with the ground armies continued, and the division was reorganized to prepare for the break-out from the bridgehead which began next day. The cost had been high, particularly in the Air-landing Brigade, whose losses in the air or on landing were between 25 and 30 per cent. However, the plan had succeeded.

Major-General Ridgway summed up the results of the operation thus:

'The airborne drop in depth destroyed enemy gun and rear defensive positions in one day—positions it might have taken many days to reduce by ground attack. The impact of the airborne divisions at one blow shattered hostile defence and permitted the prompt link-up with ground troops. The increased bridgehead materially assisted the build-up essential for subsequent success. The insistent drive to the east and rapid seizure of key terrain were decisive to subsequent developments, permitting Allied armour to debouch into the North German plain at full strength and momentum.'

From March 26 to May 2, the 6th Airborne Division took part in the advance across Germany which its action had helped to make possible. But despite the assistance of the 4th Tank Battalion, Grenadier Guards, and additional artillery and transport, the parachute and glider soldiers covered much of the 350 miles to the Baltic on foot, and fought many a fierce action on the way. Trained to fight with only light support, the airborne men were well suited to exploit the fluid situation that existed once the last great barrier to Germany was crossed. The names tell the story—Coesfeld; the Dortmund–Ems Canal; Lengerich; Lübecke; Minden; the River Weser; the River Elbe;—up to the meeting with the Soviet Army advance guard to the east of Wismar, on the Baltic coast. It was the end of the Third Reich; victory in Europe; freedom for thousands of prisoners of war and political prisoners, and for those Jews who had survived. The Red Devils had their photographs taken with the smiling Red Army

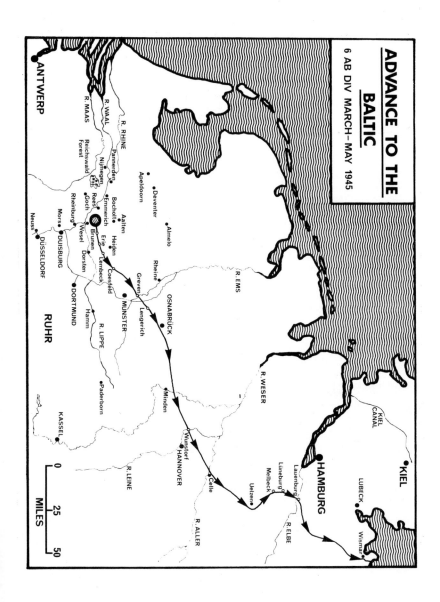

ADVANCE TO THE
BALTIC
6 AB DIV MARCH–MAY 1945

soldiers; their doctors were called away to help the victims of concentration camps. No one thought that, within a year, smiles would change to scowls as the Iron Curtain clamped across Europe, or that Jewish extremists would liken the Division to the Gestapo.

Even while the 6th Airborne were charging across half Europe in pursuit of the disordered Wehrmacht, the possibility of an operational and reconstructive force in Norway after the surrender of Germany was being mooted. This force was to include Norwegian troops in England, and 52 ('L') Division; but since the latter were committed in Germany, the 1st Airborne Division joined it instead.

By this time, May 1945, the Division had recovered from Arnhem, had been reorganized, and now included the 1st Polish Independent Parachute Brigade. But just as they were due to leave for Norway, the 1st Polish Brigade was alerted for a move overseas, and the 1st Parachute Brigade was sent to Denmark on law and order duty. So the Special Air Service Brigade, then in Germany, were flown to England

The meeting of Field-Marshal Montgomery with Marshal Rokkasovsky at Wismar on May 7, 1945, two days after the war ended. This was the first meeting between two field commanders from the Eastern and Western Allies. The other British officers in the photograph are: Back row rear L to R, Brigadier Faithfull, CRA, Brigadier Hill 3rd Parachute Brigade, Brigadier Bellamy 6th Air-landing Brigade, Brigadier Poett 5th Parachute Brigade. In centre behind Marshal Rokkasovsky is General Bols GOC 6th AB Division. The two officers on the right of the front row are Brigadier Exham the BGS and the British Intelligence Officer who acted as interpreter. (Courtesy Airborne Forces Museum.)

to take their place as part of the division. This sudden move of a brigade from one foreign country to another, via UK, and an entire division overseas, is worth more than a mere mention, for it is all of a piece with the manner in which airborne soldiers live. On this occasion, the warning order was received on May 5; Major-General Urquhart received his orders on the 6th; three days later, the division was ready to take off. By definition airborne forces are always, in a sense, at instant readiness; and yet any move is necessarily complex in its arrangements. Units have to be alerted, plans—which normally cannot be prepared in advance—have to be made, and orders formulated and issued. At the same time—for airborne forces are to this extent not self-sufficient—the air side has to be worked out. Aircraft have to be organized, crews briefed, and loads for each machine carefully calculated. Finally, battalions, with all their kit and equipment, must be transported to the departure airfields. For a force of divisional strength all this may take perhaps three to four days—days of chaos and hard work at top speed. But this ability to mount an operation in the shortest possible time is one of the Parachute Regiment's greatest assets—and one which, as we shall see, has been frequently used in the bush-fire operations of the post-war years.

The division's tasks in Norway were to maintain law and order, stop sabotage, secure the airfields, and see that the Germans observed the terms of their surrender. It was a potentially dangerous assignment, as there were some 350,000 German, but only 6,000 Airborne, soldiers.

The advance parties flew in on May 9, but on the 10th the weather clamped down, and the fly-in of the main body was not completed until May 13, 36 hours later than had been planned. On May 11, Air Vice Marshal J. R. Scarlett-Streatfield, AOC 38 Group, was killed in an air crash—a great loss to Army/Air co-operation in airborne activities. And he was not alone; accidents were frequent, and airborne forces had one officer and 33 soldiers killed and one soldier injured, and the RAF six killed and seven missing.

Until the arrival of HQ Allied Land Forces Norway, HQ 1st Airborne Division was in control of affairs in Norway. As a result, it was General Urquhart who welcomed HRH the Crown Prince when he came ashore with his Government; and the Division took part in the ceremonies to welcome His Majesty the King of Norway on his return to his country.

In addition to their main tasks, the Division helped Russian and other Allied ex-prisoners of war; rounded up war criminals; segregated German troops in reservations; and employed the Germans to 'prove safe' buildings and minefields. This, which was not popular, they achieved by making them link hands and march steadily over the charted ground. Throughout, the Division were ably assisted by the Norwegian underground organization 'Milorg', and welcomed enthusiastically wherever they went. The people were in tremendous spirits. It was during the Division's stay in Norway that the full and tragic story of Operation 'Freshman' was pieced together at last; and as a result, the Germans responsible for the murders were brought to justice.

Chapter

11

Java

S HORTLY after VE-Day, the 5th Parachute Brigade was alerted
for operations in the Far East, and moved from Germany to
Larkhill, Wiltshire. After 28 days' leave they set about the
hectic preparations necessary for a new theatre of war; tropical dress,
jungle boots, new equipment and a new rifle, the No. 5 Jungle
Carbine, all had to be drawn.

The brigade (which consisted of the 7th, 12th and 13th Battalions
the Parachute Regiment, 22nd Independent Parachute Company,
4th Air-landing Anti-Tank Battery RA, 3rd Airborne Squadron RE,
225 Parachute Field Ambulance RAMC, and detachments of Airborne RASC, REME, RAOC and CMP units) sailed for India in the
Corfu on July 19, 1945; and reached Bombay 17 days later, to start
an intensive period of training in jungle warfare. But before it was
completed, Japan surrendered.

In late August the brigade embarked in the *Chitral*, arriving off the
Morib beaches in Northern Malaya in early September. The landing
craft were manned and the assault units stormed the beaches. However, not a shot was fired; and the brigade moved inland towards
Kuala Lumpur. At this stage the monsoon broke, and the advance
through weary miles of rubber plantations continued in pouring rain.
No opposition was encountered and the brigade were later withdrawn, re-embarked in the *Chitral* and taken to Singapore. This
operation, appropriately enough, had been code-named 'Fiasco'.

In Singapore the Japanese garrison were in PoW camps, the docks
were in chaos, and the population subdued and bewildered. Between
September and December, 1945, the brigade's job was to help bring
life back to normal. This included the organization of sporting events
with the local population. One of the side-effects was to give Pte Jim
Mellow, fighting as 'Brian Aherne', and destined to become a future
British boxing champion, his early experience in the ring. Lieutenant
Eberhardie of the 12th Battalion was another outstanding athlete, and

his experiences as a young subaltern with the brigade in the coming months, he put to good use in Borneo 20 years later. Peace-keeping, however, was not all sport and goodwill; and the brigade lost several men when unrest exploded into civil disorders.

Early in December the brigade were despatched to Semerang on the North Java coast between Batavia and Sourabaya. British forces had been in the area before but had been withdrawn; and the city was in a sorry plight. There was a population of some 250,000, half of them Indonesian; 40,000 Chinese; 6,500 Dutch nationals and the remainder Javanese. Looting, arson and murder were commonplace, there was no water or electricity and no civil administration; and Nationalist extremists roamed at will, shooting at one another, or at anyone else who happened to be in the vicinity.

The Japanese had surrendered to the Indonesians; but many of them had been killed by extremists, who had taken their weapons. The Japanese local commander had, in fact, been trying to restore some sort of order. The brigade, short of troops to cope with all the tasks at hand, took a battalion of Japanese troops 'under command'; they worked very well and were most useful. Though the local population resented it, the brigade had no alternative in this odd situation.

Most of the so-called Indonesian 'Freedom Fighters' were in fact mercenary bandits working off personal scores, and out for personal gain. They were armed with a variety of weapons from Dutch, Japanese and British rifles to sharpened bamboo stakes. These groups operated from the 'Kampongs' which surround Javanese towns. The network of villages formed by these Kampongs together with the surrounding jungle provided limitless cover and hideouts for terrorist activities, and were most difficult for security forces to penetrate. However, by the end of April the brigade had restored reasonable order, and the area was under control.

The major problem was the lack of a civil administration; and the brigade had to establish a Civil Affairs Bureau, with the help of an experienced Dutch administrator assisted by a British officer. As it expanded, each branch of the Administration recruited a team from the law-abiding; but first it was essential to stamp out terrorism and re-establish the rule of law. This took time; but, at last, both Dutch nationals and the Chinese—who had suffered bitterly from the extremists, who thought they were allies of the British—came forward and offered their services.

The economic situation was equally chaotic. Food and cloth were bartered at street corners, petrol was almost unobtainable, and the black market flourished. The brigade set out to control the supply of food, and to restore the power and water supplies. Their attempt to restore confidence in the currency was less successful. The Dutch guilders issued in place of the Japanese occupation currency carried little conviction, and soap, chocolate and cigarettes, as in post-war Europe, took the place of most abstract coinage.

While the brigade engineers were busy getting the public services going again, the Field Ambulance did the same for the medical services; and the local police were re-organized and re-equipped. A complete census of the population was taken, and ration cards were issued to ensure fair distribution of food supplies and to counter the black market. The food problem was acute. At one stage, the brigade was feeding 5,000 children a day—and had to make them eat their rations on the spot to prevent them from selling them for profit! With the help of British engineers the harbour was reopened, and was in full working order when the brigade handed over to the Dutch Army and sailed for Singapore.

It was an odd assignment altogether, but one well within the traditions of the British Army; and proved, once more, that the British soldier makes an admirable ambassador. The Senior Officer of the Civil Affairs Bureau wrote to the Brigade Newspaper of—

'. . . your splendid work in the reconstruction of Semerang. All of you have done great work and thus enhanced the reputation which Great Britain enjoys throughout the world for fair play and hard work. We shall miss you; your smiling smartness, and your tenacity to create order out of disorder will forever remain in our memory.'

And the Indonesian 'City News' said much the same thing, only more picturesquely—'When the parachutists came here . . . conditions in town were awful and things were topsy-turvy. It must be said that their arrival and what they did . . . resulted in law and order being restored . . .' and went on to pray fervently that the Dutch would do as well. Subsequent events in this area speak for themselves.

Chapter

12

Palestine 1945–8

'The squalid war against the Jews.'

Winston Churchill

WHEN the war in Europe ended in May 1945, the 6th Airborne Division were at Wismar on the Baltic, and the 1st were in Norway. The 6th were now earmarked for operations in the Far East and would have gone to Malaya, and the 1st to the Middle East as part of the Imperial Strategic Reserve. But with the surrender of Japan on August 10, these arrangements were revised.

As with all the services, the end of the war brought to Airborne Forces reductions and a major dose of re-organization. The most drastic result of this was the disbandment of the 1st Airborne Division. This followed the decision that only one division should remain in the post-war regular army; and the choice fell on the 6th. So, in November 1945, after its return from Norway, the 1st Airborne Division, whose name would be forever linked with, and give an un-tarnishable lustre to, the name of Arnhem, ceased to exist. Rarely in the history of warfare can any unit of any army have achieved such glory in so short a time. It had been in existence barely three years.

There were other changes that deeply affected the structure of airborne forces in the course of the next three years. It was decided that airborne divisions would in future be all-parachute, on the German pattern, with gliders only for heavy loads and *coups de main*. Consequently, the 6th Air-landing Brigade, whose contribution to the 6th Airborne's fame had been second to none, became the 31st Infantry Brigade and severed its airborne connection. Its place was taken by the 1st Parachute Brigade, composed of the 1st, 2nd and 17th Battalions, the Parachute Regiment. Soon afterwards the 5th Brigade returned from the Far East. Eventually the division came to consist of nine parachute battalions, each of which was affiliated to a group of infantry regiments, who were responsible for supplying officers and soldiers to fill its ranks on three-year tours.

At Wismar, that May of 1945, the 6th Division formed part of the British Liberation Army. The initials BLA suggested to the brighter sparks a less rosy future. Burma Lies Ahead, for instance — and so it might have done but for the dropping of the atomic bomb. Instead, the division became part of the Strategic Reserve, and its new destination was the Middle East.

On September 21, 1945, therefore, Divisional and Tactical HQs flew out to Egypt and established themselves at Nuseirat Hospital Camp, near Gaza, to be followed by the rest of the division between then and November.

War Office policy was to keep the 6th Airborne Division clear of internal security duties; but GHQ, Middle East Forces, by deciding to base them in Palestine — where, admittedly, there were good airfields and training facilities — were unwittingly demolishing the whole purpose of a Strategic Reserve. For whatever conventional theories were cherished in Cairo concerning external threats to the British Empire, the facts of the next quarter-century were to prove that the real threats lay within, and not outside, the various colonies, mandates and protectorates. The first territory to demonstrate this was Palestine; the threat was nationalism.

Palestine in 1945 was administered by Great Britain under a mandate of the League of Nations dating from 1923. The 1939–45 War had overshadowed the 'Palestine Question'; and apart from the Mufti and irreconcilable Arab extremists, and the Jewish dissident groups, the vast majority of Jews and Arabs were too busy to pursue it. Many Jews fought in the Allied Services; and there was a Jewish Brigade in the British Army. So, by 1945, Palestinian Jewry had acquired a great deal of up-to-date battle experience — and also, one way and another, a considerable supply of arms and ammunition.

In 1939 the British Government had limited Jewish immigration to a maximum of 75,000 over the following five years, after which no further immigration would be permitted without Arab consent. The fact that Arab violence in the 1930s had helped to create this restriction cannot have gone unnoticed by the Jews. With the end of the war, they demanded an increased quota, since the 1939 total was virtually filled, and now there were vast numbers of Jews in Europe who were displaced and homeless. Nor did they allow the British to forget that, during the 1914–18 War, Lord Balfour had pledged the Government to establish 'a national home for the Jews in Palestine'. Exactly what Balfour meant by this term has never been made clear; but to the Jews it meant a Jewish State; and this was the goal towards which the fast-expanding force of Jewish Nationalism was dedicated.

By the end of 1945 the Jewish Agency, which acted as a kind of government within a government, dealing with Jewish affairs, had secretly decided that a resort to violence was necessary, both in order to convince the British Government that restrictions on immigration were intolerable, and also to gain world-wide support for Zionism.

Into this situation came the 6th Airborne Division, as open-minded a body of troops as any in the world, who had had many Jews in their ranks in the battles against Nazi Germany, and who had witnessed the terrible sufferings of European Jews under Hitler. So able a people as the Palestinian Jews could, one would have thought, easily have enlisted their sympathy; instead they chose to treat them as enemies. Even as the battalions moved into tented camps south of Gaza, in the autumn of 1945, Jewish newspapers were describing them as 'oppressors' and 'Gestapo', come to 'perpetuate Nazi anti-Semitism'. It was a poor outlook for cordial relations, and a dismal prospect for the policy of non-involvement of the division in internal security duties.

There were a number of Jewish military or para-military formations. First, there was Hagana, the Underground National Army, raised primarily for defence, but capable of more ambitious operations. Closely linked to Hagana was Palmach—the Spearhead Groups —regular, full-time soldiers, highly trained and disciplined and led by skilful and experienced commanders, who formed the elite of the army. This force was used by the Jewish authorities for specific acts of sabotage, often in connection with illegal immigration. In addition to these 'official' organizations, there were two dissident groups who answered to no authority but their own leaders. These were Irgun

Zvai Leumi (IZL) and the smaller, but even more extreme, Fighters for the Freedom of Israel, commonly known as the Stern Gang.

On the other side of the fence, Arab militarism within Palestine had crumbled during the war; and by 1945 the Arab inhabitants looked, first, to Britain, and ultimately to the armies of neighbouring Arab states, for protection.

During October the tension increased, mainly due to the immigration issue, and the 6th Airborne Division were widely deployed on internal security duties — thus, at one stroke, forfeiting their value as part of the Strategic Reserve. The 3rd Parachute Brigade were sent to the Lydda District, which included Tel Aviv; while the 6th Airlanding Brigade went to Samaria, and the 2nd Brigade, who had only just arrived from the UK, remained for the time being near Gaza. On the last night of the month Palmach sabotaged the railway — a warning shot for what lay ahead.

On November 13, a White Paper on Palestine was published in London; it dodged the issue, and caused bitter disappointment among the Jews. It was acknowledged by a 12-hour strike and rioting in Tel Aviv. The Palestine police could not cope, and the 8th Battalion Parachute Regiment was brought in. As violence spread, the whole of the 3rd Brigade became involved; and order was not restored until a curfew, lasting till dawn on November 20, had been imposed. Tel Aviv had been made to appreciate that anarchy would not be tolerated; but the airborne troops, in a thankless role, only earned themselves the nickname of 'Kalanyot' from the Jewish population. 'Kalanyot' — the red poppy with a black heart.

If the Tel Aviv riots heralded a conflict between the 6th Airborne and Zionism, the events of April 25, 1946, confirmed it. On that night, members of the Stern Gang attacked a lightly-guarded military car-park and deliberately and brutally murdered seven soldiers of the 5th (Scottish) Parachute Battalion. Far worse outrages were committed later on: the 'Car Park Murders' were shocking because they destroyed the goodwill and trust which had existed among the British troops up till then. Nothing was ever to be the same again, which was presumably what the terrorists wanted.

Because the Jewish population condoned the outrages, harboured

Men of 6th Airborne Division sorting an illegal arms cache found on a Jewish settlement in Palestine. (Courtesy Imperial War Museum.)

their perpetrators and refused to restrain their attacks, it became impossible for the Security Forces to distinguish between the patriotic, and essentially defensive, organizations, Hagana and Palmach, and the terrorists, IZL and the Stern Gang. In historical perspective we can understand Jewish resentment against settlement searches, for the weapons confiscated were a form of insurance against Arab attack; but, in the same perspective, the Israelis should understand that their support for terrorism as a political weapon was the direct cause of this failure to differentiate. Of course, one man's terrorist is another man's freedom fighter; and it was in the latter guise that the IZL and the Stern Gang were presented to world opinion by the highly-organized Zionist propaganda machine. 'Every time a British soldier is killed in Palestine,' wrote the American playwright Ben Hecht, 'I make a little holiday in my heart'. No campaign did more to project to an international audience the image of terrorism as a glamorous and legitimate form of political action; and if today the politically discontented seek redress by similar means, they are merely copying the precedent that was established in Palestine between 1945 and 1948.

Throughout 1946 and the first six weeks of 1947 the British Government still hoped to find a settlement which would satisfy both Jews and Arabs. If today it seems obvious that there was never any real prospect of it, at least hope was kept alive so long as the British governed; but on February 14, 1947, the Foreign Secretary announced that the problem had been placed before the United Nations.

All this time the terrorist campaign, punctuated now and then by more purposeful operations by Palmach, continued. The Division was trying to maintain law and order in a society that was dedicated to destroying it. The Jewish population was excellently disciplined, both in security and in hampering counter-insurgency work in every possible way. Frequently towns, villages or Kibbutzim had to be cordoned off and searched for wanted men or arms: on such occasions the women would line up before the troops and refuse to move; and it needed deep reserves of patience and self-control to move them bodily out of the way while being abused and spat upon and compared to the SS. Meanwhile, photographers would be on hand to provide the New York newspapers with fresh evidence of brutality. If the Jews made it impossible for the British to govern, they succeeded solely because the British were not prepared to get really tough. But Zionist propaganda painted a different picture.

Searches were only one aspect of the work. Road-blocks had to be established to restrict the movement of arms or wanted men; the railways had to be guarded against sabotage, so that, for weeks on end, soldiers were deployed along their length between dawn and sunset. But the most distasteful job of all was that of turning back the boatloads of pathetic refugees from Europe, the 'illegal immigrants' whose sole illegality consisted of being over and above the permitted quota. Whatever the political reasoning behind restricted immigration—and it was entirely Arab-inspired—the reality, in human terms, was pitiful.

But always the cycle of events came back to searches. In one gigantic operation, the reinforced 6th Airborne Division, with five brigades, three armoured car regiments and supporting units, searched the whole of Tel Aviv, a city of 170,000 people.

Jewish attacks were imaginative and bold, and quite unrestrained by conscience or public opinion. The IZL and the Stern Gang dealt entirely with murder. Shots in the back; electrically detonated mines on road-sides; explosive charges in various guises, left to explode inside or against buildings; raids on isolated posts; the hanging of hostages—these were their methods. Palmach's acts of sabotage were designed more to impress public opinion—such as the destruction of a number of Halifax aircraft at Qastina airfield—or in support of immigration.

But now that the future of Palestine was before the United Nations, a new danger threatened Zionism—the Arabs. Henceforth, Hagana and Palmach increasingly turned their energies towards the defence of Jewish lives and property; and in due course expanded into Zahal, the Israel Defence Forces. IZL and Stern, however, motivated more by blind hatred than patriotism, intensified their attacks on the British and later turned to massacring Arab civilians.

Of course it wasn't all bad; it never is. There was sport to be had—

Men of the 6th Airborne Division boarding the Jewish illegal immigrant ship 'Unafraid' at Haifa in Palestine. (Courtesy Airborne Forces Museum.)

swimming in the Mediterranean, and ski-ing in the Lebanon, and the routine visits to the Holy Places. There was even some satisfaction to be got out of doing a thankless job as well as possible. At a personal level, relationships with Jews as well as Arabs were often friendly and rewarding; but history is apt to lose the small, compensating details in the conflict and the bitterness.

The UN Special Committee toured Palestine in the summer of 1947, eagerly supported by the Jews but virtually boycotted by the Arabs. Their report recommended partition, and this was carried by 33 votes to 13, with 10 abstentions. Once the decision was made, the UN washed its hands of the affair, and left it to the Jews and Arabs to fight it out. For Britain, there was no reasonable alternative but to accept the ruling, and get out. The date set for laying down the mandate was May 15, 1948.

The damage done to the King David Hotel after a Jewish sabotage attack in Palestine.
(Courtesy Airborne Forces Museum.)

The final months saw the Division's role change to one of peace-keeping between the Jews and the Arabs, who were being reinforced by gangs from Iraq, Lebanon and Syria. Bus-loads of Jews were frequently rescued from ambush by the armoured cars of the 3rd Hussars or by parachute troops sent on foot. About this time, the 2nd Parachute Brigade returned to the UK to retrain as an airborne force, and the 3rd Parachute Brigade was disbanded. Amalgamations at this time reduced the battalions to six: 4th/6th, 5th and 7th forming the 2nd Brigade; and 1st, 2nd/3rd and 8th/9th forming the 1st Brigade. With the withdrawal of the 2nd Brigade the 6th Airborne Division had now only one parachute brigade, but other units and formations were placed under command.

The Commander, Royal Artillery, controlled a special 'CRAFORCE' in Galilee during the final period, and it was kept busy. In Haifa, fighting took place regularly between the rival populations, with a parachute battalion deployed between them. Eventually the Jews launched a full-scale attack, and seized control of the town. With the departure of the last parachute soldiers in mid-May, Britain's brief role in Palestine's long and troubled history was over.

The bulk of the airborne troops sailed from Haifa in April, the last airborne unit to embark being 'B' Troop, 1st Airborne Squadron RE. They were followed on May 15 by the GOC 6th Airborne Division and North Sector Palestine; and on arrival in the UK, the 6th Airborne Division was disbanded, for, in the reduction of the services to peace-time levels, it was decided that airborne forces in the Regular Army should now be reduced to a single parachute brigade group.

In February 1948, the 2nd Brigade, under Brigadier R. H. Bellamy, DSO, had joined BAOR in Germany; and it fell to them to become the nucleus of the new formation, which was to preserve the history and traditions of the earliest parachute battalions and the two immortal war-time divisions. With that vivid past in mind, the 2nd Brigade was redesignated the 16th Independent Parachute Brigade Group, the numbers 1 and 6 perpetuating those of the 1st and 6th Airborne Divisions. The brigade returned to the UK in October 1949, and was stationed partly in Wiltshire and partly at Aldershot. In 1960 the Brigade's title was changed once more by the dropping of the word 'Independent'.

Since that time, the Regular Parachute Brigade has maintained a permanent 'home' in Aldershot. In 1965, a modern barracks complex was officially opened by Field-Marshal Montgomery and named Montgomery Lines. Today the Depot of the Parachute Regiment and Airborne Forces, which also houses the magnificent and evocative museum, is in Browning Barracks, Aldershot, completed in 1968.

Chapter

13

Egypt 1951–4

I N May 1951 the Persian Government nationalized the Persian oil
industry, and thereby caused the British Government considerable concern, over both future supplies, and the safety of its
nationals. Forces in the Middle East were alerted; and in June, the
16th Independent Parachute Brigade Group, 3,500 strong, embarked
in the aircraft carriers *Warrior* and *Triumph* with its heavy equipment,
for Cyprus. However, the Persian debacle resolved itself without the
brigade being called upon: instead, they found themselves, that
autumn, in Egypt.

On July 26, King Farouk had abdicated in favour of his six-months-
old son, Faud II; but officers of the Egyptian army led by General
Neguib and Colonel Nasser, seized power. The Colonels appeared to
have no love for the British, and over the next few months political
tension mounted. In mid-October the Parachute Battalions and
Brigade HQ were flown in, and the heavy equipment, transport and
guns followed by sea. Tented camps were established in various
lonely stretches of desert and the troops stood by to await developments.

They were not long coming. In November, the Egyptian workers in
the docks, ordnance depots and workshops went on strike; and this
meant work for the British troops, of whom there were at that time
some 70,000 in the Canal Zone. The parachute battalions took over
the docks; the 33rd Parachute Light Regiment, RA, took over guard
and general duties in the Ordnance Depot at Geneifa; and 63
Company RASC were involved in general transport. Irksome though
much of it was, at least it ensured plentiful supplies of 'good cheer'
in the brigade camps at Christmas!

In January 1952, the Canal Zone itself was threatened; and two
British infantry divisions and the Parachute Brigade moved into the
desert west of Suez. If British lives in Egypt were put in jeopardy,
the 1st Battalion was ready to launch an airborne assault on Cairo in

conjunction with an attack led by the 3rd, and a squadron of the 4th Royal Tanks. The Egyptian Army advanced to within five miles of the Canal Zone border, facing the British forces; and there they halted. The RAF flew tactical reconnaissance flights daily to keep an eye on them; and by February it was obvious that they were going no further. However, Egyptian hostility towards Britain was intensified; the internal security of the Zone deteriorated, the Egyptian police refused to co-operate, terrorists were establishing themselves in the principal towns, and attacks on Service vehicles and property increased. The centre of the activity was in Ismailia. Situated at the centre of communications in the Zone on Lake Timsah, it contained the British Military HQ, was the civil administrative centre of the Zone and housed the main concentration of the staff and pilots of the Suez Canal Company. It was obvious that the town would have to be properly controlled.

So, from January 20–25, a task force, which included the 2nd and 3rd Battalions, moved in to cordon off and search the worst areas, and take over the main civil police barracks and other key points in the town. It was not done without bloodshed. When clearing a cemetery, one officer of the 2nd Battalion, and a terrorist, were killed, and 12 more terrorists captured; and the occupation of the police barracks turned into a pitched battle between the 1st Lancashire Fusiliers, with an armoured squadron, and the 95 Egyptian police. These latter were no hotheaded young fanatics, but stolid, middle-aged constables, and they fought so dourly that it took a tank, parked in the mouth of the main gate, to blast them out with its 20-pounder. By that time, half of their number were dead, and the rest wounded. British casualties were four wounded. The police became national heroes, as a result, and the 'battle' is commemorated every year by the releasing of doves in Cairo. The Parachute Brigade was next moved into camps around Ismailia and became responsible for the peace and security of the town and the area round it.

The next two years, during which the brigade were occupied with internal security duties, alternated between periods of calm and intense activity. Ambushes, theft and damage to military property, sniping and other terrorist activities, involved a round of guards, convoy escorts, road blocks, patrolling and cordon and search operations. Opportunities for relaxation were few; and in compensation, frequent exercises were held in Jordan, Cyprus and the Sinai Desert, with sight-seeing trips on their completion. Various adventure training programmes were organized, including visits to the Holy Places, St Catherine's Monastery on Mt Sinai, and to the Red Sea coral reefs.

Throughout this time the brigade had been on an 'emergency' tour, and there were no quarters for wives and families. It was left to Major J. Awdry, a bachelor, to find the solution, which was for the men themselves to build a complete village of 40 bungalows on an island in Lake Timsah near Ismailia. This, it must be admitted, turned into a scrounging operation on a heroic scale. In three months the 9th Independent Parachute Squadron RE and the Battalion Pioneers finished the job. Situated beneath the trees — and, in some cases, built round them, and close to the water's edge, the bungalows were of timber frame construction with double canvas walls stiffened by coats of paint, and contained all 'mod cons' — electric light, water, and calor gas cookers. They were passed by the medical authorities and the families started to arrive and move in. 'Pegasus Village' was opened officially by General Sir Francis Festing, the GOC-in-C, on July 31, 1953. Later another 20 bungalows were added, and, at the end of the tour, the village was sold to another formation in the Zone.

A number of changes took place in the Parachute Regiment during their tour in Egypt. One of the most radical had been the opening of the regiment the previous year to direct enlistment for other ranks. The parachute brigades had always drawn their members from volunteers from the rest of the army, and this, of course, still obtained; but now, for the first time, men could enlist straight from civil life. It was to be another five years, however, before officers could serve other than on secondment from their own regiments. In 1958 a regular cadre of officers was approved, and the first transfers took place; and in August of that year, the first officer directly commissioned into the Parachute Regiment — Second Lieutenant R. D. Penley, joined from Sandhurst. Voluntary secondment continued as before, but was now reduced to some 25 per cent of the officer requirements.

Chapter
14
Malaya 1955–7

BETWEEN 1948 and 1956, communist infiltration into Malaya created an unofficial, unacknowledged war which became known, with some understatement, as 'The Emergency'. The jungle areas became infested with roving bands of Communist Terrorists (CTs), who dominated and indoctrinated the Aborigine tribes and threw the whole country into turmoil. The 22nd Special Air Services Regiment (SAS) was formed, from the Malayan Scouts, to fight this elusive enemy on his own ground, deep in the jungle, and, particularly in the later stages, to rescue and re-educate the bewildered natives. The 22nd SAS consisted of four 'sabre' or fighting squadrons, a HQ squadron, and a large signals troop.

In 1954 the Director of Operations in Malaya was General Sir Geoffrey Bourne, who was also Honorary Colonel of the 10th Battalion the Parachute Regiment (Volunteer). 'C' (Rhodesian) Squadron of the 22nd SAS had completed its tour of duty, and he recommended that the Parachute Regiment should be invited to supply a special squadron to take its place. The War Office agreed, and volunteers were called for. The response was quick and overwhelming, and it became necessary to strike a rough balance between the units so that no battalion was favoured more than another. In all, 80 officers, NCOs and men formed The Independent Parachute Squadron.

Initial training and equipping took place at Aldershot under the command of Major E. W. D. Coventry, who was to lead the Squadron for the whole of its existence. The party flew to Malaya in the spring of 1955 for jungle training at the Far East Training Centre, Kohta Tinggi, in Southern Johore. This, in itself, was a new departure, as SAS recruits were normally trained within the regiment under the auspices of the Training Troop. The climax of the six weeks course was a seaborne exercise in the Southern Johore islands. This was a salutary experience of great value. In April, the squadron moved up to the Regimental Camp in Coronation Park, Kuala Lumpur.

Its normal organization was a HQ Troop and four fighting troops. For the last six months, and whenever the squadron was operating in the area of a Police fort, a fifth 'working' troop was formed from HQ and other selected personnel. A troop, which consisted of 14 soldiers, was sub-divided into three patrols. These patrols were usually kept together, and each became a very close-knit band of men who knew and trusted one another implicitly. A troop was always accompanied by three or four Abo (Aborigine) porters who carried the radio (62 set) and its batteries, and, when necessary, by Iban trackers from Borneo. If local inhabitants were likely to be encountered, a loyal Junior Chinese Liaison Officer was sometimes taken along to act as interpreter.

All troops throughout the regiment were serially numbered to assist recognition, especially by aircraft dropping supplies, and those of the Parachute Squadron were Nos. 11–15. The normal routine was for a squadron to be placed under command, or in support of, an infantry brigade operating along the highways and plantations near the centres of population. The squadron would penetrate, either on foot or by helicopter, and occasionally by parachute, deep into the surrounding jungle, to locate CT guerillas and report on their movements. In addition the patrols searched for terrorist cultivated areas or Abo tribes hiding, and perhaps starving, in the jungle after the communists had moved on. Surrendered Enemy Personnel (SEP) were sometimes used to lead the troops to CT camps and help to ambush their former comrades in arms.

Each patrol had a mixture of weapons; two or three Winchester repeater shotguns, normally carried by lead scouts; two ·303 Mark V rifles; an Owen gun (Australian sub-machine gun); and, for commanders, the American M1 carbine, light and convenient for jungle warfare but with poor killing power. One Bren LMG was carried for the protection of the patrol base camp. A number of new versions of the self-loading rifle, later adopted for the British Army, were issued in 1956 and added greatly to the fire power, although the stocks on early models were found to be too easily broken. Smoke and No. 36 hand grenades were also carried. All patrols were issued with panels for ground/air recognition, but because of their weight fluorescent

A patrol wading through a jungle river in Malaya during the Emergency.

panels were discarded and strips of air-drop parachutes were used instead. Each man carried rations for a week or ten days in his Bergen rucksack, and replenishment was usually by air-drop from RAF Valettas, occasionally supplemented by Bristol Freighters flown by the RNZAF. All supplies were packed and dropped by the 55th Air Despatch Company, RASC, and their integral RAOC stores personnel. For long operations a special 14-day SAS patrol ration was carried.

The Parachute Squadron's first task was a very arduous three months in the Iskander swamp area of Southern Malaya; a tangled, inhospitable stretch of country in which movement was a nightmare. It was not accurately mapped, and a maze of streams criss-crossing the region presented many navigational problems. The squadron discovered several 'Ladangs' (cleared cultivations in the deep jungle), which were ambushed for days on end with varying success, and then destroyed. At the end of this operation the squadron was withdrawn to Kuala Lumpur for a few weeks' rest and retraining, and was then sent back to the same district for a further eight weeks.

Christmas, 1955, was spent at the Regimental Rest House at Morib on the East Coast—where the 5th Parachute Brigade had landed at the end of the Japanese occupation of Malaya, ten years earlier. The squadron was then placed under command of an infantry brigade in a Southern Selangor (North Johore) swamp area known as the Tasek Bera. Their aim was to build up a general picture of all local CT activities, and then, in the last weeks of the operation, to ambush and destroy the whole organization. It was a trying time. Two troops wasted an entire fortnight escorting a woman SEP who proved quite unable to find the CT camp to which she had belonged. Plenty of evidence was found, however, on the banks of the Palong River and elsewhere, and there were several brushes with the enemy. During one of these encounters a soldier was severely wounded, and an S55 helicopter of 848 Squadron Royal Navy picked him up, under the most difficult conditions, from an emergency DZ, and whisked him off to hospital.

The next year of the squadron's tour of duty was spent in the mountainous country between Ipoh and the Cameron Highlands. Many hours of tiring, monotonous patrolling were carried out with very few contacts, and, on the credit side, only one minor casualty. A brilliant small ambush by 12 Troop resulted in the capture of an Aborigine CT organizer near the Tapah road; and another troop found a destitute Abo tribe who were escorted out of the jungle and resettled near the Kinta Waterworks. These operations were interrupted every ten weeks or so by rest and retraining periods, two of which were spent on Blaka Mati island in Singapore Harbour—a very welcome change from scaling the mountains of Northern Malaya.

Statistics for this type of campaign are extremely difficult to produce; but it was concluded that approximately 500 patrol hours were required to achieve one contact. Some troops averaged far more.

Two SAS troopers with aborigine children in Malaya during the Emergency. The SAS played a major role in winning the friendship and confidence of these primitive people who were ruthlessly exploited by the terrorists.

Undoubtedly, SAS penetration into the heart of the jungle, which the CT would normally regard as 'safe', with the consequent destruction of their vegetable patches and the removal of their Abo forced labour, had a cumulative effect. Gradually the terrorists were driven, by hunger, out of the jungle and into the plantations, where they were rounded up by Security Forces. But for the men involved it was an arduous, lonely, hazardous and often apparently unrewarding part of the Malayan campaign, which had received little recognition, and the results of which were largely invisible.

During the tour the Squadron Commander, Major Coventry, received a Mention in Despatches; and Sergeant J. McD. Ferguson was awarded a Commander-in-Chief's Commendation Certificate for his exceptional success as a Troop Commander. The squadron sailed for home in April 1957, in SS *Nevasa*, and was disbanded in May. The Parachute Regiment's association with the Special Air Service Regiment was not ended, however, and a large proportion of the SAS squadrons are still made up from officers and men of the Parachute Regiment who have volunteered for tours in them.

Chapter
15
Cyprus 1956

THE island of Cyprus, which had been part of the old Ottoman Empire and ruled by the Turks since 1560, was ceded to Great Britain in 1878 as part of a defence pact with Turkey. In 1914, when Turkey sided with Germany in the Great War, the island was officially annexed to the British Crown. In 1915 it was offered, in vain, to the Greeks as an inducement to enter the war; and finally, in 1925, Cyprus was created a British Crown Colony.

The population of half a million consisted of two distinct communities with cultural and religious links with the mainland nations of Greece and Turkey, with the Greek-speaking Cypriots outnumbering the Turkish-speaking Cypriots by four to one. As early as 1878, when the first British High Commissioner set foot on the island, the Greek Cypriots had expressed a wish for ENOSIS — the union of Cyprus with Greece. The chief spokesman for the people was then, as now, the Archbishop of the Cypriot Church, the Ethnarch.

Enosis was entirely unacceptable to the Turkish Government. The island, strategically placed close to Turkey's southern sea border, dominates her southern ports and provides a convenient jumping-off point for a potential enemy. Though lost to her because of the 1914–18 war, Turkey was not prepared to see any nation, other than Great Britain, occupying the island. She also had the interests of the Turkish Cypriot minority to protect.

The movement for Enosis continued to gain support until, in 1954, Turkey threatened annexation. A proposal for government by a condominium of her, Britain and Greece was rejected at the instigation of the Greek Government; and the Greek Cypriots, taking this to mean tacit Greek support for union, set out to pressurize Britain by demonstrations and riots.

Extremists were encouraged to form a terrorist organization called EOKA — the National Union of Cypriot Combatants — and imported an embittered professional soldier, Colonel Grivas, who had been an officer of the Greek Army in World War II, to command it. Under his direction a campaign of terror opened in late 1955.

It was noted in the chapter on Palestine how the tactics of Irgun and the Stern Gang created a paradigm of violence for those elsewhere who were seeking independence or other alterations in the status quo; and although an airborne officer who had been in Palestine gave it as his opinion that 'Irgun could run rings round this lot', the fact remains that EOKA's methods, in their cynical brutality, owed a lot to their Jewish exemplars. The object of the exercise was simply to attract world sympathy by provoking the British into actions which could be presented as the suppression, by a colonial power, of a subject people whose sole and worthy ambition was self-determination. Their choice of a leader for this despicable campaign could hardly have been bettered.

In January 1956 the 1st and 3rd Battalions were moved to Cyprus at twenty-four hours notice in order to support the security forces on the island. They went into camp, under canvas, close to Nicosia airport; but in the ensuing months they seldom enjoyed even that rough comfort.

One of their first tasks — given to 3 Para — was to arrest Archbishop Makarios, with whom the British Government had been conducting a fruitless dialogue along the lines of self-determination without Enosis. When the talks broke down, and the decision was taken to try and discover a less obdurate spokesman, the battalion cordoned off the palace, while the Ethnarch was detained for deportation to the Seychelles; for, since Napoleon was shooed off to Elba, the British have had a humane but misguided faith in exile — or gaol — as a solution to political discontent. In this case, the archbishop's apprehension went off without incident but for the discovery, within the palace, of a bricked-up chamber. Suspicious, or merely curious, the soldiers broke in, to discover nothing more alarming than the bones of an ancient skeleton walled up inside. Cyprus was no newcomer to the nastier techniques of hate; only now they were being exploited on a broader scale and with a twentieth-century thoroughness.

For despicable is not too strong a word to describe EOKA's tactics. They were aimed, in the first instance, almost exclusively at their own civilian population. Selected muktars — village headmen — and local unarmed constables were murdered, frequently by being drenched in petrol and burnt alive in front of their families. Harmless old shepherds, returning in the evening with their goats and fat-tailed sheep, were shot to pieces with Thompson sub-machine guns; and anyone who was believed to oppose, even passively, EOKA and its aims were liable to be gunned down in the street or in church, or at least threatened with a similar fate. That such methods were effective, at least in the short term, there is no question: they imposed a conspiracy of silence on the island which made the acquisition of evidence or information by the security forces virtually impossible.

This reign of terror soon spread to include the Turks. Bomb outrages increased, and military and police vehicles were ambushed, though attacks were seldom pressed home against alert and well-armed troops. In fact, throughout the campaign, there were only a few isolated occasions when EOKA were prepared to fight it out with armed opponents: they usually preferred to slip away into the obscurity of the crowd, or, if they were cornered, to surrender.

When they thought they could get away with it, they attacked British servicemen. One example typifies them all. A British sergeant, off duty and unarmed, went shopping in the outskirts of Nicosia with his four-year old son. An EOKA gunman stalked him, shot him in the back, and vanished. Later, he was actually arrested, but was acquitted through lack of evidence, since no one would testify against him for fear of reprisals.

The first major field operation in which the battalions took part was 'Pepperpot', in May, and was directed against the gangs in the Paphos forest. They succeeded in capturing one wanted man, Bouboulis; and later another, Masarides, who was armed with a Bren gun and hand grenades, was taken by ambush. For the latter, Sergeant Howse, of the 3rd Battalion, was awarded the BEM. Both these men had been in a group of four, which was working with Grivas himself; but, not for the last time, their leader just escaped. Two days later a third known terrorist, Mallas, was also captured.

It was always suspected that the Greek Orthodox Church was implicated in, or at the very least, sympathetic to, EOKA; and a search of the monastery at Kykkho confirmed it. They found no wanted men, but, in the monks' cells, plenty of evidence that they were being used as a refuge by hard-core EOKA operating in the hills.

In early June the 3rd Battalion was again in the Paphos forest, at the start of 'Lucky Alphonse'. Never was an operation more unfortunately named — though it began well enough, with the discovery of a terrorist hide and larder, and an encouraging 'scent'. But then things started to go wrong. Kykkho, searched again, kept its dark secrets secure: a Sergeant-Major of 1 Para was shot dead in an ambush when he strayed over the inter-unit boundary; and soon afterwards, Sergeant Scott, leading a patrol of 'C' Company, 3 Para, found himself within a couple of hundred yards of a bunch of men who were indisputably terrorists. He and his men were only 60 yards away when someone's foot slipped on the scree and the gang took to their heels, unharmed by the fusillade of shots that pursued them. The patrol found their hide, and it only served to compound their frustration; for, among the documents and equipment which they had abandoned were Grivas's personal diary, and his shoes.* They had been that close to EOKA's leader and his HQ group. Obviously there was useful information to be extracted from the haul — including the fact that the Colonel's arthritis was troubling him, as well as the security forces — but his skin would have been even better.

A few nights later another British soldier, a Norfolk, roaming through the forest delirious, was killed; and a week later the 3-inch mortars of 40 Commando — or so it is supposed: Grivas claimed the 'credit' for himself — started a forest fire which burnt for a week and swept through the district. Moving through the dry pines like a flame-thrower, it gobbled up a score or more of British soldiers' lives, including those of Captain Michael Beagley and Private Hawker of 3 Para.

The 2nd Battalion and the balance of the Brigade sailed to Cyprus in early July, and were soon involved, like the rest, in anti-terrorist operations. These included continual village cordon and search, road

---

* The rest of Grivas's uniform is now in the museum.

blocks, curfews, and the preservation of law and order in Nicosia. The old walled city was roughly divided into two areas, Greek and Turk. When inter-racial fighting increased, it was divided by an actual barbed wire line, nicknamed by the soldiers 'the Mason–Dixon Line', and patrolled by troops to enforce separation between the two communities.

It had been established that three mountain terrorist groups were active in the East Kyrenia range, and in early October a large operation, 'Sparrow-Hawk', was mounted to destroy them. This involved the entire Parachute Brigade, and was highly successful. A total of some 20 hard core terrorists were using villages in the area as their supply and communication centres. On the night of October 2, a cordon was thrown round the district by a mixed force of gunners and infantrymen with the Navy carrying out the seaward cut-off to the north. Early the following morning, the three parachute battalions, with the Guards Independent Parachute Company under command of the 2nd Battalion, moved in and set up HQ at Halevga Forest Station in the heart of the mountains. Village curfews were enforced, and all farmers were rounded up and sent home. Observation posts were set up, and planned arrests were made. Platoons were sent off, with two days' rations, on a systematic search, patrolling by day and setting up light machine gun ambushes in section groups by night. Houses were combed from roof to cellar.

At 0900 hours on the second day, a patrol from the 2nd Battalion was searching a farmhouse near Trapeza, when a soldier accidentally dislodged a rock. Beneath it were two holes packed with arms and ammunition, and further investigation disclosed a dugout, carefully camouflaged and concealed in the hillside. It was empty, but gave every sign of having been recently and hurriedly abandoned — plates of half-eaten food, a pile of discarded blankets, a watch left hanging on a nail. Eventually, six men were found hiding in a byre beside the farmhouse, and two more arms caches were unearthed. Altogether this was the biggest haul, in men and material, since the beginning of the Cyprus emergency, and most of it was from this one farmhouse.

In between the major sweeps of this kind, each unit waged its own private war against the EOKA thugs in its area. With information almost impossible to get, owing to the grip of terror on the villagers, it became a matter of hard work and guile, with the essential pinch of luck required for success. Luck did not always run; but one particular company deserved better than they got. They were after a singularly unpleasant bunch of killers who were as elusive as they were ruthless. The company commander, knowing EOKA's weakness for ambushing any vehicle that made a regular run, laid a bait for them in the shape of an apparently harmless stores truck, which he arranged should take the same route at the same time on the same day every week. It travelled alone; it looked quite harmless; but in the back, behind sandbags, were ten heavily-armed men; and behind it, half-a-mile or so, came two other vehicles, equally well-armed.

For six weeks nothing happened. Then, one evening, the supporting vehicles heard shots ahead. They raced to the spot, to find a truck damaged and on fire. The terrorists had indeed struck at last — but not at the decoy. A lorry had strayed in from another area unannounced, unknowing and totally unprepared, and had sprung the trap. One officer was wounded; one terrorist had been killed; the rest escaped. And weeks of patient hard work had gone to waste.

While engaged on 'Foxhunter' in the Troodos mountains at the end of October — an operation which was beginning to yield information, suspects and arms — the brigade was recalled to camp at Nicosia in order to go to Suez, as described elsewhere in this book; and afterwards, in December, the 1st and 3rd Battalions returned to England, leaving the 2nd in Cyprus.

The 2nd Battalion left Nicosia just before Christmas and moved to Platres in the Troodos mountains where they took over a large area from the Gordon Highlanders. Early in January, 1957, the battalion scored their first success. Information was received about two hides near Yerakies; and a patrol from 'C' Company, led by Captain Peter Field, went to investigate and captured Nicos Ioannan, who had a price of £5,000 on his head, and two other terrorists.

In mid-January, in operation 'Blackmac', another major blow was struck against the Troodos area terrorists. It started with the capture of three men in a secret room in the village of Kannavia; rapidly followed by that of Karadimas, the EOKA QM, and others in a hide in Sarandi. Finally, Spanos Polycarpos, the EOKA Intelligence Officer, was added to the bag with six of his associates. The total for the month was 21 hard core terrorists, 46 weapons and a large amount of ammunition. Early in February the battalion sailed from Limassol for home.

The effective work by British troops brought EOKA to its knees and it was saved, as it were, by the gong, when a truce was agreed to enable politicians to try once more for a settlement. This relatively calm period lasted until the early summer of 1958, when EOKA, restored and reorganized, resumed its terror offensive. At about the same time, events elsewhere in the Middle East brought the parachute soldiers back to Cyprus. The activities of the brigade in Jordan are described elsewhere; but when the 2nd and 3rd Battalions flew off from Nicosia, the 1st Battalion stayed behind and, while awaiting events, resumed the hunt for terrorists.

Their most notable success was operation 'Filter Tip'. It was known that gangs were active in the Kyrenia hills, but conventional methods had failed to discover them. Lieutenant-Colonel G. G. Reinholt, MC, the Commanding Officer, devised a scheme of constant surveillance that made it virtually impossible for anything that happened, however trivial, to go unobserved. Pairs of soldiers concealed themselves everywhere, watching, recording, waiting. A mass of information was painstakingly assembled; and every mistake made by the terrorists, as their nerves cracked, was noted and used. At last the jigsaw was completed, pinpointing a house on the lower foothills, and here Matsis, Grivas's second-in-command, was found hiding beneath the stone floor. He was braver than most. Rather than surrender he chose to fight it out and was killed by a grenade. For the second time, EOKA was close to defeat.

In March 1959, the 1st Battalion returned to the UK. Three months later the fighting ceased, at least for the time being. The Greek Cypriots decided to forget ENOSIS, for which they had spilled so much unnecessary blood, and opted for independence, which they could have had, without bloodshed, five years earlier. They chose to call it 'victory'.

Chapter
16

Suez 1956

I N July 1956, President Nasser of Egypt arbitrarily nationalized
the Suez Canal, and, despite international pressure, refused either
to withdraw, or accept the principle of free and uninterrupted use
of the Canal by ships of all nations. The British Government laid
plans for possible military intervention; but meanwhile war broke
out between Israel, who felt herself particularly threatened, and
Egypt. This changed the whole situation.

The Israelis decisively defeated the Egyptians near their borders
and pursued them across the Sinai Desert. An Israeli parachute battalion was dropped at the Mitla Pass to cut them off, and it was clear
that fighting would soon affect the Canal Zone. The British and
French Governments issued ultimatums to both sides, ordering them
to draw back from the canal. The Israelis, though in hot pursuit of
the defeated Egyptians, and with most to lose by halting, agreed: the
Egyptians, who had everything to gain, refused.

Although there was a complete airborne division in the post-war
regular army order of battle — reduced in 1948 to a brigade group —
there were few Transport Command aircraft available to lift them.
Consequently, plans for the invasion of Egypt had to be based on an
amphibious assault, supported by relatively small numbers of British
and French parachute troops.

On October 31, 1956, the RAF and the FAA began their attacks
on the Egyptian Air Force, and virtually wiped it out in 48 hours.
The plan, however, being geared to the speed of a naval task-force,
there was no way of accelerating the actual occupation of the Canal
Zone; and during the three days that elapsed between the air strikes
and the landings, world opinion hardened against the Anglo–French
action.

The seaborne landings were timed to begin on November 6 and
were to coincide with the airborne drop; but at the last moment the
latter was brought forward 24 hours. This meant that the parachu-

CAPTURE OF EL-GAMIL AIRFIELD 5th NOV. 1956
3 PARA GROUP

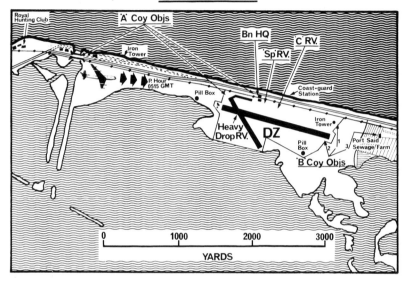

tists would have to forgo the benefit of supporting fire from the destroyers of the naval task-force. Instead, strike aircraft of the Fleet Air Arm were to form a cab-rank above the DZ, and provide aerial artillery on call.

The drop itself was a double one, part British and part French. The former were to land on El Gamil airfield at 0715 hours on November 5 and secure it for future use; that done, their orders were to clear the area between the airfield and the town of Port Said, seal off the native quarter and link up with the RM Commandos — who would have by then come ashore — and, finally, to capture and demolish the bridge to the west of the airfield. The French, on the other hand, accompanied by part of the 1st (Guards) Independent Company, were to drop south of Port Said and to the east of the canal, seal off the southern approaches to the town, and capture the bridges that linked the town with the two roads south. Thereafter,

The first lift of 3 PARA arrives at El Gamil airfield, Port Said, during the Suez operations November 5, 1956. (Courtesy Airborne Forces Museum.)

they were to set off as hard as they could go and secure the canal itself. They were to drop from their own aircraft.

The RAF could muster at this time only enough Hastings and Valettas to lift 668 men—3 Para, commanded by Lieutenant-Colonel P. E. Crook—seven jeeps, four trailers, six 106 mm anti-tank guns, and 176 supply containers. The initial odds were expected to be five to one against the parachute force, and the task-force would still be a day's steaming away.

At 0415 hours the first aircraft taxied out on to the Nicosia runway. The drop began over El Gamil on time, and in ten minutes, despite some flak and casualties in the air, the whole force was on the ground, bar one or two containers and a very few men. Two trailers 'candled' in; but in spite of the very heavy loads the men were carrying, there was only one parachuting injury. The Egyptians reacted promptly and vigorously with 120 mm guns, mobile Russian-built, multi-barrelled rocket-launchers, small arms, and machine gun and mortar fire, but it was not as dangerous as it sounded, luckily. The black spots which had suddenly appeared on the Tac/R photographs just before the force took off, and which had been thought to be mines, turned out to be nothing more threatening than 40-gallon oil drums distributed to prevent aircraft landing, and presented no problem.

A parachute soldier, on landing, other than the initial DZ clearing force, is faced with an uncomfortable dilemma if he is being shot at. He is burdened with a considerable weight of weapons and equipment on his person and in the containers that drop with him. To unload these takes a short time, but, once unloaded, their contents have to be carried to the RV. With all this to shift the last thing he can do is run; and therefore the first few minutes after a drop often have a curious, slow-motion air about them at a time when everyone concerned might be expected to be moving at full speed. This forced leisureliness particularly impressed the French liaison officer, François Collet, who dropped with the 3rd Battalion at El Gamil. The

The CO 3 PARA (Lt-Col. Paul Crook) and his Tac HQ moves off the DZ at El Gamil Airfield, November 5, 1956. (Courtesy Airborne Forces Museum.)

only thing which caused them to move fast, he observed, was the mystical rallying-cry 'Char Up!'—and then he said, he was almost trampled to death in the rush. Collet's call-sign was 'Ici Robert'; and since he was tough and likeable, as well as being a commander in the French Navy and a member of the Légion d'Honneur, 'Ici Robert' became a catch-phrase among the 'Toms'.

'A' Company quickly captured the control building and tower, and silenced a pill-box with rockets, killing two and capturing nine of its occupants. 'B' Company, which landed on top of the Egyptian positions, cleared the coastguard building and the eastern end of the airfield, while the mortars engaged enemy positions behind the sewage farm. Fifteen minutes after 'P' Hour, the first Fleet Air Arm strikes came in.

Within half-an-hour the airfield was in British hands. 'B' Company, with 5 Platoon in the lead and supported by a medium machine gun (MMG) section, now set about clearing the area of the sewage farm.

A parachuted 3 PARA 'Jeep' being de-rigged after the drop on El Gamil Airfield during the Suez Operations. (Courtesy Airborne Forces Museum.)

A 106 mm anti-tank gun demolished a house that was being used as an observation post.

No. 4 Platoon pushed forward through the thick reeds on the right-hand edge of the sewage farm, clearing snipers, and then came under heavy fire from the cemetery. No. 6 Platoon advanced to the left-hand edge of the farm, and the two platoons contained the Egyptians while plans were made for 'C' Company to attack the cemetery. Meanwhile, by 0915 hours — only four hours after the landings — the airfield was ready for use.

At 1028 hours an air strike of Naval Sea Venoms and Sea Hawks was launched on the cemetery; and two minutes later 'C' Company attacked, supported by mortars and MMGs. They were extremely successful, and after fighting at close quarters around the tombstones through to the far end, were able to call for accurate air strikes on the large block of flats facing them, which was being used as an observation post. The battle continued into the afternoon and ammunition, particularly for the 3-inch mortars, was running short. It was decided to pull them back and hold firm in the sewage farm for the night; a counter-attack could not be ruled out.

During this time, Major Stevens, commanding 'B' Company, had been twice wounded, in the hand and then in the leg. He bound up the first himself, and it was not until his shattered leg made it impossible for him to continue in command, that he agreed to be evacuated. He was awarded a Military Cross.

As the second lift was arriving, the French dropped another battalion at Fort Fuad. Soon afterwards, on the invitation of the Military Commander of Port Said, Brigadier M. A. H. ('Tubby') Butler and the Brigade Major left to arrange a cease fire; but Cairo intervened and negotiations broke down. At least it meant that the night was relatively quiet, though the morning of the 6th opened with a lone MIG fighter strafing at low level.

The amphibious assault force was now about to land on the beaches at Port Said, and as the landing-craft ran on to the shore, MMGs from 3 Para gave covering fire along the beaches. At 0510 hours 'C' Company re-occupied the cemetery without opposition, and moved forward to attack and capture the coastguard barracks and some flats that were occupied by snipers. Then a patrol sealed off the native quarter. Throughout the morning, in spite of reports of another cease fire, desultory mortaring and shelling continued. It was clear that the Egyptians were prepared to fight in the native quarter; and after the hospital was captured, a four-man patrol entered the maze of narrow streets to try and link with 45 RM Commando. They soon ran into rocket and sniper fire, and all four of them were wounded. They were extricated under fire by Captain Malcolm Elliott, of the 23rd Parachute Field Ambulance, who happened to be in the area looking for an anaesthetic machine. He was later awarded an MC. One of the battalion's anti-tank guns was then brought up and effectively silenced the opposition. In the process it demolished half of shanty-town, which then caught fire. After this, the parachute soldiers and 45 Commando succeeded in linking up, though sniping continued throughout the day.

A 3 PARA soldier ensures that no one remains in a Russian built Egyptian S.U.100 tank overrun during the fighting at Port Said November 1956. (Courtesy Airborne Forces Museum.)

Aerial view of the Port Said fighting by 3 PARA. The burning outbuildings of the airfield control tower can be clearly seen. The large white blobs near the runway are the 60 foot parachute clusters used for the 'jeeps' and anti-tank guns. Immediately below the airfield is

the sewage farm. The causeway then narrows — the cemetery is in the centre of the photograph
followed by the 'flats' and the suburbs of Port Said. To the right of the road are the Coast
Guard Barracks and on the left of the picture is the felucca harbour. (Courtesy Airborne
Forces Museum).

At 2359 hours on November 6 a general cease fire was ordered; thereafter the 3rd Battalion spent a few days patrolling the town, clearing and rounding up scattered Egyptian forces, and supervizing the flow of refugees who were leaving Port Said from the felucca harbour. The 3rd Battalion's casualties were four killed and 36 wounded.

The 2nd Battalion the Parachute Regiment came ashore during the afternoon of November 6 near the de Lesseps statue in Port Said, and moved through the town and down the causeway to the south. There was no opposition, but plenty of evidence of the accuracy of the airstrikes by naval aircraft. The battalion halted for the night at El Cap, and dug in. Defensive positions were improved on the following day; the Egyptians were digging in a few hundred yards down the road. The 2nd Battalion dealt with sporadic sniping south of El Cap during November 8 and 9, and on the second night 'A' Company of the 3rd Battalion occupied El Tina, between the 2nd and Port Said.

World opinion, and pressure from friends and enemies alike now caused the British and French governments to call a halt, and eventually to withdraw their troops. El Cap marked the limit of the advance. When the 1st Battalion landed, they moved west along the coast and dug in. A week after their arrival in Egypt, the parachute troops embarked in MV *New Australia* and returned to Cyprus. Operation 'Musketeer' was over.

If it was indecisive the reasons were political, not military. As far as the handful of paratroops who took part in it were concerned, they had no professional cause to feel ashamed. They had done their work well even if, as Cairo radio claimed, they had been wiped out to the last man!

Chapter

17

Jordan 1958

IN the summer of 1958 the normally tranquil state of Lebanon erupted into civil war. Since there was no evidence that the attempted take-over by left-wing extremists had any real support from the people, the United States and Britain made preparations to help restore order if necessary. The 16th Independent Parachute Brigade Group was flown, at traditionally short notice, to Cyprus; while US Marines and paratroops, serving with the 6th Fleet and in Germany, were alerted.

Then, on July 14, there was a *coup d'état* in Iraq, in which the King, most of the Royal family and the Prime Minister were murdered. A junta headed by General Kassim seized power, and quickly showed itself unfriendly to the West, opposed to the Arab Union, and hostile to King Hussein of Jordan. Iraq and Jordan had previously been united by treaty; but now General Kassim and President Nasser of Egypt openly supported anti-government factions threatening to overthrow King Hussein. Stability in the Middle East depended to a large extent upon responsible leadership in Jordan; and on July 16 the King and his Prime Minister appealed to the British Government for the immediate despatch of troops to Amman, the capital.

Consequently, while the Americans went to help the Lebanese, the British went to Jordan. It was necessary to fly across Israel to get to Amman, and although permission was obtained, there was some delay in the air lift due to confusion between government officials concerning the over-flying rights. The advance party, consisting of the Brigade Commander, Brigadier T. C. H. Pearson, DSO, OBE, and a small Headquarters and Signals element, were isolated on Amman airfield for several hours on July 17, much to the surprise and embarrassment of the Jordanian authorities, who knew nothing of the plan.

The main body arrived in due course, and by July 20 the force was complete. It consisted of the entire Parachute Brigade except for the

1st Battalion, which had remained in Cyprus in case of another emergency and 208 Squadron RAF, with its ground attack Hunters and maintenance staff. Its task was threefold, and it was divided into three groups. First, the security of Amman airfield was entrusted to the 2nd Battalion: the 3rd Battalion and much of the 1st (Guards) Independent Company formed a mobile force for the other two — the protection of HM King Hussein and his government, and of British and friendly residents in Jordan. Lastly, a reserve was formed from the minor units. All dangers were guarded against, from internal strife to full-scale invasion.

From July 17 until August 10 there was an enormous airlift of men and stores, much of it in Globemaster transports of the United States Air Force. The brigade was kept busy unloading, reconnoitering and preparing positions. There was very little transport available and vehicles were borrowed from the Jordan Arab Army, with whom relations remained cordial throughout. The brigade was allowed the use of several large barrack blocks around the airfield for offices, stores, messes, canteens and a certain amount of accommodation, but for the most part the troops bivouacked in the surrounding sand. Cooking and sanitary arrangements had to be improvized, and life was made as comfortable as could be expected.

On August 7, the 1st Battalion the Cameronians (Scottish Rifles) arrived at Aqaba from Kenya aboard the commando carrier HMS *Bulwark*, and came up to Amman to strengthen the very thin defences of the airfield. The final reinforcement, the 17th Field Battery Royal Artillery, arrived on August 22.

After a time the situation became less tense, and training and recreational trips were possible. Rifle companies spent two or three days in the wooded hills to the north of Amman; and many expeditions set out for places of interest, Petra being the most popular. Aid was given to some of the half-million refugees, and hospitals were helped where possible. Games were played, and hospitality exchanged, with the Jordan Arab Army. A display was laid on at the airfield, and a remarkably well turned-out Guard of Honour was formed by the 3rd Battalion, for King Hussein when he paid a ceremonial visit to the brigade. Behind the ceremonial and the sport, however, the brigade remained at instant readiness in case of trouble, right up to the moment it left.

Dr Hammarskjold, the then Secretary General of the United Nations, came to Amman at the end of August; and a month later the King told parliament that British forces would start to withdraw on October 20. The Cameronians left first, and the Parachute Brigade flew out between October 25 and 29, returning to Nicosia and then to the UK.

Not a very dramatic operation, perhaps; but military action must be judged by its political consequences, and on this basis the intervention in Jordan in 1958 was entirely successful. There is no doubt that good planning and rapid action in a potential trouble spot can avert not only unnecessary loss of life, but hostilities which, in this particular case, might have escalated to unforeseeable dimensions. The good fireman is not judged by the size of the fire, but by the speed with which it is extinguished. In this operation the concept of a 'Fire Brigade' was fully justified.

Chapter 18

Cyprus Again 1964

W HEN Cyprus finally achieved independence, in 1960, her new Constitution laid down certain measures for the protection of the Turkish Cypriot minority, and was guaranteed by Britain, Greece and Turkey, who each stationed troops on the island. The Government was to consist of 70 per cent Greeks and 30 per cent Turks, with similar representation in the Civil Service and legislature; and the six main towns were to have separate municipal authorities for Greeks and Turks.

The Greek Cypriots were not satisfied for long with these arrangements, and by 1963 were complaining that the proportional representation required by the Constitution was holding back some of their ablest administrators. Once again, the atmosphere in Cyprus became tense and acrimonious.

On Christmas Day, 1963, a group led by Nichos Samson stormed into the Ormophita district of Nicosia and attempted to capture the Turkish political leaders by force of arms. This attack sparked off disturbances in Larnaca and Famagusta, in which shops were looted and atrocities committed by both sides, while the police force, its loyalties divided, was indecisive and virtually ineffectual.

Within hours of the initial outbreak of violence, the two British battalions stationed in the Sovereign Base areas—the 1st Battalion the Gloucestershire Regiment and the 3rd Royal Green Jackets— were moved into Nicosia to impose a rather uneasy truce. It soon became clear to the military authorities that more troops would be needed, and standby units of the 3rd Division were despatched from the UK to augment the small British force.

The 1st Battalion the Sherwood Foresters and 2nd Regiment RA both arrived before the end of December; but the 1st Battalion the Parachute Regiment was, for once, enjoying Christmas block leave, and widely scattered. On New Year's Eve the CO, Lieutenant-Colonel P. D. F. Thursby, received the order to be ready to move at

24 hours' notice; and recall telegrams were sent to every man in the battalion. The QM arrived from the north of Scotland to find he was with the advance party, and had only two hours in which to pack; and there are some apocryphal stories of how soldiers on leave in Europe managed to get back in time to catch the last aircraft. But such is the way in Airborne Forces.

They reached the RAF station at Akrotiri between January 2–4, and made the long drive to Dhekelia and their first temporary home. The camp was sited on a wind-swept headland four miles east of the town, in the eastern of the two Sovereign Base areas. At once, tents were erected, vehicles were drawn from the stockpile, and the soldiers were ready to tackle the problem of a country in the throes of civil war.

After a week in Dhekelia, the battalion moved to Episkopi in the Western Zone and occupied the Glosters' barracks during their absence in Nicosia. From this comfortable base, they and the Guards Independent Company patrolled the administrative districts of Limassol and Paphos. Meanwhile, HQ 16th Parachute Brigade took over responsibility for operations in Nicosia from the rather cramped confines of the Nicosia Club.

As the only major unit in the Western Zone, the battalion found itself running what amounted to a Brigade Operations Room. There were three large towns and about 350 villages in the area, containing both Greek and Turkish Cypriot communities. For the next six weeks, a very active patrol programme enabled every village to be visited at least twice a week. It was not long before *agents provocateurs* from the capital brought trouble to these rural outposts; and the Greek Cypriots' stock of small arms was supplemented by more sophisticated weaponry. Patrols had to intervene almost daily, to settle inter-racial disputes and to prevent bloodshed.

In February, the pressure on the Turkish communities isolated outside the main enclaves in Nicosia, Famagusta and Lefka began to increase. On February 11–12, Greek Cypriots, using armoured bulldozers and a Stuart tank with an improvized turret, carried out a determined and well-planned attack on the Turkish quarter of Limassol. This was perhaps the most difficult day the battalion faced, as more than 130 British families lived in the battle zone and any action might lead to reprisals against them. However, after hours of fighting, a cease fire was achieved, and the families evacuated to safer areas. Similar disturbances occured in Paphos and Polis during February, although not on so large a scale.

On the 28th, the battalion moved to Nicosia, taking with it memories of a thousand small dramas, and the satisfaction of having saved many lives. When the Western Zone 'Ops' room was handed over to HQ Royal Artillery of the 3rd Division, the IO and his little team were surprised to see not fewer than 11 officers as their replacement.

In Nicosia, the battalion occupied a variety of buildings, from ordinary bungalows to a five-storey flour mill, from a block of luxury flats, to the legendary Cyprus Cold Store. No-one liked the change to city life, after wide-ranging patrols and a good deal of independence. An incident which in the Western Zone would have been dealt with by a junior officer or NCO, now had usually to be referred to Brigade HQ.

Daily routine consisted of maintaining a constant watch on both Greeks and Turks, and in settling arguments before fighting broke out. Both communities were very touchy, and violence was never far away. The basic drill was to place a representative on each side and fill the middle with as many men and vehicles as could be mustered. This led to anyone being pressed into service, and occasionally visitors to the battalion found themselves mixed up in various alarms and excursions. Reporters were particularly valuable, since neither side liked being described as the aggressor, and so restrained their actions when the Press were present.

There was usually an outbreak of shooting during the night; but this often started by accident, and in any case was quickly stopped by finding and disarming the leaders of both sides.

When the original cease fire was negotiated by General P. G. F. Young, CB, CBE, he drew a line on the town plan with a green chinagraph pencil, to represent a truce line between the two communities, who were not allowed to cross it. Shortly after the battalion's arrival in Nicosia, it was noticed that empty houses near the 'Green Line' were beginning to fill with Greek Cypriot irregulars.

Reports filtered in that at least two armoured bulldozers were concealed in the area in preparation for a major assault on the Turkish quarter. Within hours, the battalion had deployed all its support weapons, with anti-tank guns covering likely approaches. This had the desired effect; tension diminished, and the attack never materialized.

World interest had been focussed on Cyprus from the outset, and the crisis assumed international importance when Greece and Turkey began war-like preparations. At this stage the United Nations proposed that an international truce force should take over from the British troops.

Early in March 1964, a Canadian contingent arrived, and on March 25 the United Nations Truce Force UNFICYP officially took over the thankless task of keeping the two communities apart. An armada of aircraft poured in Irish, Swedish and Finnish troops, and the majority of the British units were withdrawn.

The 1st Battalion replaced their red berets with the light blue United Nations berets and remained with UNFICYP. During the first week in April they were relieved by the Canadian 22nd Regiment, and left Nicosia to go into reserve as an emergency force. They spent the rest of the month dealing with many threatening situations throughout the island.

On May 5, the battalion withdrew to Dhekelia, took off their blue berets and flew home. Their contribution to the maintenance of peace had been considerable, and was recognized by the award of an OBE to the Commanding Officer and an MBE to Captain G. J. Brierley. All ranks who served in UNFICYP were permitted to wear the UN medal commemorating the Cyprus Peace Force.

Chapter
19
The Persian Gulf 1961–7

IN June of 1961 Kuwait was threatened with invasion by Iraq.
Britain had been closely linked with Kuwait since 1899 when the
territory accepted British protection; and 40 per cent of Britain's
oil came from the Kuwait Oil Company, which was jointly owned
by British Petroleum and the Gulf Corporation of America.

It came as no surprise, therefore, when the ruler, Sheik Abdhullah-
Al-Salim, called on Britain for help. HMS *Bulwark* was there within
24 hours, landing 600 men of No. 42 Royal Marine Commando; and
other units, summoned from Bahrain, Kenya, Aden and Cyprus, soon
followed. Among the contingent from Cyprus was the 2nd Battalion
the Parachute Regiment Group, commanded by Lieutenant-Colonel
F. King, MBE. The Brigade Group was under the command of
Brigadier D. Horsford, CBE, DSO; and this was the first time that
the Strategic Reserve 'Fire Brigade' had been deployed.

The 2nd Battalion Group were landed at the local airport with
instructions to push forward to the Matla Ridge some 40 miles from
the capital of Kuwait. They had expected a parachute drop, and were
short of transport, so any vehicle on 4, 8 or 12 wheels was commandeered for the journey.

All forces converged on the Matla Ridge, which is approximately
2,000 yards long and lies astride the only good tank approach from
Iraq, whose border can be seen from the summit. Within 48 hours of
the request for help, 3,000 troops were in the area, and at the close
of the fifth day 7,000 were in position on a defensive line 80 miles long.

The rapid deployment of the brigade was a sufficient deterrent to
the Iraqis, and the invasion was called off. It was a notable, and blood-
less, victory for the concept of 'Peace Keeping'.

The real enemy proved to be the heat, with shade temperatures
between 120° and 149°F. Soldiers were drinking an average of 20
pints of liquid a day. By the end of the second week they were more
or less acclimatized, and companies began training with supporting

units. A rotation system was then started, allowing everyone three days at the seaside in Shaiba rest camp, where for the first time in weeks the men were able to bathe and relax.

The Kuwait Oil Company also opened its most generous doors. Soldiers enjoyed the hospitality of Hubara, the oil town, and sporting fixtures were arranged between the battalion and the Company.

By mid-July the political situation was quiet enough to begin reducing the force. The 2nd Battalion moved to the island of Bahrain, an hour's flying time down the Persian Gulf, and set up a temporary camp on a corner of Muharraq airfield, where a comprehensive training programme was begun.

In August they returned to Kuwait and Matla Ridge, relieving the 1st Royal Inniskilling Fusiliers, and carried out various exercises including one with the Kuwait Commandos. Relieved in turn, they were pleasantly surprised to find Bahrain much cooler and the transit camp greatly improved. During their absence, 2 Troop of 9 Squadron had been working on it, and had even provided electricity.

However, after only five days, the 3rd Battalion began flying in to relieve them, and by October 27 the change-over was completed and the 2nd Battalion were back in Cyprus. It had not been without incident — as the last aircraft touched down a saboteur's bomb demolished a Beverley parked on the Muharraq runway.

The 3rd Battalion's tour in Bahrain lasted until May 1962, when the 1st Battalion took over. During these combined tours the pattern of life in the Gulf was established.

One company group guarded the airfield, at the same time being available for quick moves. At least one company did construction work on a new permanent camp for the battalion at Hamala, 15 miles from Manama on a stretch of rock-hard desert. Contractors supplied the main services and specialized work, but the task of erecting all the 'Twynham' huts fell to the soldiers. They set about this seemingly endless job with good-humoured determination — and some pertinent comments — and by the time the 2nd Battalion relieved the 1st, in April 1963, the camp was virtually complete.

Battalions were accompanied by their affiliated artillery batteries, engineer troops and RASC platoons, together with smaller detachments from other arms and services. One company was usually free for training, which was varied and valuable. Combined exercises were carried out with the Navy and the RAF; patrols worked with the Trucial Oman Scouts, or with the Sultan of Muscat's Armed Forces. It was hot work. The soldiers sweated in Bahrain, roasted on Yas Island and sizzled in the Trucial States. When Beverleys took off on parachute exercises on summer days, and nosed up into the climb, rivers of sweat literally poured down the floor towards the tail doors.

During its 1962 tour the 1st Battalion established a camp near the Jebel Ali, south of Sharjah, to which one company at a time went to train, swim and exercise. It had an airstrip and dropping zone, permitting rotation by parachute 'in' and air recovery 'out'. Parties of soldiers also travelled to Aden, Kenya and Cyprus for sports, adventure training and leave.

The experience was excellent in many respects. Battalion Groups have seldom been fitter for war, or higher in morale, than at the end of their Bahrain tours.

The other side of the coin was, however, less attractive. Socially, Bahrain was alien and uninviting. The climate was extremely uncomfortable for eight months of the year; and the air-conditioned camp appropriate to the station was not ready for some time. Worst of all, tours were initially unaccompanied. Service away from its families was no new experience for the regiment, but usually it arose from some crisis when the conditions clearly precluded them. Here, in Bahrain, the soldiers were on routine duties, and all around them were the staffs and base units provided with married quarters.

When, therefore, the 3rd Battalion took over from the 2nd in April 1964, accompanied by 80 lucky families, it was a considerable step forward. The numbers rose gradually, as accommodation and facilities improved; but Bahrain never became, for the Parachute Battalions, a fully-accompanied station.

Events outside the Persian Gulf affected tours. In early 1964, 'D' Company Group of the 2nd Battalion stood by in Aden during the Communist-inspired uprising in Zanzibar. But they were not called in—and in consequence 8,000 lives were lost. Companies of the 1st and 2nd Battalions took part in the Radfan Campaign, described in the next chapter, and were in Aden while the situation in that area deteriorated towards the final shambles of independence.

Nor was Bahrain itself always tranquil. During the 1965 handover between the 3rd and 1st Battalions, violence broke out and local police clashed with rioters. A pipeline was blown up and 12 oil company buses burned. The battalions were not called upon to intervene, although the 1st stood to for some weeks. It was the families who saw the action, living as they did in the heart of a riot-torn city; and an odd reversal of form for the parachute soldiers to be safe in camp while their wives and children were at the 'sharp end'.

There was time during the last two years for ceremonial and festivity as well as active service. In October 1965, the 1st Battalion laid on an impressive tattoo, in which the Red Devils free-fall team displayed their skill before a crowd of 3,000 including the Colonel Commandant, General K. T. Darling, the Political Resident, Sir William Luce, and the Ruler of Bahrain himself.

In April 1967, the 2nd Battalion handed over to the 1st Battalion, the King's Own Royal Border Regiment, and Airborne Forces ended six years of service in the Gulf. These tours will be remembered with mixed feelings. They were years of hard work and discomfort; of comradeship and adventure. But, whichever memory is uppermost, every man who took part can be proud of his contribution to the cause of peace in a volatile corner of the world.

Chapter
20
The Radfan 1964

IN the spring of 1964, the sniping war which was perennially waged in the hinterland of the South Arabian Federation, flared up. The campaign which followed was sharply reminiscent of the pre-war fighting on the North-West Frontier of India.

The Radfan is about 50 miles north of Aden, a mountainous tract of country and extremely hot. The Radfanis normally recognize the Amir of Dhala as suzerain, but they are fiercely independent; and warfare between the tribes practically amounts to a way of life. Caravans, passing through the Radfan along the Dhala road to the Yemen — one of the traditional routes to Mecca — were forced to pay tribute, and this was a constant source of friction.

In 1963 the Qutaibis, the main tribe of the Radfan, once again began to cause trouble on the Dhala road. Under new laws, they had been forbidden to levy tolls; and so they resorted to the traditional expression of dissatisfaction. They started shooting up the road, and this time mined it as well. This happened to coincide with civil war in the Yemen. Nasser, with Yemeni co-operation, and as part of a general policy of subversion in the Federation, backed them. Fomenting trouble, in these circumstances, was simple. The British authorities decided that it was time to intervene.

At last light on April 30, 1964, No. 45 Royal Marine Commando set out on foot to capture the high ground on the north side of the Dhanaba Basin; later the same night, 'B' Company, the 3rd Battalion the Parachute Regiment, based in Aden, was to drop on the Wadi Taym; while the Federal Regular Army advanced into the western part of the Dhanaba Basin in order to dominate the Rabwa Pass from the north.

In the event the DZ marking party from 22 SAS was discovered by the enemy and the drop had to be cancelled. The small 10 man SAS patrol was surrounded by 90 tribesmen and had to fight its way out assisted by ground attack Hunters. In the process they killed

Thumier 'base' in the Radfan Operations, 1964. A Belvedere helicopter with suspended load takes off to supply the troops in action. Typical Radfan terrain is clearly seen in the background. (Courtesy Commandant General Royal Marines.)

some 25 of the enemy but lost their commander and radio operator whose bodies had to be left behind. These were decapitated and the heads displayed in the Yemen, a gruesome incident which caused anger and shock throughout Britain. There was now no chance of a surprise drop and 'B' Company were brought up from Aden to Thumier by road to start operations on foot. By 0400 hours on May 1 the Marines had secured their objectives without opposition, though this involved a stiff climb at night up and onto 'Coca Cola'.

Three nights later the Commando, with 'B' Company under command, advanced once more to capture the peaks known as 'Cap Badge' and 'Gin Sling'. The troops were heavily laden with water and ammunition and the final approach involved climbing steep cliffs: however two of the Commando companies reached the top without running into trouble. They had, however, arrived before the dissidents who had spent the night in the village below. When they

RADFAN OPERATIONS
3rd PARACHUTE BATTALION 1964

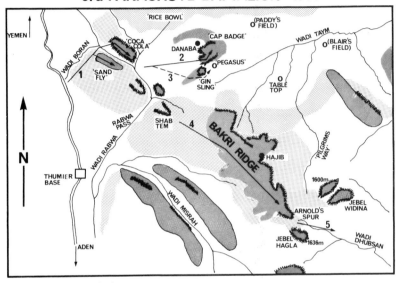

RADFAN OPERATIONS

1. 45 Cdo
2. 45 Cdo
3. 'B' Coy 3 PARA
4. 3 PARA
5. 3 PARA & 'X' Coy 45 Cdo

0 1 2 3 4
Miles

returned at dawn to their positions they were driven off after a brisk exchange of fire. 'B' Company on the longer eastern approach through the Wadi Taym were less fortunate. The apparently easier route took longer than expected and they were still on the low ground at dawn. They soon came under accurate small arms fire from the forts and buildings of the village of El Naqil on the lower slopes of Cap Badge.

The Company Commander, Major Peter Walter, led the leading platoon to clear one fort while the rest of the company assaulted the village. They drove the dissidents out, killing several in the process.

A determined group of the enemy then managed to move in behind the leading troops and assembled to put in a surprise attack. They were themselves then ambushed by the rear element of the company under the Company Second in Command, Captain Barry Jewkes. All of this enemy party were killed. This fierce battle lasted about an hour and was followed by a lull in which the company reorganized itself in the village.

Enemy snipers from the slopes above the village now opened accurate and incessant fire, causing several casualties. These snipers were in dead ground to the Marines above who were unable to help and ground attack Hunters were called in. Despite this, casualties continued to mount. Captain Jewkes was killed while helping a badly wounded sergeant and another soldier was killed and six more wounded. Ammunition and water began to run low and the company was out of range for accurate close fire support from the guns. The RAF Hunters performed magnificently, strafing as close as 150 yards in front of the troops; so low and close, in fact, that one soldier was injured by a spent cannon case! Two Beavers of 653 Squadron AAC made re-supply sorties, dropping their loads accurately despite intense rebel fire which damaged one aircraft.

Meanwhile the reserve Marine company had been flown forward by helicopter to the top of Cap Badge. The Marines now moved down to outflank the rebels from above. The enemy withdrew under this pressure and the firing gradually ceased by mid-afternoon.

'B' Company then reorganized rapidly, the casualties being flown out by Belvedere, and climbed the steep slopes to their original objectives on Cap Badge. They had been in action for a continuous 30 hour period including an 11 hour march and a 10 hour battle. To mark this achievement El Naqil was thereafter called 'Pegasus' Village.

They now commanded the Rabwa Pass and overlooked the Wadi Taym, the largest fertile tract in the Radfan. Control was thus imposed on the Dhanaba Basin and the Wadi; few enemy were encountered, but stocks of food, arms and ammunition were destroyed.

The Bakri Ridge was the next objective. This has a sheer cliff running the length of its eastern flank, sloping comparatively gently up from Shab Tem, through Hajib, up and on to Arnold's Spur,

'Pegasus' village with 'Cap Badge' beyond in the Wadi Taym. Scene of the 'B' Coy 3 PARA battle on May 5, 1964. The fort like structure of the houses can clearly be seen. (Courtesy Commandant General Royal Marines.)

5,000 feet high. Below this the land drops 3,000 feet sheer to the Wadi Dhubsan, which was known to be the headquarters of the dissidents. The Ridge is 10 miles long, and hard going despite its comparatively gentle slope.

The advance of the 3rd Battalion (less 'B' and 'D' Companies) was delayed awaiting the arrival of 815 Squadron RN, with its Wessex helicopters. Patrols, however, discovered that the ridge was not in fact held as strongly as supposed and better still, discovered a route up onto it from Shab Tem. The CO, Lieutenant-Colonel A. H. Farrar-Hockley, determined to take advantage of this information, turned one company into fighting porters and advanced with the others. In this way the battalion was able to keep itself supplied with the help of two scout helicopters. In addition to their arms the soldiers carried some 5,500 lb between them, an average load of 90 lb per man. They advanced 10,000 yards during the night of May 18 and by dawn on the 19th were well established on the ridge. The 'porters' then dumped their stores and returned for further loads to the bottom of the hill—a considerable feat of endurance.

The Bakri Ridge. The difficult nature of the ground can be seen despite the gentle slope. The fort like buildings are sited to cover the approaches. (Courtesy Commandant General Royal Marines.)

When the advance was continued on the evening of the 19th a forward patrol had a brush with a group of seven rebels and surprise was now lost. They covered a further 10,000 yards up onto the Hajib escarpment, and half the ridge was now in their hands. The advance on the 20th was led by the Anti-Tank Platoon under their forceful Company Sergeant Major 'Nobby' Arnold. They surprised a party of 12 dissidents and captured three with their arms — the first time this had been achieved in the campaign so far. In recognition of his leadership the ridge was promptly named 'Arnold's Spur'.

The main force now halted to recoup and reorganize before the final assault on the ridge. Patrols in this period made only light contact with the enemy who had developed a lamp signalling system giving warning of all patrol movements. The advance was resumed on May 23, 'C' Company clearing a number of villages. They were finally held up by accurate fire from the fortified village of Qudeishi, situated on the highest point of the Bakri Ridge, where it appeared the rebels were at last prepared to make a stand. Some 50 tribesmen in strong positions armed with several automatic weapons now gave battle. RAF Hunters were called in and demolished some of the forts.

The enemy fought with great determination and courage, withdrawing only when, under cover of the fire support, 'A' Company outflanked their position while 'C' Company stormed the village. By May 24 the parachutists were in complete control of the whole ridge and overlooked the Wadi Dhubsan. This fine achievement was due almost entirely to their initiative and determination, coupled with an outstanding example of resourceful self-help. This, according to the GOC, advanced the campaign by a whole week.

It was believed that the rebels would bitterly oppose any invasion of the Wadi Dhubsan, which was regarded in the Radfan as an impregnable stronghold, and had never been entered by Europeans. For this very reason it was decided to continue with the operation; and the CO was ordered to suppress enemy resistance, search the houses of leading dissidents for documents, destroy foodstuffs and arms and generally take over the Wadi for a limited period.

The obvious route down into the Wadi along the Wadi Dura'a was bound to be guarded. Patrols found a precipitous track down the 3,200 foot drop from Arnold's Spur which included a 30 foot sheer cliff at one point involving a rope descent. This offered surprise and the CO determined to use the route, despite the problems facing the heavily laden soldiers on such a descent at night.

By first light on May 26 the 3rd Battalion and 'X' Company of 45 Commando had descended successfully into Wadi Dhubsan, achieving complete surprise. Indeed, rebel tribesmen were seen hurrying back from guarding the easy route, though too late to retrieve the situation: they had been completely caught out by this bold move. The Jebel Haqla was firmly picketed and held, thus securing the right flank for the early stages of the advance and for the eventual withdrawal. For the first 1,500 yards there was no opposition. Then 'X' Company were fired upon by 40–50 enemy tribesmen with automatic weapons from the high ground. The fire was heavy and accurate and the Company Second in Command was killed and a Marine wounded.

The CO then went forward to reconnoitre in a Scout helicopter. They overshot the leading troops and were promptly shot down; 11 bullet holes being later counted in the machine. The pilot managed

The Wadi Dhubsan from Arnold's Spur. 3 PARA and X Coy 45 Cdo climbed down 3000 feet at night to advance along the wadi bottom. They came under fire from the hills in daylight. The shell and smoke bursts in the picture indicate enemy positions. X Coy seized the small house on the pinnacle to right of the first shell burst while 3 PARA then made a flank attack to clear the dissidents. (Courtesy Commandant General Royal Marines.)

to bring the helicopter down safely and the occupants escaped under fire back to the cover of the leading troops, though the IO was wounded. REME fitters were brought in and working under most difficult conditions in the battle area made an excellent recovery job, enabling the helicopter to be flown out the next day.

A full scale battle now developed with 'A' Company moving round to the higher ground on the left of 'X' Company while a platoon of 'C' Company did the same on the opposite side. Fire support from medium artillery and the battalion's 3-inch mortars was effectively employed. RAF Hunters performed incredible feats of flying in the narrow confines of the Wadi to add their support to the troops below. The attack was pressed home and the rebels withdrew leaving six of their dead and 11 rifles on their positions.

At a cost of one killed and seven wounded an area of 200 square miles had been secured and the 'impregnable' stronghold had been taken — a serious blow to the morale of the Radfanis. The troops were now in complete control until their withdrawal the following day. On the 28th the 3rd Battalion returned to Thumier and then to Aden.

On June 8, 'D' Company the 3rd Battalion arrived in the Radfan to relieve the main body, and from the 14th to 18th carried out a reconnaissance in force down the Shaab Lashab in company with the Royal Scots. Opposition was restricted to sniping, and at the end of the sweep the Company returned to Bahrain. It was the end of the Battalion's work in the Radfan; a tough couple of months which earned their CO a bar to his DSO, and the remainder, five medals, three Mentions in Despatches, and six C-in-C's Commendations.

Chapter

21

Confrontation : Borneo 1965

A T the end of 1964, President Sukarno of Indonesia spiked his policy of 'confrontation' against the young Malaysian Federation with the threat of invasion. Since he had 400,000 men under arms, and an Air Force and Navy equipped with modern Russian and American weapons—including MIGs, Tu-16s and missiles —this could not be dismissed as bluff; and the 2nd Battalion, commanded by Lieutenant-Colonel C. E. Eberhardie, MBE, MC, found themselves recalled from Christmas leave, rushed out to Singapore, and promptly immersed in the Jungle Warfare School. The curriculum included tracking, helicopter drills, snap shooting, jungle navigation, signals, medical duties and Malay language classes, and exercises under jungle conditions with a 'live' enemy.

During this period, 'C' Company, whose history can be traced back to the Bruneval Raid, was converted into a special patrol company to operate in an SAS role organized into four main patrols with an Operations HQ. The Company was to supplement the Guards Independent and Gurkha Parachute Companies already operating in a similar capacity. Its members were all volunteers, selected from a special course run by 22 SAS Regiment. The Company, 85 strong, moved direct to Brunei and operated throughout Borneo as Corps troops. The four-man patrols consisted of commander, linguist, radio operator and medical orderly, and were supported by two RN Fleet Air Arm Squadrons, Nos. 845 and 846. Only one incident marred the success of their work —a tragic mid-air helicopter collision in which five of the Company and the Naval air crews perished. This was the first of the patrol companies which later formed part of each battalion in the regiment.

The battalion itself embarked at Singapore on March 9 in HMT *Auby*, and docked at Kuching in Sarawak on March 12. They were at once moved by rail to Balai Ringin, and flown by helicopter to the Indonesian border to relieve the 1st Battalion the Argyll and Suther-

Jungle fort in Borneo. Gunan Gagak, the HQ of D Company 2 PARA 1965. (Courtesy Airborne Forces Museum.)

land Highlanders. The various bases which the companies and battalion HQ occupied were separated by miles of virgin jungle, were dependent entirely on helicopters, were within 2,000 yards of the border, and fortified. Fields of fire were cleared, barbed wire was erected, punjis and Claymore mines laid, and they were flood-lit at night. Patrols by platoons were constantly out and lasted anything from three to ten days, leaving company HQ and one platoon in the base location.

Mortars in action during a night attack by Indonesian troops on a 2 PARA Company in Borneo, 1965. (Courtesy Airborne Forces Museum.)

The battalion's arrival coincided with a full moon—and a period of intense Indonesian activity, culminating on April 27 in one of the biggest battles of the Borneo war. It was launched by a Javanese TNI* Battalion assisted by IBT† Dyak trackers and guides. The enemy bombardment began at 0505 hours. It was a dark, dismal, rainy night and the enemy formed up in dead ground at the foot of the hill. They were about 150 strong with a support platoon and an engineer detachment armed with Bangalore Torpedoes. The opening burst of fire was short, sharp and heavy, and came from Jugoslav 44 mm rocket launchers, 50 mm mortars, Armalite rifle grenades and Russian RPD machine-guns. The rocket launchers caused most casualties. This initial barrage killed or wounded the section facing the enemy, and their first assault penetrated the wire and carried a mortar position. They were immediately ejected by a section counter-attack which led to a close-range small arms fight in which three or four more men were wounded. The enemy were beaten back but the

* TNI = Tantura National Indonesia. Mobilised conscript units supported by regular army elements.
† IBT = Irregular Border Terrorists.

bombardment continued. Twenty minutes later another, stronger assault developed in the same area, and this again penetrated the inner wire and reached the trenches before being beaten off with heavy losses. The enemy then withdrew, leaving many of their weapons and two dead, but carrying the remainder of their dead and wounded with them. Throughout the battle 'B' Company's remaining mortar fired continuously with its barrel nearly vertical, bringing its bombs almost in to the perimeter wire; and the 105 mm howitzer from 'D' Company fired DFs* and harassed likely withdrawal routes.

At this point two enemy patrols were sighted, presumably searching for the two dead left behind — they were invariably scrupulous about this — and a patrol set off after them. The enemy made off so quickly that the three platoons which roped† down from helicopters to cut off their escape were too late. Only the trails of blood showed where they had split up and crossed back within their own frontier.

The Company was credited with 50 enemy casualties, for the loss of two of their own men killed and seven wounded.

After this attack, the enemy continued to show a close interest in the area, which suggested a further and more powerful onslaught to come. On May 15, Sergeant Barker's platoon was sent out to follow up an enemy reconnaissance party seen near Mongkus. That evening they were in an ambush position when an enemy party moved across their front, but only one enemy soldier entered the ambush area. Fire was opened and he was seen to fall followed by movement nearby. A follow up was attempted but by this time it was dark; during the night it rained heavily and no useful tracks could be found next morning. On the following day the villagers of Mujat reported that 70 Indonesians had been in the village the previous night. They did not want information or food, and so it looked like an ambush. Lieutenant Gavin Coxen's platoon went in, took them by surprise, and opened fire. One man fell and was dragged away. This was

---

* DFs — Defensive Fire Tasks. Pre-arranged target areas for artillery or mortars in case of attack or emergency. These can be called for over the radio link by use of a codeword or number.

† Roping areas — in difficult country, where even a helicopter may not be able to land, troops may be disembarked by climbing down a rope suspended from the helicopter as it hovers above the ground.

obviously the 'Come on Party', with the main enemy body waiting further up the track. By this time Captain Collinson-Jones had arrived from Battalion HQ by helicopter with the Reconnaissance Platoon and a tracker team, and took command.

The tracker team set off, following the blood trail left behind by the wounded Indonesians. After a few hundred yards the track divided into three: Sergeant Murray led his team down one — a good choice, as it happened, since it took them right into the enemy ambush, but from a flank on which they were protected by the slope and hidden by the bush. The enemy loosed off several thousand rounds; but firing almost blind, caused only one casualty. Whereupon the two platoons charged, and the enemy broke and fled. The ambush which misfired had been carefully laid, and consisted of 70 men.

The follow-up continued until last light, when a halt was called. At moonrise they set off again, with an Iban tracking with his hand*, until eventually the smell of the enemy became overpowering, and the party stopped. But at dawn, when they continued, the enemy had left. At the border there were signs that over 200 Indonesians had crossed and recrossed.

A week later, locals again reported Indonesians in the area of Mongkus and Mujat. Immediately seven platoons were lifted by helicopter, and roped down into the bush. One section heard movement and waited, ready. Soon, 40 Indonesians broke cover and came towards them, laughing and waving, obviously thinking they were friendly. They were in for a nasty shock. The section held their fire until they were only ten yards away, then opened up with rifle and Bren. The enemy scattered and tumbled down the slope, leaving 15 of their number behind. But there were more in the trees; a 50 mm mortar started firing, followed by a flanking attack, but the section escaped without loss.

A month later, on June 24, the same platoon ambushed an enemy party of 50 to 60. The leading enemy scout was very cautious; possibly he heard the radio operator, who had not seen the 'enemy alert' signal, sending morse; for suddenly he spun round and opened fire

---

* Native trackers often use their hands to 'feel' for track marks when following a trail in the dark.

with his Armalite rifle. The ambush was then sprung, and approximately ten of the enemy were killed.

They fought back bravely, however, and the platoon began a fighting withdrawal, with the enemy following up hard. The platoon were out of radio contact with base, but managed to send a short message for artillery fire via a helicopter, and five rounds were enough to enable them to slip away unscathed. As usual, there was a follow-up by helicopter; and, as usual, the enemy disappeared back over the border before he could be caught.

This was the battalion's last battle in the Borneo jungle: so ended the first Far East tour by a Parachute unit since the 5th Brigade's spell in Java just after World War II, a tour which earned them a DCM, two MMs and three Mentions.

Chapter

22

British Guiana 1965–6

IN October 1965, the 3rd Battalion was sent to British Guiana to relieve the 1st Battalion the Lancashire Fusiliers on internal security duty.

Guyana, as it is now known, is on the northern coast of South America, and a land of violent contrasts. Four great rivers sever it; the coastal strip is below sea level; while 100 miles inland the Potaro river rolls down from the high savannahs, to drop a sheer 786 feet over the Kaieteur Falls into the tropical jungle below. Gold, diamonds, bauxite and timber inland, sugar on the coast, supply the country's wealth; and of these, sugar is king. One of its by-products which most interested the battalion was rum—at four shillings a bottle.

The people are as varied as their land, but Negroes and Indians—with some Chinese—make up the bulk of the population. The Indians largely support the communist Peoples Progressive Party, and the Negroes the socialist Peoples National Congress. The two groups are approximately equal in size, which meant that, in 1964, there were only small election majorities, and the struggle for power had produced a great deal of racial unrest. However, by the time the battalion flew in, the situation had calmed down; and, apart from the occasional minor incident, it remained that way.

The battalion were responsible for West Coast Demerara and the Courantyne, and for maintaining a company in reserve. Company areas were very large, and a platoon, living on its own in requisitioned houses on the sugar estates, might be 60 miles from Company Headquarters. Patrolling, and long hours on guard, were most of the soldiers' lot; but the local population invariably looked to the Army when disaster struck. They had an implicit faith in the skill of the medical orderlies, and frequently a badly wounded man would present himself to be patched up after a brawl in a rum shop.

The Drums Platoon were greatly intrigued by the native steel

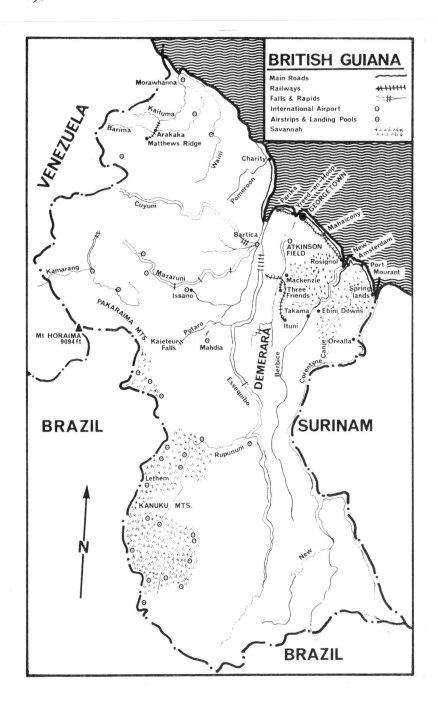

BRITISH GUIANA

Main Roads	
Railways	
Falls & Rapids	
International Airport	O
Airstrips & Landing Pools	Ⓞ
Savannah	

VENEZUELA

Morawhanna

Kaituma

Barima

Arakaka
Matthews Ridge

Waini

Charity

Pomeroon

Cuyuni

Parika

Vreed-en-Hoop

GEORGE TOWN

Bartica

Mahaicony

ATKINSON
FIELD

Rosignol

New
Amsterdam

Kamarang

Mazaruni

Issano

Mackenzie

Three
Friends

Port
Mourant

Spring
lands

PAKARAIMA MTS.

Potaro

Takama

Ebini Downs

Ituni

Mt HORAIMA
9094 ft

Kaieteur
Falls

Mahdia

Essequibo

DEMERARA

Berbice

Corentyne

Canje

Orealla

BRAZIL

SURINAM

Rupununi

Lethem

KANUKU MTS.

New

N

BRAZIL

drum music, and set about turning themselves into a 'Steel Band', under the guidance of a local musician called Dan the Pan. The early stages of their transformation were a trial to 'B' Company Head-quarters, on whom they were billeted, but eventually they became very proficient, and were much in demand for entertainments when the battalion returned to England.

Every four weeks the companies changed locations. These moves, of anything up to 200 miles, involved a great deal of organization, but enabled the soldiers to see as much of the country as possible in the time available. The reserve company was stationed at Atkinson, and here training was carried out every day. The ranges were cut out of the jungle and the ground was white sand, blistering in the glare of noon. In compensation, it was near enough to Georgetown to be able to go there for the evening and enjoy the 'flesh pots' of the capital.

The battle camp was in the savannah around Takama, a jetty on the Berbice river and two huts, one of which was a rum shop and general store. The camp was five miles away, in a disused cattle staging station on what was known as the Rupununi Cattle Trail. In days past the herds were driven cowboy fashion from the hinterland down to the coast for sale, but now the same trade is done by aircraft deliveries of already slaughtered meat. Here companies carried out extensive and ambitious field firing exercises, often with the support of the mortar platoon. There were no range restrictions and one could just step out of the camp and start shooting, being careful not to hit 'Lulu's ranch' from whence came oranges, grapefruit and fresh meat. Takama was linked to Atkinson Field by a jungle track 120 miles long, and the MT platoon fought an endless battle to keep it open, improvising bridges, and coping with foot-deep sand and mud after the rains.

One of the battalion's tasks was to prepare the Guyanese Defence Force for their responsibilities after independence. Towards the end of their platoon training, they moved to Takama for an Internal Security exercise organized by the Air Adjutant and the Drill Ser-geant Major. The camp was used to simulate a terrorist village, and, with all Guyanese officers and sergeants out of the way, the soldiers were allowed to stage a riot. This was all too convincing, especially when the Drill Sergeant Major, acting as a policeman, was hit on the head.

A highlight of the tour was the three-day visit of Her Majesty the Queen and Prince Philip to British Guiana, from February 4, 1966, as part of the Independence celebrations. Georgetown was a riot of colour and steel bands, and hordes of people came to the capital to cheer the Royal party and to join in the fun.

On February 10, the first chalk* left for England, and by the 20th the whole battalion was back and on leave. The tour had lasted only four months, but it had been full of interest and challenge, and in spite of being unaccompanied by families it was generally voted as 'one of the best yet'.

---

* 'Chalk'—a term used to denote a plane-load of parachute soldiers. On operations aircraft are serially numbered by the airfield liaison staff so that each plane-load of troops can easily identify the aircraft in which they are to travel. This is usually done by means of a chalked numeral on the side of the fuselage.

Chapter
23
Aden 1967

Eᴀʀʟʏ in January 1967, the 1st Battalion, under Lieutenant-Colonel M. J. H. Walsh, was sent to Aden to cover the final withdrawal of British troops from the South Arabian Peninsula. The threat was unspecified, but could include military attack from the Yemen or civil disorders within the colony of Aden itself, or both. The battalion's directive, therefore, was to prepare itself for 'any contingency'. It was not to be disappointed.

At 0001 hours on May 25, the paratroops took over the districts of Al Mansura and Sheik Othman which together made up Area North, under the command of HQ Aden Brigade. Their instructions were to keep open the north–south route from the border to Aden, and to prevent the use of Sheik Othman as a terrorist base.

It was the practice of the rival political parties in the colony to call a general strike from time to time, in order to clear the civilian population from the streets so that their gunmen could get to grips with Security Forces. The battalion had hardly settled in when they were involved in a typical example of one of these affrays. Leaflets and police reports gave overnight warning, and at 0200 hours on June 1, 'D' Company and 8 Platoon 'C' Company took up positions in a series of eight observation posts (OPs) in the heart of Sheik Othman commanding the principal thoroughfares and the main mosque, which had been the scene of many previous disorders. Three hours later, a grenade attack outside the mosque signalled the start of hostilities, and all OPs came under heavy and well-co-ordinated fire, some at only 50 yards' range.

The shooting continued for some hours, during which two troops of 'C' Squadron, Queen's Dragoon Guards, patrolled the streets, engaging targets indicated to them by the OPs. At 1100 hours the main mosque broadcast instructions to the terrorists to change their positions, and a lull of 20 minutes followed. This was the turning point of the battle, as the Company Commander took advantage of

ADEN
1st PARACHUTE BATTALION POSITIONS 1967

Map labels:
DHALA
DARSAAD
STATE BOUNDARY
GOLF
SHEIK OTHMAN
JULIET
GC
FW
LIMA
AL MANSURA
MANSURA PICQUET
PENNINE CHAIN
LITTLE ADEN
BRAVO
SALT PANS
RADFAN CAMP
KILO
SALT PANS
CHARLIE
CAUSEWAY
AIRFIELD
SLAVE ISLAND
KHORMAKSAR
LEGEND
O   CHECKPOINTS
FW   FORT WALSH
GC   GRENADE CORNER
=== ROADS
STEAMER POINT
MAALLA
PASS
GOV'T HOUSE
CRATER
MOUNTAINS
0   ½   1   2
Miles (approx)

the pause to bring down harassing fire on all known, and likely, enemy positions, forcing them 300 yards further back. It was not until late that night, however, that the situation was brought under control.

This strike, which became known within the battalion as 'The Glorious First of June', was the most violent ever experienced in Aden, and set a pattern for future operations of a similar nature.

After this, Area North returned to normal, and for a day or two it seemed that peace had been restored. But on June 5 it was announced on the BBC midday news that Israel had invaded Sinai. It was difficult to anticipate what Arab reaction would be, but one thing was certain, there would be trouble in Sheik Othman—and there was. The Commanding Officer immediately decided to re-occupy the OPs, which had proved so successful, and to move his tactical HQ and one platoon into the disused Scottish Mission Hospital. This group of buildings dominated the main road to the border and the east side of the town. 'C' Company and the Anti-tank Platoon fought their way in, and by nightfall had secured these vital positions in the face of heavy opposition.

During the night every off-duty man back in 'Radfan' camp was out filling sandbags, without orders, as his personal contribution to the battle up front, which could be heard still raging in the distance. By dawn the sandbags had been moved forward, and the newly occupied buildings, known as 'Fort Walsh', were quickly becoming well defended strong-points capable of resisting any attack. Fort Walsh was occupied by 1 Para until they were relieved three months later.

On June 20, after a comparatively quiet spell, the Commanding Officer was warned of serious disorders in the South Arabian Army and Police Force, and a detachment was sent to the Police barracks at Champion Lines, close to the battalion's living area at Radfan camp, to secure the main arms store. This was done with great dash and vigour against fierce opposition. Unfortunately, a few weapons were already in the hands of dissident soldiers, who used them indiscriminately against people, vehicles, tents and huts in Radfan camp. Everyone there, including cooks, clerks and QM staff, stood-to in slit trenches on the perimeter. In order not to inflame an already dangerous situation, they were forbidden to return the fire. It is a tribute to the courage and discipline of the battalion that this unpopular order was obeyed implicitly, and events proved it to be right.

In just under one month, they had faced three general strikes, the effects of the Arab–Israeli war, and an armed mutiny. They were now secure in well-fortified positions, and every man was toughened by hard fighting. Life settled down to an endless round of patrolling, manning checkpoints, and cordon and search operations, with companies taking turns of four days at a time in the forward positions in Sheik Othman and Al Mansura. On July 13 the 1st Battalion the Lancashire Regiment came to Area North and assumed control of Al Mansura, enabling 1 Para to concentrate on Sheik Othman. From that date until September 24, when both battalions were relieved, they fought side by side, displaying the highest degree of co-operation, even to the extent of sharing the same radio command net.

Once British responsibilities had been handed over in the South Arabian Federation, the safe evacuation of troops, stores, arms and equipment was of prime importance. During the night of September 23–24, 1 Para was relieved in Sheik Othman by the South Arabian Army and given the task of holding a close defensive line to protect Khormaksar airfield. With the possibility of a fighting withdrawal, no chances could be taken, and the battalion worked hard to make the line — later known as 'The Pennine Chain' — impregnable against any attack. Fortunately, it was never put to the test; but it was ready, and stood as an example of the battalion's professional approach and efficiency.

Their tour came to an end on November 27, when they handed over responsibility for the defence of Khormaksar to 42 Commando. Their departure was soon followed by the final withdrawal of all our forces, ending 128 years of British rule in Aden.

Decorations awarded after these operations included a DSO for the CO, Lieutenant-Colonel Walsh, and one MBE, four MCs, one MM, 16 Mentions in Despatches and one C-in-C's Commendation.

Chapter

24

Summing Up

'To their officers, and among themselves, they were always The
Toms, just the latest in line of generations of amateur soldiers.
But no one whose ancestors have at one time or another fought
most of the nations in the world can be quite unmilitary. If you
select a bunch of such men for their determination and aggressive-
ness, train them hard, give them tough and experienced leaders
and the best available equipment . . . then the result is bound to
be extraordinary. A parachute battalion.'

Sandy Cavenagh: *Airborne to Suez*

THE Parachute Regiment is just (at the time of writing) 28 years
old; airborne forces as a whole, dating their formation from
the setting-up of Central Landing School in June 1940, two
years older. Their history, as outlined in the preceding chapters, is as
compact and glorious as that of any unit in the British Army; the
names they bear upon their regimental colours, from Bruneval to
Athens, bear witness to their pride and prowess. What distinguishes
the airborne soldier, whether parachutist or glider-borne, from his
comrades in other infantry regiments?

On a superficial view, one might say, only his mode of going to
battle. But the pilot's life-saving parachute, adapted to become the
parachutist's vehicle, like the towed glider, both enabling him to drop
far behind the enemy's lines, have imposed their own requirements
and disciplines on those who use them. The actual dropping by parachute has always been no more than a means to an end, and therefore
only a small, though vital, part of an airborne soldier's training, like
learning to drive.

The drama of the men in their bulky kit, passing the time on the
flight as best they may, reading, snoozing, smoking; the red and green
lights; the door opening on to that chasm of air; the leap into space —
these capture the imagination as they did from the beginning. But in

doing so they tend to obscure more important and relevant facets of the airborne soldier's task, for it is the conditions he has to cope with on landing, his isolation, the odds against him, that set him and his comrades apart. The fact that he may well find himself separated from his unit, and possibly alone, miles from his objective, makes his selection and training different from those of other soldiers, and so important. For in the field, every man bears the responsibility of being able to act decisively and on his own. This resourcefulness was demonstrated time and again during World War II, in actions as different and far apart as Bruneval and North Africa, and never more vividly than during the great airborne actions in Sicily, in the water-meadows of Normandy, and in the fire-swept streets of Arnhem. It will continue to be required for as long as men land in small parties behind their enemies' lines. For this reason, now, as for many years, less than half the men who apply to join airborne forces are accepted. The process of selection is designedly extremely tough, taking men to the limits of physical and psychological endurance and then demanding that extra ounce of effort that only a stubborn will can summon up. The result, after intensive training, is, as Sandy Cavenagh, who as a Medical Officer served with 3 Para, remarks, bound to be extraordinary.

As a corollary to this, the parachutist is a first-class fighting man, a master of his trade. That this has been so from the beginning is proved by the number of times he was employed as an infantryman during a crisis such as occurred in Tunisia, at Monte Cassino or in the Ardennes: that it is so still is amply shown by his presence at most of the post-war trouble spots from Cyprus to Malaya.

On a broader view, the inseparable link between the soldiers and the men who fly and supply them is unusual in the relations between the Services. No history of airborne forces can pretend to be complete or just without special acknowledgement not only to the glider-pilots of the Army Air Corps but to the squadrons of the RAF — 38 and 46 Groups during World War II, Air Support Command today — who carry them into battle, and are frequently shot down or badly-damaged in the process. Notes on the histories of 38 and 46 Groups, and of Air Re-Supply, will be found in the appendices.

In 1945 Field-Marshal Montgomery, who had recently been appointed Colonel-Commandant of the Parachute Regiment, summed up the value of Airborne Forces, and much of what he had to say then remains true today.

'*General*
Airborne Forces form an essential part of a modern army, and there will often be occasions in which they can play a vital role: particularly in deliberate operations. Apart from their participation in the battle, the threat of the use of airborne forces can also be used to great advantage, and experience has shown that the enemy can be led by these means to make considerable and even vital dispersion of his front line forces; in addition, there is always the need to lock up troops in guarding vital areas and installations when an opponent is known to have airborne troops at his disposal.

Under European conditions of warfare, employment of airborne forces during highly mobile operations has been shown to be limited; large airborne operations require considerable time to plan, and the ground troops are liable to overrun Dropping Zones before the airborne project matures.

In undeveloped countries, especially against a second-rate enemy, airborne forces may play a highly important role, particularly since conditions may sometimes permit of their being dropped and maintained in areas well in rear of the enemy's main front.

Airborne Forces in Deliberate Operations
The employment of airborne forces has proved a battle winning factor in deliberate operations such as the major sea-borne assault and the assault across a major obstacle.

In Sicily (June 1943), in spite of mistakes and disorganization due to the inexperience of those early days, airborne troops played an important part in the capture of Syracuse and of the group of airfields in south-east Sicily.

In the Normandy invasion, British airborne forces secured intact crossings over the Orne river and canal, which were to prove of great importance in the subsequent development of operations, and their action in the first days of the invasion caused confusion and delay to enemy forces at the most vital time.

US airborne forces played an essential part in the establishment of the Utah beaches, by drawing enemy forces to themselves while the seaborne troops were establishing a foothold, and their employment greatly facilitated cutting off the Cotentin Peninsula and launching the assault northwards to Cherbourg.

Airborne Forces were employed in Holland in September 1944, to seize a series of crossings over the water obstacles between the Meuse–Escaut Canal and the Neder Rhin. By their action a series of crossings were seized intact, and although the Arnhem bridge was subsequently lost, possession of other bridges, and particularly those at Grave and Nijmegen, had a decisive bearing on the subsequent development of our operations.

At the crossing of the Rhine, airborne forces greatly facilitated the seizure and rapid expansion of the bridgehead, and the speed of the subsequent breakout.

In all these examples the chief advantages which accrued from the employment of airborne troops were secured as a result of their descent from the air. In the case of seizure of intact bridges, no alternative method could have ensured success.

Value of the Threat of Airborne Forces

It has been shown that the threat of employing airborne troops can be made a major factor in determining both the strategical and tactical layout of the enemy's forces.

The airborne threat, used in conjunction with other factors, was material in causing the Germans to retain major formations in the Pas de Calais area during the initial period after our landing in Normandy.

Uncertainty as to our intentions, combined with the use of dummy paratroops, caused the enemy considerable alarm and despondency in the tactical area of the landings, and delayed the arrival on the battlefield of some of his forces at the most vital time.

Both during the Battle of the Rhineland and the Crossing of the Rhine, the airborne threat was again used to inspire uncertainty and confusion in the enemy's mind, and to upset his planning.

We have learnt that the Germans always believed us to have more airborne formations than we actually had, and the possible use of them had constantly to be considered and guarded against.

In the early days of the war, it will be recalled that the Germans made much of the threat of airborne invasion, and that this greatly affected our dispositions in the United Kingdom between 1940 and 1942, and led to a vast expenditure of material and effort.

In north-west Europe even the threat of a small suicidal drop by enemy paratroops in the Antwerp area caused us to maintain troops in a constant state of readiness.

Limitations to the Use of Airborne Forces

Airborne forces are subject to limitations in their use, the chief of which is the uncertainty of the weather.

The degree, however, to which weather will influence airborne operations in the future is a matter of speculation; the rapid development of scientific methods designed to facilitate the use of aircraft under adverse weather conditions will undoubtedly continue. It may be expected therefore that this factor will become less important in the future.

Conclusion

A nation without airborne forces will be severely handicapped and at a great disadvantage in future warfare. There can be no doubt that airborne forces will continue to have an important role in battle, and they definitely justify the expenditure of effort which they involve'.

The duties and adventures that have befallen Airborne Forces during a quarter of a century are described in the various chapters. Whilst valuing tradition it had always been the primary concern of Airborne Forces to look forwards and not back. Further changes are inevitable as tasks, methods and problems alter, but the standards for selection of the parachute soldier do not. Whatever challenges the future may hold, one thing is certain—the airborne soldiers will meet these with the same confidence and certainty that has hallmarked a short but not uneventful history.

Appendix A

Chronology of British Airborne History

Mr Churchill's call in June 1940, for 'a force of at least 5,000 parachute troops', raised many problems. There was no first-hand knowledge or experience, nor were there military parachutes, gliders, or transport aircraft. The Nation's resources were already fully stretched in raising forces and manufacturing arms necessary to defend Britain against attack and sustain overseas theatres of war. An experimental and training centre, known as the Central Landing School (later expanded as the Central Landing Establishment RAF, and subsequently renamed Airborne Forces Establishment) was set up at Ringway Airport, near Manchester, on June 21, 1940. Men of No. 2 Commando received parachute training, the first parachute descents being made on July 21, 1940. The unit name was changed on November 21, 1940 to No. 11 Special Air Service Battalion and then, on September 15, 1941, to the 1st Parachute Battalion. Converted Whitley bombers were used both for parachuting and towing gliders.

The first military gliders came off production in April 1941 (Hotspur and Horsa fuselages may be seen in the Airborne Forces Museum) and volunteers trained by the RAF were taught to fly. This system proved inefficient and on December 21, 1941 the Army Air Corps was formed and within it, the Glider Pilot Regiment. Although soldiers flew gliders, the Royal Air Force became entirely responsible for parachute training and despatching trained troops from aircraft.

In September 1941, the 1st Parachute Brigade under Brigadier R. N. Gale was formed and by November 1941 two more parachute Battalions — the 2nd and 3rd — were in process of completion. These, and the 4th Battalion that followed, were manned by volunteers from all parts of the Army.

It was appreciated that Glider-borne or air-landed troops would be necessary to support the parachute troops, in anything other than very limited operations, with heavier equipment than could be parachuted. On October 10, 1941 therefore, 31 Independent Brigade Group, recently returned from India and trained in mountain warfare, was selected to form the 1st Air-Landing Brigade Group. The brigade consisted of the 1st Battalion The Border Regiment, 2nd Battalion The South Staffordshire Regiment, 2nd Battalion The Oxfordshire and Buckinghamshire Light Infantry, 1st Battalion Royal Ulster Rifles, a Reconnaissance Company, 223rd Anti-Tank Battery RA, 9th Field Company RE, 181st Field Ambulance RAMC, a Workshops and Field Park RAOC, a RASC Vehicle Company and other Brigade Troops. It was decided that this hazardous occupation called for little special individual training and it was thought unnecessary for the soldiers to be volunteers. Consequently the main limiting factors in raising air-landing units lay in the production of gliders and the training of pilots.

The need for a separate airborne headquarters was also recognized, to supervise and co-ordinate all aspects of training and development and to organize the expansion of the airborne force to divisional level. On October 29, 1941 Brigadier F. A. M. Browning was selected for appointment, with rank of Major-General, as 'Commander Para-Troops and Airborne Troops'. A HQ was formed and expanded progressively to become HQ 1st Airborne Division. As the new force expanded, a separate formation HQ was later established. First, in April 1943 as 'HQ Major-General Airborne Forces' and later in December 1943 to, 'HQ Airborne Troops'. The rank of the Commander, who was to exercise command over all airborne forces was then raised to Lieutenant-General. A Depot to hold and train all reinforcements for the airborne formations had been unofficially established at Hardwick in April 1942 and was officially approved by the War Office in December. In June 1942 a further far reaching step was taken with the establishment of an Air Directorate at the War Office, headed initially by Brigadier Gale.

On July 17, 1942, the 2nd Parachute Brigade was formed. This expanded the Divisional organization to two parachute brigades, the air-landing brigade and divisional troops. The 4th Parachute Battalion was transferred to join the 2nd Parachute Brigade and in August, 7th Battalion The Cameron Highlanders and 10th Battalion The Royal Welch Fusiliers became the 5th (Scottish) and 6th (Royal Welch) Parachute Battalions respectively. In August too a second Glider Pilot Regiment was formed.

On August 1, 1942, in conjunction with the formation of the Division, the Parachute Battlions which had until now no parent regiment or corps were formed (by the War Office) into the Parachute Regiment as part of the Army Air Corps.

On November 5, 1942 the formation of the 3rd Parachute Brigade was authorized, raised as follows: —

10th Battalion The Somerset Light Infantry, becoming
7th (Light Infantry) Battalion The Parachute Regiment
13th Battalion The Royal Warwickshire Regiment becoming
8th (Midland) Battalion The Parachute Regiment
10th Battalion The Essex Regiment, becoming
9th (Eastern and Home Counties) Battalion The Parachute Regiment
3rd Parachute Squadron RE
224th Parachute Field Ambulance RAMC

In November 1942, the decision was also taken to form the 4th Parachute Brigade in the Middle East. The Brigade began forming at Kabrit in December with the 151st Parachute Battalion (renumbered 156th Battalion) from India as its first unit. The 10th and 11th Parachute Battalions were then raised from

From left to right:

British parachutist 1944/45 with the 'Leg Kit Bag'. In this was carried a variety of heavy loads, ammunition, wireless sets, medical stores, etc. After jumping the quick release straps were pulled and the bag lowered on a 20 foot rope to hang below the parachutist leaving him free to steer the chute with both hands. (Courtesy Imperial War Museum.)

Parachutist with the Light Machine Gun (LMG) valise. The attachments can be clearly seen. After jumping the quick release was pulled and the gun in its thick felt container, butt down, was lowered on a suspension rope. A sleeve to prevent rope burns was used and can be seen on the soldier's right hand. (Courtesy Imperial War Museum.)

Parachute Rifleman WWII. The rifle was carried in a valise similar to the LMG and lowered in the same way. The soldier's personal equipment was worn on his chest for jumping covered by a 'Jump' Jacket to prevent equipment catching in the rigging lines or falling away during flight. The parachute harness was then fully extended to fit over the load as is shown here giving the 'bulbous' appearance. Once on the ground the 'Jump' jacket was discarded and the equipment worn in the normal manner on the back. (Courtesy Imperial War Museum.)

volunteers throughout the theatre. In February 1943, the Brigade moved to the Ramat David area in Northern Palestine and in May, less the 11th Battalion joined the 1st Airborne Division in North Africa. The 11th completed its training, carried out a small successful airborne operation against the Island of Cos (September 15–25) and sailed in December 1943 to rejoin the 4th Brigade now in England.

While the 1st Division was expanding the RAF were endeavouring to keep pace by providing the necessary transport lift and training establishment. In September 1941, the Airborne Forces Establishment was reorganized and between November 1941 and February 1942 Flying and Glider Training Schools, No. 1 Parachute Training School (Ringway), Parachute Exercise and Glider Exercise Squadrons and a Technical Development Section were in operation. On January 15, 1942 the need for an RAF HQ to co-ordinate the army/air problems of training and operations were recognized and HQ 38 Wing RAF was formed under Group Captain Sir Nigel Norman. This HQ was to work direct with HQ 1st Airborne Division.

After two small raids in 1941 and 1942 (Tragino Aqueduct and Bruneval), the 1st Parachute Brigade fought in North Africa from November 1942. The fighting exploits of this Brigade in this campaign earned them the name of 'Red Devils' from their German opponents. Accepted as a compliment the name has remained to this day the unofficial title of British Airborne Forces. In April 1943, Major-General Browning was appointed Major-General Airborne Forces and Major-General Hopkinson succeeded him as the divisional commander. The remainder of the 1st Division, less the 3rd Parachute Brigade, completed mobilization by May 1, 1943 and shortly after units sailed for the Middle East to join the 1st Brigade. The first Divisional Operation was in Sicily, followed by seaborne landings in Italy.

Concurrent with the expansion and development of the 1st Airborne Division the foundation of the Special Air Service (SAS) was also being laid in the Middle East. In January 1941, a commando formation known as 'Layforce' arrived in the Middle East. Among them was a young lieutenant, A. D. Stirling, who developed unconventional methods of raiding behind enemy lines. In July 1941, Stirling, now a captain, was empowered to raise a unit from 'Layforce' for this purpose called 'L' Detachment, SAS Brigade. By August it consisted of seven officers and 60 men all trained in parachuting.

Between this time and the end of the war the SAS developed their own highly effective and unorthodox techniques. They operated with tremendous success in the Western Desert, throughout the Middle East and in Europe both before and after D-Day. By 1945 they had expanded to Brigade strength. Their value was out of all proportion to their size and made a significant contribution to the final victory in Europe.

Meanwhile, the 6th Airborne Division was being raised in England, to be ready for the invasion of Europe. The orders for its formation, under Major-

General Gale, were issued on April 23, 1943 on a phased programme, the number '6' being chosen for security reasons. The 3rd Parachute Brigade, left behind by the 1st Airborne Division, was transferred complete to the 6th Division. The 1st RUR and 2nd Oxfordshire and Buckinghamshire were also transferred, to form the 6th Air-landing Brigade. Divisional troops and a new 5th Parachute Brigade were to be formed on June 1, 1943. Two new parachute battalions, the 12th and 13th were formed from the 10th Battalion The Green Howards and the 2nd/4th Battalion The South Lancashire Regiment respectively. In July, the 1st Canadian Parachute Battalion arrived in the UK and joined the 3rd Parachute Brigade, releasing the 7th (Light Infantry) Parachute Battalion to transfer to the 5th Brigade as its third battalion. The 53rd (Worcestershire Yeomanry) Air-landing Light Regiment RA formed on July 1, 1943 and was followed in September by the 12th Battalion The Devonshire Regiment joining the 6th Air-landing Brigade as the third battalion.

Throughout all this time the Prime Minister, Mr Winston Churchill, took an active and direct personal interest in the training and development of the new force, encouraging and making policy decisions to further the pace of progress. In two years airborne forces had grown from nothing to a force of two divisions and an independent Brigade, with its own HQ which had full authority and world-wide responsibility in airborne matters.

The 6th Division's operations on and after D-Day — June 6, 1944 — secured the left flank of the Allied Invasion Force. While they were still fighting in Normandy, the 1st Division, less the 2nd Parachute Brigade which remained in the Middle East and fought in Italy, the South of France and Greece, returned to England, for action in the forthcoming battles in Europe. At this time the 1st Air-landing Brigade was reinforced by the addition of the 7th Battalion The King's Own Scottish Borderers. They were warned for 16 operations, all cancelled, then, on September 17, they flew to Holland for the Battle of Arnhem. In this valiant struggle, the Division was virtually destroyed. Seven months later the Rhine was crossed again, this time near Wesel, by the 6th Airborne Division, in the last airborne operation of the war.

In India, the 50th Indian Parachute Brigade was raised in 1941 consisting of 151 Parachute Battalion (British) which was later withdrawn for service in the Middle East, 152 Indian Parachute Battalion, 153 Gurkha Parachute Battalion, and 411 (Royal Bombay) Parachute Section Indian Engineers. By the summer of 1945 this had been expanded to full divisional strength into the 44th Indian Airborne Division which included the 15th and 16th (British) Parachute Battalions and the 2nd Battalion The Black Watch. Although there were no airborne operations in the Far East (except those of General Wingate) on anything approaching the scale of those in Europe there were some smaller actions by brigade groups or smaller formations, by glider or parachute. These included the dropping of a Gurkha Parachute Battalion to clear the Japanese positions covering the approaches to Rangoon Harbour. In all of these the

The scene at the bridge at Arnhem at 5 pm on the second day, September 18, 1944, depicted in a 'Cameo' in the Airborne Forces Museum, Aldershot. (Courtesy Airborne Forces Museum.)

Indian airborne troops proved, as had their counterparts in Europe, what can be achieved by well-trained soldiers of high morale even under the most adverse conditions.

The end of the war in Europe in May, 1945 found the 6th Airborne Division at Wismar on the Baltic. In the Pacific the war against Japan was gathering momentum, but there was as yet no sign of the enemy capitulating. Plans had been drawn up for operations to clear the Japanese from Malaya and Singapore, actions in which the 6th Airborne and 2nd Indian Airborne Divisions would have played important parts. The 1st Airborne Division had been earmarked as part of the Imperial Strategic Reserve in the Middle East.

Early in August atomic warfare was opened against Japan which was soon followed by the Japanese capitulation. In the reorganization that followed it was decided that only one regular airborne division would remain and that this would be the 6th. The choice fell to this Division because it was up to strength, and the age and service groups of its soldiery were less likely to cause an immediate man-power problem due to post-war demobilization. At this time the 1st Airborne Division was in Scandinavia following operation 'Doomsday', the liberation of Norway. It contained a high proportion of the original parachute volunteers who would now be due for release from military service, and, though reinforced by new drafts, had not fully recovered from Arnhem. The 1st Airborne Division returned to the UK in August 1945, and set up its HQ at Longford Castle near Salisbury. The division was disbanded in November 1945, certain elements having by this time been transferred to the 6th Division.

The 6th Division therefore now stepped into the Imperial Reserve role and plans were made for its despatch to the Middle East. As the 5th Parachute Brigade was already in the Far East, its place was taken by the formerly independent 2nd Parachute Brigade. Within the 3rd Brigade the 1st Canadian Parachute Battalion returned to Canada and was replaced by the 3rd Battalion Parachute Regiment, from the 1st Brigade: in the 6th Air-landing Brigade, the 12th Devons were replaced by the 1st Argyll and Sutherland Highlanders.

On September 21, 1945 Divisional HQ and a Tactical HQ flew out to Palestine and was followed by the remainder of the Division between September and November 6, 1945. Divisional HQ was established at Nuseirat Hospital Camp near Gaza and the Brigades were also located in the Gaza District.

Although the Division was drawn into counter-insurgency, it continued to train for its strategic reserve role. Exercises were carried out in Iraq, Trans-Jordan and the Sudan, and a Divisional Training Centre consisting of a Battle School, Vocational Training Wing and Airborne Training Wing, was set up. It was now decided that airborne divisions would in future be all-parachute, on the German pattern, with gliders only for heavy loads and *coups de main*. Consequently the 6th Air-landing Brigade, whose contribution to the 6th Airborne's fame had been second to none, became the 31st Infantry Brigade and severed its airborne connection. Its place was taken by the 1st Parachute Brigade, composed of the 1st, 2nd and 17th Battalions, The Parachute Regiment. Soon afterwards the 5th Brigade returned from the Far East. Its 7th Battalion replaced the 17th in the 1st Brigade and its 12th and 13th Battalions, together with the 17th, ceased to exist in the regular army, although they were soon reformed in the Territorial Army. As part of post war reorganization amalgamations of some parachute units also took place during the Division's tour. The 2nd and 3rd Battalions and the 8th and 9th Battalions were amalgamated to form the 2nd/3rd and 8th/9th Battalions, The Parachute Regiment. The Division now consisted of the 1st, 2nd and 3rd Parachute Brigades, 3rd King's Own Hussars (who had replaced the Armoured Reconnaissance Regiment), 53rd Light and 2nd Anti-Tank Regiments RA, Divisional Engineers, Signals, Glider Pilots, RASC, RAMC, RAOC, REME and the Training Wing.

Each of the nine Battalions of the Parachute Regiment was affiliated to a group of infantry regiments, who were responsible for supplying officers and soldiers to fill its ranks on three-year tours.

During this period the 3rd Parachute Brigade was disbanded and in early July 1947, the 2nd Parachute Brigade was withdrawn from the 6th Division and moved to Perham Down on Salisbury Plain. It was here, in December 1947, that the 4th and 6th Battalions of the Parachute Regiment amalgamated to become the 4th/6th Battalion. In February 1948, the 2nd Brigade under Brigadier R. H. Bellamy, DSO, moved to Germany to join BAOR, the 4th/6th Battalion to Lübeck, four kilometres from the East-West border, the 5th (Scottish) Battalion to Husum and the 7th Battalion to Itzehoe.

Further changes in post-war policy now had far reaching effects upon Airborne Forces. With the reduction of the Services to peace time levels it was decided that only one parachute brigade group would be retained in the Regular Army. In consequence, the 6th Airborne Division (whose last remaining Airborne element consisted only of the 1st Parachute Brigade and supporting units) was now on its return from Palestine in 1948, also disbanded.

During the war it had been found both necessary and advantageous to form small groups of parachute soldiers into 'pathfinder' units, to parachute onto the selected operational DZ ahead of the main force. Their tasks were to mark the drop zone, establish directional wireless beacons to enable the transport aircraft carrying the main assault force to 'home' in on the exact drop point and to clear and protect the zone itself as the main force parachuted or air landed. They served also as an early warning agency, should the selected drop zones prove to be heavily defended at the time of the operation. The main force could then be warned or diverted to an alternative and less dangerous DZ. Once the main force had landed these sub-units provided the formation commander with a small reserve or reconnaissance force. Each of the 1st and 6th Airborne Divisions had formed a sub-unit of pathfinders, the 21st (1st Division) and the 22nd (6th Division) Independent Companies the Parachute Regiment. The disbandment of the divisions and the reduction to a parachute brigade group did not alter the requirement for such a sub-unit, or the tasks it performed. The responsibilities for this were taken over in 1948 by the Brigade of Guards which thereafter provided the officers and men for the 'pathfinder' element of the parachute brigade, known as the 1st (Guards) Independent Company, the Parachute Regiment.

The Airborne Force remaining in the post-war regular army was to be initially stationed in Germany. Consequently it fell to the 2nd Brigade to become the nucleus of the new formation which was to preserve the history of the wartime divisions and of the earliest parachute battalions. In June 1948, therefore, the 2nd Battalion the Parachute Regiment was re-formed on the existing 5th (Scottish) Battalion and adopted the blue lanyard as its unit colour designation. In July 1948, the 1st Battalion the Parachute Regiment was reformed on the 4th/6th Battalion adopting the red lanyard; the 3rd Battalion the Parachute Regiment was re-formed on the 7th Battalion with the green lanyard as its unit colour. The 2nd Brigade was now re-designated the 16th Independent Parachute Brigade Group, the number '16' being chosen to perpetuate the numerals of the 1st and 6th Airborne Divisions. In September 1948, the brigade moved to the Hannover District and Brigadier W. F. K. Kempster, DSO, OBE, assumed command. The brigade returned to the UK in October 1949, the 1st and 2nd Battalions to be stationed at Aldershot in Albuhera and Talavera Barracks and the 3rd Battalion at Chisledon Camp in Wiltshire. Later, the 3rd Battalion rejoined the brigade by moving to Waterloo Barracks in Aldershot. From this time the Regular Parachute Brigade has maintained a permanent 'home' in Aldershot.

During the war all airborne training units were under the command of the Commander Airborne Establishments (CAE). At their peak these comprised the Depot (first established at Hardwick and later moved to the Isle of Wight), two Parachute Regiment Infantry Training Centres, the Parachute Reserve Battalion, an Army Air Corps Holding Battalion, the Parachute Course administrative Unit, the Army Air Transport Training and Development Centre (AATDC) and elements of the Glider Pilot Regiment. The HQ of the Airborne Establishment (HQ AE) was located first at Amesbury Abbey and then at Aldenbury House near Salisbury. In 1946 the Commander, Brigadier C. H. V. Pritchard, DSO, who had recently returned from command of the 2nd Brigade, decided that as far as possible all training units should be centred at Aldershot. The HQ AE was therefore moved to Knollys House, Aldershot, in October.

In May 1947, a branch of HQ Airborne Establishments was created, consisting of a DAAG and Staff Captain who were to be responsible for liaison with all the Infantry Brigade Groups which provided the seconded officers and soldiers to their affiliated parachute battalions, and for all the internal domestic affairs of the Parachute Regiment. This branch was called HQ the Parachute Regiment. On the reduction of Airborne Forces to one Parachute Brigade Group in 1948, HQ Airborne Establishments was disbanded. The responsibilities of the CAE were transferred to the Commandant of the Depot at Maida Barracks, Aldershot, whose rank was upgraded to colonel for this purpose. The DAAG and GSO2 from HQ AE were transferred to the Depot strength as The Officer In Charge of HQ the Parachute Regiment (later the Regimental Adjutant) and as the Air Training Officer to assist with these additional duties. The first Commandant in this capacity was Colonel K. T. Darling, DSO, OBE, appointed in 1948. In 1959 a Depot Commander was added to the establishment with the rank of Lieutenant-Colonel. The Commandant became the Regimental Colonel with a Regimental Adjutant and a staff for RHQ the Parachute Regiment as a separate entity, though sharing the same accommodation. The Depot and RHQ remained at Maida Barracks until moving to the newly-built Browning Barracks which were opened officially by Lady Browning (Daphne Du Maurier) widow of the late Lieutenant-General Sir Frederick (Boy) Browning, the 'Father' of Airborne Forces, on June 6, 1968.

During the 1950s a significant decision was taken regarding the status of the officers and soldiers of the Parachute Regiment. During the war volunteers for service with the Parachute Regiment had been accepted from officers and men of all arms and corps. Territorial and war-time soldiers had been transferred to the Army Air Corps, and Regular Soldier volunteers had been accepted on secondment from their parent regiments. Many volunteers were received from corps other than the infantry. After the war a large number of the regular soldiers and officers on secondment had continued to serve in this way (though post-war secondments were restricted to infanteers), and by the early 1950s many stalwarts had 10 to 12 years continuous service with the Parachute Regiment and Airborne Forces. During this time they had remained on the permanent strength of their own parent regiments though in many cases the soldiers had been promoted to senior rank within the Parachute Regiment's establishment. To maintain continuity and regularize the anomalies which existed, direct enlistment into the Parachute Regiment for other ranks was introduced in 1953. The transfer of volunteers was accepted, and men from civil life could for the first time enlist direct into the Regiment. Officers, however, continued to serve on secondment terms until 1958 when a regular cadre of officers was approved and the first transfers effected. In August 1958, the first directly-commissioned officer for the Parachute Regiment, Second-Lieutenant R. D. Penley, joined the Regiment from the Royal Military Academy, Sandhurst.

In order to provide an avenue for officers and soldiers of other infantry regiments to continue to be trained as parachutists and in airborne techniques, a proportion of the Parachute Regiment's establishment was retained for volunteer secondments. The arms and services within the brigade continued to be manned by officers and soldiers from the parent Corps serving on secondment tours which have in some cases, not infrequently, lasted for many years.

In 1962 a modern complex of barracks was begun in Aldershot, on the site of the original barracks, to house the Parachute Battalions and Brigade HQ. This complex was opened officially by Field Marshal Montgomery in 1965 and named 'Montgomery Lines'. In 1960 the brigade's name was changed once again to the 16th Parachute Brigade, dropping the title 'Independent', when the British Army adopted the brigade as the basic organizational unit.

Certain other important changes took place at this time. The 33rd Parachute Light Regiment RA, for long the brigade's tireless close-support artillery was replaced by the 7th Parachute Regiment, Royal Horse Artillery. The brigade's anti-tank capacity was improved by the inclusion of the Parachute Squadron, Royal Armoured Corps, equipped with anti-tank guided missiles. Later, the Arms and Services were also reorganized. The Royal Corps of Transport, the

Royal Army Ordnance Corps, and the Royal Electrical and Mechanical Engineer elements were combined to form the 1st Parachute Logistics Regiment. In 1968, a further change in defence policy decided that the air assault element of the brigade could be reduced to a Parachute Force consisting of two parachute battalions and reduced supporting arms and services. The third parachute battalion, not forming part of the Parachute Force, was then made available for overseas garrison duties.

The reduction of the regular units of Airborne Forces in the post-war years has been paralleled by the history of the Territorial Army. After the end of World War II the Territorial Army was reconstituted. As part of this reconstruction, and to compensate for the disbandment of the wartime parachute units, a Territorial Airborne Division of three brigades was established on January 1, 1947. This was commanded by Major-General R. E. Urquhart, CB, DSO (Commander of the 1st Airborne Division at Arnhem) and included many other famous Airborne 'names' amongst its commanders. The three brigades were the 4th (Brigadier S. J. L. Hill, DSO, MC), centred on London, 5th (Brigadier A. H. G. Ricketts, DSO), at York, and 6th (Brigadier G. P. L. Weston, DSO, OBE), at Liverpool. The division raised nine parachute battalions, the 10th to the 18th inclusive, spread throughout the length and breadth of the UK, mostly from volunteers who had served with Airborne Forces in the war years. Of these battalions, the 11th, 14th, and 17th Battalions were formed direct from other units, the 8th Battalion The Middlesex Regiment (DCO) TA, the 4th Battalion the Royal Hampshire Regiment TA and the 9th Battalion The Durham Light Infantry TA, respectively. This Division also took the number '16' to perpetuate the numerals of the original 1st and 6th Airborne Divisions.

Subsequently, in 1956, its brigades were renumbered the 44th, 45th and 46th Parachute Brigades (TA), respectively. But further post-war policy changes were still to come, and with the reduction of the Territorial Army later in 1956 the 16th Division was reduced to one brigade group. This brigade, the 44th Independent Parachute Brigade Group (TA) retained initially five battalions: the 10th (City of London), 12th (Yorkshire), 13th (Lancashire), 15th (Scottish) and the 17th (Durham Light Infantry) Parachute Battalions (TA). This too lasted only for a very short time as the 12th and 13th Battalions were then amalgamated in October 1956, to become the 12th/13th (Yorkshire and Lancashire) Battalion reducing the brigade to four battalions. In 1967, this was further reduced to three battalions, by the amalgamation of the 12th/13th and 17th Battalions to form the 4th (Volunteer) Battalion, and the formation and unit designation were changed once more.

From this time therefore, in common with the Regular Army, the Territorial Army had only one Parachute Brigade Group, the 44th Parachute Brigade (Volunteers) consisting of three Parachute Battalions, the 4th (Volunteer) Battalion with its HQ at Pudsey near Bradford, the 10th (Volunteer) Battalion centred in London, the 15th (Scottish Volunteer) Battalion based in Glasgow with its companies spread throughout Scotland, the 16th (Lincoln) Independent Company, the Parachute Regiment (Volunteers), and the various supporting arms and services drawn from the Royal Horse Artillery, Royal Signals, Royal Engineers, Royal Corps of Transport, Royal Army Medical Corps, Royal Army Ordnance Corps, Royal Electrical and Mechanical Engineers and the Royal Military Police.

In an era of uncertainty further changes will doubtless occur in the future. One thing is sure, whatever the future holds, the problems will be faced and overcome with that same determined spirit and initiative which has become the hallmark of Airborne Forces.

Battle Honours of the Parachute Regiment

'Utrinque paratus' — ready for anything

BRUNEVAL	DJEBEL AZZAG 1943
NORMANDY LANDINGS	DJEBEL ALLILIGA
PEGASUS BRIDGE	EL HADJEBA
MERVILLE BATTERY	TAMERA
BREVILLE	DJEBEL DAHRA
DIVES CROSSING	KEF EL DEBNA
LA TOUQUES CROSSING	NORTH AFRICA 1942–43
ARNHEM 1944	PRIMOSOLE BRIDGE
OURTHE	SICILY 1943
RHINE	TARANTO
SOUTHERN FRANCE	ORSOGNA
NORTHWEST EUROPE 1942, 1944–45	ITALY 1943–44
SOUDIA	ATHENS
OUDNA	GREECE 1944–45

(Those underlined are borne on the Queens' Colour)

Colonels Commandant the Parachute Regiment

1942–44	Field-Marshal Sir John Dill, GCB, CMG, DSO, LLD
1944–56	Field-Marshal The Viscount Montgomery of Alamein, KG, GCB, DSO, DL.
1956–61	General Sir Richard Gale, GCB, KBE, DSO, MC.
1961–65	General Sir Gerald Lathbury, GCB, DSO, MBE.
1965–67	Lieutenant-General Sir Kenneth Darling, KCB, CBE, DSO.
1967–	Lieutenant-General Sir Mervyn Butler, KCB, CBE, DSO, MC.

Appendix B

History of No. 38 Group RAF

When Major-General Browing was appointed, in October 1941, to co-ordinate the expansion of airborne forces to divisional strength, he was faced with a variety of problems not least of which was that of training his growing command in airborne exercises at unit level. The RAF had anticipated the inevitable expansion in September 1941, by ordering the reorganization of the Airborne Forces Establishment. By November 1, this reorganization was completed, the new self-contained units were ready to be formed and the RAF assumed full responsibility for the training of parachute troops, all Army instructors being replaced by RAF personnel. The first course under the new system began on November 3, and consisted of 18 officers and 237 soldiers.

On November 28, 1941, the Air Ministry stated that the RAF training organization for airborne forces would be: —

(1) *For individual training of glider pilots :*
  One Elementary Flying Training School;
  Two Glider Training Schools (No. 1 School already existed);
  Two Glider Operational Training Units.

(2) *For individual training of parachute troops :*
  One Parachute Training School (in existence at Ringway).

(3) *For collective training :*
  One Parachute Exercise Squadron;
  One Glider Exercise Squadron.

(4) *A technical Development Section* (in existence at Ringway).

Immediate steps were taken to implement this new organization and No. 1 Glider Training School opened at Weston-on-the-Green on December 1. No. 16 Elementary Flying Training School turned over to glider training on December 31, and Nos. 1 and 2 Glider Operational Training Units opened at Netheravon and Kidlington on January 1 and February 1, 1942, respectively. Of the two exercise squadrons formed at Netheravon during January 1942, No. 296 (Glider Exercise) Squadron (Squadron Leader P. B. N. Davis) was to have eight plus a reserve of three Hectors, 20 plus six Whitleys, 30 plus 10 Horsas and 16 plus 14 Hotspurs, and No. 297 (Parachute Exercise) Squadron (Wing Commander B. Oakley) was to have 12 plus four Whitleys. Aircrews were immediately available but aircraft and gliders were slow in arriving and the squadrons were still not up to establishment by April 1942. The numbers of aircraft in the two exercise squadrons would, in any case, have been inadequate for their task.

On February 15, 1942, the Airborne Forces Establishment ceased to exist and No. 1 Parachute Training School became a self-contained unit remaining at Ringway. The HQ, the Technical Development Unit and the Experimental Flight were merged into a new unit known as Airborne Forces Experimental Establishment under Group Captain L. G. Harvey, whose charter was 'to carry on the Technical Development programme in conjunction with the RAF side of Airborne Warfare'.

It soon became obvious that some form of headquarters was necessary to co-ordinate the activities of Nos. 296 and 297 Squadrons, and to work with HQ 1st Airborne Division on the common problems which would have to be solved jointly. On January 15, 1942, therefore, HQ No. 38 Wing was established. Wing Commander Sir Nigel St V. Norman, Bt, who had been directly connected with the formation of airborne forces since September 1940, was promoted to Group Captain as its first commander. HQ No. 38 Wing was opened alongside HQ 1st Airborne Division at Syrencote House, Netheravon, and was to be responsible to Army Co-operation Command for the air training of the division and for any operations that took place in the future. The Wing was given a small operational staff whose duties were to include the evolving of a technique of training that could be applied to Bomber Command aircrews and squadrons as they became available as, at first, the Air Ministry would not permit the squadrons of the Wing to become operational. Airborne operations were to be carried out by aircraft loaned from Bomber Command.

One of the first problems confronting Group Captain Norman was the air training of troops and particularly that of the glider pilots. No. 38 Wing was desperately short of aircraft and gliders and Bomber Command could not at this time spare aircraft or crews for training. The only resources available were the few aircraft at the Airborne Forces Experimental Establishment and No. 1 Parachute Training School already fully committed to individual training and technical development. The allotment and best use of the available aircraft, therefore, were problems that taxed the ingenuity of the Wing to the utmost.

Almost immediately the Wing was plunged into the preparations for the Bruneval Raid (Operation 'Biting'). No. 51 Squadron of 4 Group Bomber Command, consisting of 16 'Whitley' aircraft commanded by Wing Commander P. P. S. Pickard, DSO, DFC, was placed under command of No. 38 Wing for the operation.

The raid (described in Chapter 1) took place on the night of February 27–28, 38 Wing acting under the command of the Naval Commander-in-Chief Portsmouth. The first aircraft took off at 2215 hours on February 27, the troops being heard to cheer as the aircraft left the ground. Fighter cover was provided by No. 11 Group. The aircraft were engaged by German flak ships off the French coast with considerable accuracy and three of the Whitleys were damaged, though not sufficiently to prevent them from reaching the target on time. With the exception of two aircraft ('Nelson' Group) all drops were made on or close to the Dropping Zones. All aircraft returned safely to base and landed by 0230 hours February 28.

Parachuting with the soldiers was RAF Technician, Flight Sergeant C. W. H. Cox, who dismantled the enemy radio direction-finding apparatus and ensured that the vital sections were safely returned to England.

The succeeding months of 1942 were spent in training and participating in airborne exercises with the Division. On June 26, 1942, the first complete battalion parachute drop by daylight was successfully executed followed by a night drop on the evening of the following day. On August 22, a further successful exercise was held in conjunction with the Polish Parachute Brigade.

On October 3, 1942, No. 1 Mobile Parachute Servicing Unit began forming at RAF Netheravon within the Wing. This unit, the first of its kind, was designed to handle all the RAF equipment needed by a parachute battalion (parachutes, containers and container packs) and to be capable of independent operation anywhere in the country.

In addition to their involvement with the Airborne Division, and in accordance with new Army Co-operation Command directives the Whitley squadrons of 38 Wing now also undertook operational sorties. These were designed to contribute to the efforts of Bomber Command and to give the aircrews of the Wing valuable operational experience. In October the Wing carried out 34 operational sorties, mainly leaflet dropping raids, over Northern France.

During this initial year the Wing received many distinguished visitors including Their Majesties The King and Queen, Lord Louis Mountbatten and the Prime Minister, Mr Winston Churchill.

The early months of 1943 saw a continuation of training and airborne exercises interspaced with operational bomber sorties. On February 19, 1943, Whitleys and Halifaxes of Nos. 295, 296 and 297 Squadrons attacked transformer and electrical installations in France, losing three aircraft by enemy action. Throughout February, March and April, operations — including leaflet dropping raids over France and the Channel Islands — were continued.

In April, the Wing's first Commander, now Air Commodore Sir Nigel Norman, CBE, Bt, was posted to the Special Duties List. He was tragically killed a few weeks later when a Hudson aircraft carrying him and a 38 Wing detachment crashed in Cornwall on May 19, 1943.

During May and June 1942, as part of the build-up for the invasion of Sicily, the Wing was engaged in Operation 'Beggar', the ferrying of 36 Horsa gliders to North Africa. This involved a flight of over 1,400 miles mostly over the sea, a distance never before attempted with gliders on tow. The flight presented difficulties. The Halifax aircraft would be at full load with petrol and gliders had not hitherto been towed in this condition. Petrol could not be jettisoned and forced landings would be hazardous. Favourable weather was required since the combinations had to avoid cloud. Over a six week period 30 combinations set out. One glider, breaking its tow rope in cloud over the Bay of Biscay, crashed into the sea, the pilot being picked up by naval destroyer. The latter stage of the journey also proved hazardous since low cloud was often encountered over the mountains of North Africa and the conditions were extremely bumpy and tiring for the pilots. Nineteen gliders finally reached Kairouan, near Sousse in Tunisia, the final destination. Of the others, four landed in the sea, three crashed in the mountains and four crashed near Sale in Morocco, the airport at which they first arrived in North Africa after their ten-hour flight over the sea.

The aircraft and gliders of the Wing were now involved in the airborne operations against Sicily as part of the invasion plan (Operation 'Husky'), and the subsequent land battle. The first operation, the airborne assault on the Ponte Grande bridge and the port of Syracuse took place on the night of July 9–10. The Wing contributed 28 Albemarle and seven Halifax aircraft from Nos. 296 and 297 squadrons as glider tugs. The operation, mounted from Kairouan, was not entirely successful. Time for training had been insufficient. This, combined with inexperience in glider towing techniques and anti-aircraft fire encountered over the coast contributed to an unhappy start. A large number of the 137 gliders which took part, towed by Dakota aircraft of the 51st US Troop Carrier Wing, were released too early and landed in the sea or were scattered over the countryside. Of the 35 gliders towed by the Wing, 26 landed in the correct areas.

The second operation in Sicily was the airborne assault on the Primosole Bridge over the River Simeto on the night July 13–14. One hundred and seven aircraft (Dakotas and Albemarles) were involved in parachute dropping and 17 gliders were towed by Halifax and Albemarle aircraft. Twenty-seven of the parachute aircraft were lost and many damaged, 19 returned to base without dropping and one tug aircraft was lost due to intensive and accurate enemy flak. Of the 17 gliders, 13 landed in the correct place, two were shot down and two were damaged on take-off. The violence of the enemy flak was, in this instance, primarily responsible for the scattered drop of the airborne troops who, none the less, managed to achieve their task.

In August, the Wing was again involved in ferrying glider reinforcements from the United Kingdom to North Africa (Operation 'Elaborate'). Twenty-three Halifax–Horsa combinations set out: 15 gliders reached North Africa, three landed in Portugal and five landed in the sea due to bad weather and enemy action. One Albemarle was also shot down in this period.

The Wing took no further part in the operations in the Middle East and were returned to the UK. However, as a result of the experience now gained in airborne operations it was apparent that the Wing would need to be both expanded and reorganized.

On October 11, 1943, it was enlarged to Group status under the command of Air Vice-Marshal L. N. Hollinghurst, CB, OBE, DFC. The new Group absorbed all the stations of No. 38 Wing and a new strength of nine squadrons

A Hamilcar glider on tow as seen from the tug aircraft. (Courtesy Imperial War Museum.)

was authorized, comprising four Albemarle, one Halifax and four Stirling squadrons. These squadrons were to consist of 16 front line and four plus four reserve aircraft each, all to be ready for operations by February 1, 1944. Reorganization was completed by November 22, 1943, and the Group was then placed under the command of HQ Allied Expeditionary Forces.

The early months of 1944 saw the squadrons of No. 38 Group continually engaged in bomber operations against the enemy, though in April the Group was switched to special missions including the dropping of supplies to the Resistance movements and transporting agents to the occupied countries of Europe. This continued into May when some 200 sorties were flown for the loss of two aircraft.

By early March 1944, No. 38 Group comprised the following squadrons:—

Squadron	Aircraft	Glider	Location
190	Stirling	Horsa	Fairford
196	Stirling	Horsa	Keevil
295	Albemarle (later Stirling)	Horsa	Harwell
296	Albemarle	Horsa	Brize Norton
297	Albemarle	Horsa	Brize Norton
298	Halifax	Hamilcar	Tarrant Rushton
299	Stirling	Horsa	Keevil
570	Albermarle (later Stirling)	Horsa	Harwell
620	Stirling	Horsa	Fairford
644	Halifax	Horsa	Tarrant Rushton

Throughout March and April the Group were engaged with the Airborne Division in exercises and training practices in preparation for Operation 'Overlord'—the invasion of Europe. Training was completed by the end of April but continued at a reduced tempo in May. The last major exercise took place on the night of May 1, when 74 gliders were landed on a small landing zone at Netheravon.

D-Day June 6, 1944

Nos. 38 and 46 Groups RAF were charged with the task of conveying the 6th Airborne Division to Normandy. The operation was divided into three subsidiary operations — 'Tonga', the dropping of two parachute brigade groups in the early hours of June 6, — 'Mallard', the landing of the main glider force on the evening of June 6, and 'Rob Roy', the subsequent re-supply missions.

On June 5, the first pathfinder aircraft, carrying men of the 22nd Independent Parachute Company, an Albermarle piloted by Squadron Leader Merrick, DFC, with Air Vice-Marshal Hollinghurst as passenger, took off at 2303 hours from Harwell. There is today a memorial standing at the end of the old runway, now part of the Atomic Energy Research Establishment, Harwell, to mark the spot where the first aircraft and soldiers took off for the invasion, and where a service of remembrance is held annually by members of the No. 38 Group and Airborne Forces Associations.

The Pathfinder and *coup de main* parties were due over their targets at 0020 hours June 6. The advance parachute parties met with mixed success in finding their drop zones, but the *coup de main* operation was an unqualified success. The gliders, with one exception, landed within a few yards of their objectives, the swing bridge over the Caen Canal and the road bridge over the River Orne, both of which were captured intact. Throughout the night aircraft of the Group conveyed personnel and equipment of the 6th Airborne Division to their dropping zones. Altogether they dropped 4,310 parachutists and towed gliders carrying 493 soldiers, 17 guns, 44 jeeps and 55 motorcycles. Seven aircraft and 22 gliders were lost.

In support of the attack by the 9th Battalion the Parachute Regiment on the German battery at Merville, three Horsa Gliders towed by Albemarles of No. 297 Squadron and piloted by volunteers undertook the highly dangerous task of crash landing on the battery. One glider broke its tow rope and force-landed in England, the other two gliders reached the French coast, both being hit by flak. As the 9th Battalion's mortars were missing, the signal flares could not be fired from the ground. One glider managed to land about 350 yards from the target, but the second tug aircraft mistook the village of Merville for the battery and released its glider. At 500 feet the glider pilot realized the mistake but was unable to correct and landed some distance away. The battery was, however, captured, as related in Chapter 6.

'Mallard', the landing of the main glider elements of the division was completely successful. Of the 256 gliders taking part, only 10 failed to land on the correct areas. The Group's part in 'Rob Roy' was, however, marred by weather although 12 of the 18 aircraft from the Group dropped their loads accurately.

With the successful conclusion of the D-Day landings the aircraft of the Group were switched to support of the Special Air Service (SAS) and Special Operations Executive (SOE) missions designed to hinder the movement of enemy reserves into the invasion area at the early stages of this battle. These

RAF Stirlings drop supplies to the troops at Arnhem, September 1944. The 'flak' bursts can be clearly seen. (Courtesy Imperial War Museum.)

missions continued throughout June and July. In the latter month a total of 4,080 hours on night operations were flown during which three enemy aeroplanes were destroyed by the airgunners of 38 Group aircraft.

Arnhem (Operation 'Market-Garden')

For Operation 'Market', the airborne part of Field-Marshal Montgomery's plan to advance across the Rhine in 1944, Nos. 38 and 46 Groups were given the task of pathfinder dropping and all glider towing and subsequent re-supply missions in the Arnhem sector. No. 38 Group was also charged with the responsibility of towing the gliderborne British Corps HQ to the Nijmegen–Grave area. For this task, scheduled for September 1944, the Group had available 10 squadrons comprising two Albermarle, two Halifax and six Stirling, together with Horsa and Hamilcar gliders.

The early morning fog which had been forecast for the first day of the operation September 17, 1944, did not delay the take-off of the 353 glider/tug combinations comprising the first lift. Of the 205 gliders provided by the Group, 187 made successful landings. Unfortunately, bad weather delayed the take-off of the second lift on September 18 for five hours and became one of the main contributory causes in the failure of the operation. The lift itself was successful but due to heavy opposition from the now fully-alerted German defences many gliders were burnt out in the landing. The last glider operation in the Arnhem battle was undertaken successfully with the landing of the glider elements of the Polish Parachute Brigade on September 20, in 35 Horsa gliders.

During the afternoon of September 19, 100 aircraft of No. 38 Group and 63 aircraft from No. 46 Group undertook the first of the large scale re-supply missions. Thirteen aircraft were lost and 97 were damaged by anti-aircraft fire. On the following two successive days the story was repeated. Determined to support the, by now, hard pressed airborne troops the aircrews displayed remarkable courage and resolution in the execution of these missions. Flying into a concentrated and deadly zone of enemy anti-aircraft fire at only 1,000 feet the aircraft maintained a straight and level course until their loads had been released. On one of these missions Flight Lieutenant David Lord, DFC, was awarded the Victoria Cross.

On September 23, the final re-supply mission from the UK to Arnhem was undertaken. A fighter escort of 854 aircraft was provided. Though enemy aircraft were kept at bay the flak was so severe that more than half of the RAF transports were lost or damaged. Overall, during Operation 'Market' — in what has become perhaps the most historic of all airborne operations — 12,997 British and American aircraft and 2,598 gliders were involved. No. 38 Group casualties in this period were 21 killed, 159 missing and 12 wounded.

For the remainder of 1944 the Group was heavily engaged in SAS and SOE missions to support the land operations. By the end of November, 1,700 troops, 41,000 containers, 2,500 packages, 650 panniers and 86 jeeps had been dropped in these operations.

A further operation ('Molten') to ferry gliders to the Middle East was also undertaken. This comprised 33 aircraft and glider combinations which took off from Fairford on October 9 for Pomigliano Airfield in Italy. Twenty-seven of the gliders were successfully delivered.

On October 18, 1944, Air Vice-Marshal J. R. Scarlett-Streatfield, CBE, was appointed Air Officer Commanding the Group in succession to Air Vice-Marshal Hollinghurst, who was posted to South East Asia with the rank of Air Marshal.

Land operations in Europe were now moving eastwards and the distances for support operations mounted from the UK were rapidly increasing. It was decided, therefore, to move the squadrons of the Group to airfields in East Anglia. This move took place in early October 1944, when the Group was established in Essex with

its Headquarters at Marks Hall,
all Brize Norton units at Earls Colne,
all Fairford units at Great Dunmow,
all Harwell units at Rivenhall, and
all Keevil units at Wethersfield.

During the first three months of 1945 the squadrons of the Group were heavily engaged in SAS, SOE and tactical bomber operations to harass the enemy's movements and communications. During one of these missions unidentified aircraft were observed flying at great speed and burning a very bright orange light; these are thought to have been the first glimpses of enemy jet aircraft, though no attacks were made on the bombers.

In March 1945, the final planning and training with the 6th Airborne Division for the crossing of the Rhine (Operation 'Varsity') was commenced. No. 38 Group's task in this, the final and completely successful airborne operation of the War, was to provide the glider towing lift to six dropping zones. The operation took place in perfect weather on March 24, and all but one of the 320 glider/tug combinations were despatched within one hour. The journey was uneventful and no enemy fighters were encountered, doubtless because of the vast fighter cover provided. Thirty-one of the aircraft and gliders, for one reason or another, failed to reach the target. Over the landing zone intensive and accurate enemy flak was encountered. As a result there was a high percentage of casualties amongst the gliders and the Group lost four aircraft shot down, 39 damaged with two listed as missing. The Group casualties were seven aircrew killed and 16 missing.

A 'Locust' light tank emerges from a Hamilcar glider. This glider, the largest wooden aircraft built, carried the heavy equipment which could not be carried or parachuted from the types of aircraft in use in WW II. (Courtesy of Cyril Peekham F.R.P.S.)

During April, the Group again reverted to SAS and SOE operations, the largest of which (Operation 'Amherst') involved the dropping of two parachute regiments of the Canadian Army on to zones in the Low Countries. The drop was undertaken by 47 Stirling aircraft of 38 Group in very poor weather on the night of April 7–8. Because of extensive cloud and fog, the troops were dropped from 1,500 feet, the aircraft using GEE fixes* to find the targets. The drop was successful and no aircraft were lost.

With the war in Europe now rapidly drawing to its close the number and intensity of operations began to diminish. On VE-Day, May 8, the Group flew the 1st Parachute Brigade to Copenhagen (Operation 'Schnapps') to assist with the maintenance of law and order in Denmark. On the following day, May 9, the Group commenced the fly-in of the 1st Airborne Division to Norway (Operation 'Doomsday') involving the move of 7,000 troops and 2,000 tons of stores.

The jubilation following the victory in Europe was, however, marred for No. 38 Group by the tragic death of its Air Officer Commanding, Air Vice-Marshal Scarlett-Streatfield, his crew and 17 passengers from the 1st Airborne Division. Their aircraft crashed on May 10, 1945, on a flight to Oslo; the wreck· was not discovered until the last week in June. The funeral of those killed was held in Oslo with full Service honours on July 2, 1945.

Throughout the remaining months of 1945 aircraft of the Group were engaged in a wide variety of transport tasks between Europe and the UK. These included the return of prisoners of war, ferrying replacement troops to the Continent, the repatriation of others and the movement of displaced persons. Personnel of all arms, including many of our Allies were transported at this time, involving a total of 415 million passenger miles flown by the end of the year. In October 1945, a regular mail and freight delivery service to India was commenced.

The early months of 1946 saw, in conformity with the other Services, the reduction of the RAF until by April 1, No. 38 Group retained only two first-line squadrons. Later in the year, however, the Group strength was increased by the addition of two squadrons, No. 47 and No. 644, from overseas, both based at Fairford.

Throughout 1946 the Group continued the Indian mail service and took part in minor airborne exercises. In May, Group HQ moved to RAF Upavon and on June 8 four Halifaxes from the Group took part in the Victory Fly Past over London. The exceedingly severe winter of 1946–47 saw the Group involved in dropping supplies to villages and livestock isolated by snow, during which a Halifax of No. 47 Squadron crashed in Staffordshire, killing the crew.

The pattern of exercises established in 1946 continued throughout 1947, culminating in September with a major airborne exercise ('Longstop'). This

---

* A radio-navigational aid using prepositioned ground transmitting beacons.

consisted of parachute and glider operations with re-supply missions and was observed by the Minister for Air, the members of the Imperial General Staff, the Chief of the Air Staff and foreign Armed Forces representatives.

For No. 38 Group the year 1948 started in similar fashion to the previous year, but on June 25 the Russian blockade of Berlin commenced. To relieve the city a gigantic airlift (Operation 'Plainfare') was mounted to supply Berlin from the air. The 'Berlin Airlift', as it became popularly known, continued for 323 days until May 1949. Two squadrons of the Group, Nos. 47 and 297, were deployed to Germany for the airlift and operated from Schleswig during most of the period.

In August 1948, the Group strength was again cut to two squadrons, Nos. 47 and 297, which were now re-equipped with Hastings aircraft and moved to Dishforth, Yorkshire. In 1949 three more squadrons were added and RAF Abingdon, Lyneham and Bassingbourne were transferred to No. 38 Group control. The Group was engaged in minor exercises and scheduled route services throughout 1949 and 1950, the major highlight of the period being Exercise 'Oil King' in which the whole of the 16th Independent Parachute Brigade was dropped in Norfolk in October.

During the remainder of 1950 many of the Group tasks were transferred to RAF Transport Command until, on February 1, 1951, as an economy measure, the Group was disbanded.

Re-formation

On January 1, 1960, Headquarters No. 38 Group under the command of Air Vice-Marshal P. G. Wykeham, DSO, OBE, DFC, AFC, re-formed at RAF Upavon with an establishment of 17 officers and 20 airmen. In May the HQ moved to RAF Odiham, Hampshire, the Group comprising by this time of RAF Lyneham, Abingdon, Colerne, Dishforth and the Transport Command Parachute Servicing Unit located at RAF Bicester, Oxfordshire.

The new Group was charged with the task of 'planning and ordering all tactical transport tasks, close liaison with the Army and the development of tactical air transport and airborne assault techniques'.

Throughout the 1960s No. 38 Group worked in direct co-operation with the 16th Parachute Brigade Group developing, practising and improving airborne assault techniques. Technical developments in transport aircraft design have permitted considerable progress to be made in heavy drop techniques thereby increasing the range and scope of airborne operations. In addition to the routine training of parachute troops and numerous minor exercises carried out annually within the UK, many major tactical exercises have been mounted overseas. These have been both widespread and have embraced all aspects of airborne operations taking place as far afield as the Jutland Peninsula 1960, Cyprus and Cyrenaica in 1961, Greece 1962, Libya and Cyprus 1963, Libya 1964, North Africa 1965, the UK 1966 and West Germany 1967.

During this period the Group's activities have not been entirely confined to airborne warfare but have also included a variety of unconventional tasks. During the severe winter conditions in the early months of 1963 the aircraft of the Group were engaged in relief operations in the West and South West of England carrying animal fodder, foodstuffs and solid fuels to isolated areas. In April 1967, the Group participated with the 16th Parachute Brigade in demonstrating typical land/air offensive operations to Her Majesty the Queen and HRH The Duke of Edinburgh during their visit to the Brigade in Aldershot. This consisted of a parachute and helicopter assault combined with heavy drop, re-supply, photographic reconnaissance and offensive strike support by aircraft controlled by the Group.

Later, in April 1967, Hunter aircraft of No. 38 Group from RAF West Raynham together with Naval strike aircraft bombed the SS *Torrey Canyon*, an oil tanker which had gone aground on the Seven Stones Reef, south east of the Lizard. Oil from the tanker had polluted the coast nearby and was threatening to contaminate the whole of the Cornish Riviera and most of the South Coast. The British Government decided that the ship was to be bombed in an effort to set fire to the oil. Napalm was successfully used and the operation ('Mop-Up') provided valuable experience for the Hunter pilots in affording them a 'live' target for bombing practice. Involved also in this operation were the Wessex helicopters from RAF Odiham which lifted freight and cleaning-up personnel to the affected beaches.

As part of the reorganization of the RAF Command structure, Transport Command was renamed Air Support Command on August 1, 1967. On this day too, Air Vice-Marshal H. B. Martin, DSO, DFC, AFC, was appointed to the command of the Group. Air Vice-Marshal Martin was, at this time, the last serving member of the famous No. 617 Squadron (the 'Dam Busters') which destroyed the Mohne and Eder dams in World War II.

During mid-1967 the Group was occupied with Exercise 'Unison', part of a series of Commonwealth Defence studies, during which two Air Days were held. These were designed to demonstrate to Commonwealth and foreign staff officers the operational effectiveness of British Service aircraft and tactical support weapons. This was demonstrated by simulating operations at a main base airfield, a forward airhead and in a combat zone. A parachute assault operation was staged with the troops of the 16th Parachute Brigade and the RAF Regiment. This was followed by a series of typical airhead operations including tactical landings by transport aircraft delivering men and equipment, together with casualty evacuation procedures and current air delivery techniques. These Air Days were highly successful, demonstrating the high degree of Army/Air co-operation achieved between No. 38 Group and the military units involved. The highlights included demonstrations by the Harrier vertical take-off and landing (VTOL) aircraft and spectacular air-to-ground strikes by Hunters at Larkhill.

R

Since 1960, No. 38 Group has achieved remarkably high standards of operational and technical efficiency and in passenger safety. In the course of millions of air-miles flown, carrying many thousands of troops on airborne exercises, there have been only two aircraft crashes involving loss of life. Judged in the context of the often hazardous nature demanded by operational flying techniques this is a record of which any civilian airline might be justly proud.

Girls of the (WW II) W.A.A.F. pack the chutes under a constant reminder of the responsibilities of their task. A tribute to their care and devotion in this respect is the fact that a parachute failure (or 'Candle') was an extremely rare occurrence. (Courtesy Imperial War Museum.)

Appendix C

Air Re-supply

Historical

One or two small-scale emergency re-supply missions flown during World War I gave a hint that the military aeroplane had a logistical as well as a tactical and strategic role to play in war. Peace-time exercises with troop-carrying aircraft and re-supply missions in the course of minor military campaigns in various parts of the world subsequently dispelled any doubt about the aeroplane's logistical role, but it was not until World War II that the role was fully recognized and exploited.

The first recorded attempts at re-supplying ground forces by air took place in 1916 when nine aircraft of the Royal Flying Corps flew 140 sorties in six days in a bid to sustain the ill-fated British garrison beseiged at Kut-al-Amara during the Mesopotamian campaign. However, the limited size and range of the aircraft restricted the scale of the operation and the valiant effort failed to achieve its purpose. Two years later another relief operation was entirely successful.

This took place in October 1918, when elements of Belgian and French divisions were cut off in the area of Houthulst Forest and could not be re-supplied from the ground. The troops appealed for help to the Belgian Air Force (BAF) who, in turn, requested support from the newly formed Royal Air Force.

No. 82 Army Co-operation Squadron (2nd Brigade) equipped with Armstrong Whitworth FK8 aircraft, and No. 218 Squadron (5th Group) equipped with de Havilland 9 aircraft, were assigned to the operation. Rations and ammunition were placed into sandbags filled with earth to be dropped in specified areas from 300 feet. Five to 10 rations (tins of bully beef, stew, jam, hard 'tack' biscuits etc. . . .) each weighing approximately 1 lb were packed and the total weight of each bag was about 18 lb. Boxed ammunition was also dropped.

Between October 1 and 4, 1918, these two squadrons made 193 sorties dropping 1,202 sandbag loads and some 60 boxes of ammunition. Each aircraft carried two boxes of ammunition and six sandbags, or 11 sandbags, per sortie. These had all to be dropped over the side by the observer who had also to manhandle the loads. Probably no more than two loads could be dropped on each run-in over the target, necessitating five runs per aircraft to dispose of the load. During this time the aircraft were undoubtedly in range of enemy small arms fire. Nevertheless, they also undertook bombing, strafing, spotting for the artillery or reconnaissance tasks as part of these sorties, but only one air-

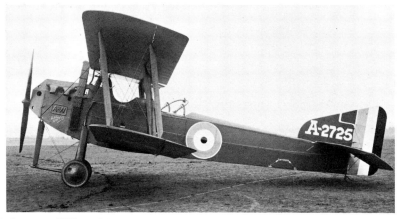

Armstrong Whitworth FK8.

De Havilland 9a.
These two aircraft of Nos 82 and 218 Squadrons RAF carried out the first recorded success-
ful supply drop missions to troops in action in October 1918. 10 tons of supplies in four days
is an astonishing feat, considering the limited load and carrying capacity of aircraft at this
date. (Courtesy Royal Air Force.)

craft, of No. 218 Squadron, is reported missing in this period (the crew presumed killed) in the squadron records. In all some 10 tons of containers were dropped successfully and the squadron documents record the congratulations of the Belgian Commander who indicated that they had 'saved the situation'.

Aeroplanes were used by the RAF between the wars to transport troops and, in some cases, to drop supplies to isolated parties, particularly in the numerous small minor campaigns that took place on the NW Frontier of India. However, the load capacity and range of the between-wars aircraft still normally precluded this type of operation on anything other than a very minor scale. The Russians, in 1936, startled Western observers with a mass parachute drop of 1,500 men and equipment, but it was left to the Germans to develop this technique to practical proportions. This they were to demonstrate, to the consternation of the Allies, so effectively in 1940.

Troops emplaning in a Vickers Valentia for a practice air-transported move between the wars. Due to the shortage of modern aircraft in the early days of World War II a number of Valentias were pressed into service at the Middle East and Indian Parachute Schools. Their slow speed and stable flying characteristics made them an ideal jump platform for training purposes. Many early parachutists were trained on this aircraft. (Courtesy Royal Air Force.)

The fate of many supply aircraft. A Curtis 'Commando' of the USAAF shot down while dropping supplies at the Rhine Crossing, March 1945. (Courtesy Imperial War Museum.)

As the range and cargo capacity of aircraft increased, so the means to supply large formations in battle by air became a reality. With a measure of air superiority and the necessary availability of transport aircraft, large forces can be maintained for long periods, though cut off from ground re-supply routes. General Wingate proved this in the Burma Campaign, and though he was not the first to use aircraft for this task his operations proved the practicability of large scale missions of this type. A classic example is the Berlin Airlift, when the Allied sectors of the city were maintained over a period of 323 days solely by air-supply.

The growth of air re-supply, which played so vital a part in many of the later campaigns of World War II and, subsequently, in post-war emergencies such as Malaya and Borneo, is an aspect of Airborne History which has gone generally unsung and unrecorded. It has, in so far as the British Army is concerned, grown and developed out of the close co-operation between the Army and Royal Air Force Transport Command (now Air Support Command). What is perhaps not appreciated, except by soldiers on the ground in desperate need, is the vital and dangerous task that is undertaken by the men of the Royal Corps of Transport Air Despatch Units (formerly Royal Army Service Corps) and the RAF crews of the transport aircraft. A lumbering, heavily laden transport aircraft, which must fly low at near stalling speed on a straight and level course when despatching its container and parachute supply loads, often into a confined area, becomes the target for every enemy anti-aircraft gun or small arms weapon in the vicinity. This requires deliberate, calculated courage and devotion to duty which is often beyond praise and, more often than not, unrecognized. It was this devotion to duty, and the desperate needs of those on the ground, that won for Flight Lieutenant David Lord, DFC, RAF, the Victoria Cross at Arnhem.

The casualties suffered by those responsible for air-supply have, in proportion to unit strength, frequently been higher than those of the ground units they have so ably supported.

Definition

Supply by air in its broadest sense means the maintenance by air of a force which, for some reason, cannot be sustained by conventional routes. The term covers both the air landing of supplies at forward airfields or airstrips and the dropping of loads from an aircraft in flight. Dropping from the air may be by parachute — for the more fragile stores — or by free drop where this is feasible. Flour and sugar for example, may be free-dropped in double sacks without great harm to the contents. New methods are under constant experiment and plastic containers for the free-dropping of water and petrol are now practicable. Whatever the means of despatch, it entails using specially trained personnel who are adept in the rapid and often tricky procedures required. The term also embraces the control and executive agencies needed to co-ordinate the demands, issue, packing, movement to the airfields, loading and finally the delivery of stores at the right place, at the right time and in the right order of priority.

The War Years

At the commencement of World War II no such organization existed in the British Army. Indeed, little thought had been given to air-supply and any that had was concerned with purely emergency measures. An example of this was the attempt to supply the British Expeditionary Force at Dunkirk in 1940, using converted airliners and some obsolescent RAF Hector bi-planes. This was true, too, of German thinking at the time. Though far ahead of the British in this field, the Germans were mainly pre-occupied with the air-supply of the immediate needs of their parachute forces in action. Little thought had been given, or indeed thought necessary, for the protracted supply of an isolated force. The concept of sustaining large forces in the field, not as an emergency or even supplementary means of supply, was conceived in the Far East theatre. Here, Major-General Orde Wingate devized a plan for raiding deep into enemy territory and maintaining his force entirely independent of the normal ground lines of communication. So successfully was the technique developed that by the end of the war almost the whole of the Burma theatre was given over to supply by air as the primary means of sustaining troops in the field. The scale of this may be judged from the fact that in 1945, during its final victorious advance, the 14th Army received no less than 96 per cent of its requirements from the air.

Logistical requirements between the Far East and the European theatres differed in important aspects. In the former, the very difficult and under-developed terrain prevented the deployment of large, heavily-mechanized forces; consequently, the quantities of fuel and ammunition required were less. In addition, ground opposition to transport aircraft was less intense.

In Europe, where normal communications were highly developed, mechanized armies consumed vast quantities of stores of all kinds. Anti-aircraft measures against transport aircraft were co-ordinated and intense. In this theatre therefore, with the notable exception of airborne operations, air-supply was planned as an emergency measure rather than, as in Burma, the normal means of supply. These factors still pertain today and are sometimes not fully appreciated when planning what is possible rather than practical. The Germans were faced with this lesson in their attempt to sustain Field-Marshal Von Paulas's army invested by the Russians at Stalingrad. The logistical resources supplied from the air proved too little, and too late, to prevent the army's eventual annihilation.

When in early 1944 the British 21st Army Group, in action in Europe, stated a firm requirement for supply and maintenance by air, the tonnages envisaged were so great that it became necessary to establish a new and large organization to carry out this task. There existed at this time only a small organization which had grown up with, and was part of, the airborne divisions. This consisted of two Royal Army Service Corps (RASC) air composite companies, one serving the 1st, and the other the 6th Airborne Divisions. These companies were not organized on special establishments but were normal transport companies, RASC. Their method of operation was for the drivers to pack and load stores for their division, drive to the airfield, load the aircraft, accompany the stores in flight, despatch these over the drop point, return to the airfield and drive their vehicles home. These companies could produce only 50 despatch crews of four men. Related to the estimated requirements of an airborne division at that time (270 tons per day) requiring some 130 aircraft, their task became well nigh impossible. They were, therefore, sensibly pooled in due course with the new organization.

War establishments were now agreed for a HQ RASC (Air Despatch), an air despatch company and an air loading platoon. In March 1944, HQ of No. 36 Lines of Communication Transport Column and No. 233 Troop Carrying Company, RASC were released by the 21st Army Group for conversion to air despatch duties. They moved to Swindon, Wiltshire, into the vicinity of the airfields occupied by No. 46 Group RAF. Their task was set at 170 tons of stores delivered by air drop, and 700 tons by air-landing each day. Later, these figures were revised to 350 and 3,000 tons, respectively, resulting in an expansion of the air despatch organization which was then increased to three companies, with a total of 12 dropping platoons each of 74 all ranks. These additional companies, Nos. 749 and 799, were formed in May 1944, from members of the permanent staff of the 8th Training Battalion, RASC.

NCOs and soldiers attended air despatch courses and underwent flying training with the RAF. Training was chiefly based on the roller conveyor type of despatch, designed for large-scale supply drops, and partly on the manual ejection method for small drop zones. Apart from the purely air despatch units, the Group also had under command transport, petrol, ordnance and pioneer units.

For their primary task the Group was able to provide sufficient air despatch crews to man 205 Dakota aircraft (four-man crews to despatch panniers), or 410 Stirling aircraft (two man crews only, since half their load was carried in bomb cell containers slung beneath the aircraft). The Group's secondary task was the airfreighting of stores from local depots or dumps—normally without special packing—to forward airfields in the operational area. The final strength of this new organization in the European theatre consisted of some 5,000 men and 1,500 vehicles.

From the outset the air despatch organization was involved in many exciting and hazardous operations. Over and above the daily maintenance requirements of the 21st Army Group were superimposed the requirements of the Special Air Service Brigade (SAS) and French Resistance fighters in enemy-occupied territories. There were too, many emergency calls for supplies for liberated French territories, special deliveries of fuel to American forces, air maintenance of units in the Falaise Gap operation and for those on Walcheren Island. On average, some 1,000 tons a day became the normal requirement. These loads consisted in the main of fuel, ammunition and composite rations, but as time went on the cargoes became more varied and included almost the full range of ordnance stores.

Undoubtedly the most testing period for the air despatch organization was during the battle at Arnhem. The background and development of this battle are well known, but the plan envisaged the maintenance by air of the 1st Airborne Division, by the whole Air Despatch Group, for a period of 48 hours until relieved by the ground forces. In the event the division was forced to withdraw into a contracting perimeter and the battle lasted for nine days. In these circumstances the Air Despatch Group was stretched to its utmost as the heroic efforts of the RAF aircrews and despatchers became daily more difficult. The drop zones fell into enemy hands and less than 10 per cent of the total supplies dropped were received by the division. Nonetheless, as long as there was a chance of aiding the men on the ground, the air supply missions continued. The measure of the sacrifice made by the air despatch organization at this time is that, had the battle lasted a further three days the last air despatch crew would have been used up by attrition. It is difficult to describe, in words, the holocaust into which these airmen and soldiers were prepared to fly— sufficient to say that of the 900 trained air despatch officers and men, 264 were shot down in the four days that air supply missions were flown—of these 116 were killed and 148 taken prisoner. A total of some 600 sorties were flown, during which all despatchers completed two missions and the majority three.

A distinctive emblem consisting of a yellow Dakota aircraft on a blue background had been adopted by the Air Despatch organization and was displayed on all unit notice boards and directional signs. As a result of the Arnhem operation, official recognition of this emblem as the formation sign to be worn on the uniform sleeve was granted in Army Council Instructions, 'for the good work done by the Air Despatch Group over Arnhem'. This is believed to be the first instance of a formation sign being officially granted as an operational award to a RASC unit, and the badge is worn today with great pride by all air despatchers.

The development of the Air Supply organization in South East Asia Command (SEAC) reflects great credit on the vision of those involved. At a time of defeat, retreat and disaster in 1941 there was established at Delhi an Air-Landing School. Its charter was to study airborne operations and tactical air supply. From this school was developed the Airborne Training Establishment, an Army Air Transport Development Centre, and an Air Despatch Centre located at Chaklala. No. 1 Company Royal Indian Army Service Corps (RIASC) became the first company to be trained in air-supply duties. Their first large-scale operation took place in 1942, when the Company was sent to Assam to drop 3,000 tons of foodstuffs to refugees in Burma.

In the period between 1942 and 1945 a total of 10,000 all ranks of the RIASC were trained in air supply duties. Parallel with this expansion was the progress made in this theatre in the development of techniques for handling awkward loads. This included the air dropping of mules on platforms without, apparently, adverse effects on the animals themselves.

Air-supply in this theatre varied from the support of an advanced patrol to that of a complete army, requiring finally the deployment of nine RIASC air despatch companies and one RASC. The real vindication for its adherents, and confirmation of the soundness of their vision, came on the Arakan front in early 1944. Here the 7th Indian Division was surrounded by the Japanese and for the first time in this theatre a British force was able to stand its ground and beat off all attacks, firm in the knowledge that its needs could be supplied from the air. The event was significant, both to the morale and confidence of the British forces, and went far to dispel the Japanese image of invincibility. Soon after, hundreds of miles to the north, powerful Japanese forces surrounded the 4th British Corps. The story of the defence of Kohima and Imphal is well known, and it was in no small part due to the air-supply organization that the defenders were able to hold until relieved. The flexibility that air-supply offered to the 14th Army was possibly crucial to its successful operations from 1944 onwards. Certainly without a similar organization the Japanese were unable to produce an effective defence. As an illustration of the scope which a sound air-supply organization offers to ground operations, more than 60,000 tons of stores and 48,000 reinforcements were flown into Burma and 11,000 casualties were flown out in March 1945, alone.

The Post-War Years

Inevitably the immediate post war years saw the contraction of air despatch units until only two companies remained—Nos. 749 and 799 Companies RASC. The former was to serve principally as a training centre in the UK and the latter as an operational unit in the Far East.

The final pattern of the air-supply organization evolved in Burma was initially accepted as the design for future possible operations in the post-war era. This organization was put to the test in 1948, when the Allied sectors of Berlin was isolated by the Russians. A massive air-supply operation was mounted by RAF Transport Command, the US Air Force and chartered aircraft of civilian airlines. The British operations were controlled by an Army Air Transport Organization (AATO), based on the executive nucleus of No. 799 Air Despatch Company, RASC. This organization handled some 40 per cent of the total tonnage supplied to the city. The aircraft memorial, built by grateful Berliners at Tempelhof airport in 1950, pays mute tribute to those who, by means of air-supply, won a significant victory for freedom.

As a result of this operation, and in the light of developments in the post war political scene, it became apparent that the AATO organization was not in itself flexible enough to be geared to operations likely to result from a 'cold war'. From this developed the concept of an Army Air Supply Organization (AASO). Two such groups were therefore brought into being in 1950, No. 1 AASO in the UK and No. 3 AASO in the Far East. These were almost entirely manned by the RASC, but were organized to be capable of commanding and controlling units of other arms involved in the air-supply system. When, in 1965, the Royal Corps of Transport was formed from the RASC the titles of No. 1 and No. 3 AASO where changed again to No. 14 and No. 15 Air Despatch Regiments, RCT.

In the post war years air despatch (AD) companies or squadrons have been formed and disbanded as the need arose. Apart from No. 749 and No. 799 companies, both retitled during the ensuing years and kept in continuous existence, there have been: —

No. 16 AD Squadron — In Kenya and Aden.

No. 22 AD Squadron — in the UK as a training cadre and in support of the strategic reserve.

No. 69 AD Squadron — raised for the confrontation in Malaysia.

No. 73 AD Company — the former No. 233 Company employed in the post war years in Egypt.

It has, however, been principally in the Far East that the major operational post war tasks of air-supply have been carried out. In this theatre it has been, in the main, undertaken by No. 55 Air Despatch Squadron, RCT. This Squadron (originally No. 799 Company, RASC, renumbered No. 55 Air Despatch Company RASC in 1953 and, subsequently, to No. 55 Air Despatch Squadron Royal Corps of Transport in 1965) whose history dates back to May 1944, has been engaged in almost continuous operations since the end of the war and is probably the most widely known and famous of all air despatch units.

Having served in the European Theatre throughout 1944 this unit was transferred, in early 1945, to the Far East. It undertook air-supply missions in Burma until the end of the war and was then engaged in similar missions in

An Auster of the Army Air Corps drops supplies direct into a jungle clearing in Malaya. The static line is just about to pull the parachute from its container. (Courtesy Royal Air Force.)

Java during the turbulent period of 1946. It returned to Burma and spent the next two years in Rangoon assisting with that country's reconstruction during the handover period to the Burmese Government. In addition to air-supply missions — in one period 600 tons of rice was dropped to Karen villagers in remote areas who were starving because of drought and crop failure — the unit undertook internal security operations in an era of civic disorder. Returning to Singapore in early 1948, it was almost at once plunged into operations as a result of the Malayan emergency. It continued in this fully operational role for the next 12 years — until July 1960.

As the emergency developed the air-supply requirement grew and rapidly became a major feature of the campaign. This finally totalled some 90 per cent of the air support effort. An efficient anti-terrorist campaign could not have been conducted without the widespread use of air-supply; patrols would have been unable to penetrate the thickest and remotest areas of the jungle which contained the terrorist base camps and arms dumps. The security forces soon came to accept that, wherever they might be in this wild country, they could rely on an aircraft arriving over an agreed point at a pre-arranged time to drop to them food, arms, ammunition, medicine, mail, newspapers or whatever else they required.

This demanded great skill on the part of the aircrews. The right spot had to be located in an endless jungle scene not over well mapped. In the humid climate thick cloud often covers wide areas, creating a formidable hazard in mountainous country. A further hazard that faced pilots who descended into a small valley to locate a drop zone, was the possibility that it might prove too small for the aircraft to climb out of again. Great accuracy in dropping, and a high degree of skill on the part of the despatchers, was essential. Supplies falling only a short distance from the drop zone might be caught up in 200 feet tall trees, or it might take a patrol hours, even days, to hack its way through to the spot.

During this period the Company built up a tremendous reputation for efficiency, and for its flexible approach to the handling of all types of loads. These included, in addition to normal items, such cargoes as somewhat startled dogs and cats to isolated rat-infested police posts, barbed wire and defence stores, Ferguson tractors, pre-fabricated houses, iced beer on Anzac Day to New Zealand troops and, on one occasion, fresh lobsters packed in ice for a patrol commander celebrating his birthday deep in the jungle. The Company also undertook relief operations for the World Health Organization, dropped supplies to Malayan villages on behalf of the Government and medical equipment to a ship at sea to save the life of the Captain who had had to undergo an emergency operation. The variety and scope of the tasks requested of the unit were multitudinous and no request, however small, was ever rejected unless proved impracticable.

An instance of the odd situations in which members of the unit often found themselves is perhaps best illustrated by the 'Amethyst Affair'.

In May 1950, HMS *Amethyst* was trapped by Chinese Communist shore batteries in the Yangtse River. It was decided that a Sunderland flying boat should drop supplies to the beleaguered ship. Men of the Company, on detachment in Hong Kong, packed the stores and two members of the unit flew with the aircraft. In the end the Sunderland actually landed in the river alongside the *Amethyst*! The first sortie was followed by a second, the aircraft coming under heavy fire on both occasions. The two despatchers concerned both qualified for the Naval General Service Medal for this operation.

Throughout the Malayan emergency every soldier and unit that took part in the anti-terrorist operations must, at one time or another, have received supplies packed, loaded and despatched by the Company. Their brilliant but hazardous work was officially recognized at the end of the emergency when, on October 26, 1960, the Deputy Prime Minister of Malaya, Tun Abdul Razak bin Hussein, handed to Major B. H. Bradbrook, the Officer Commanding No. 55 Company, a ceremonial kris on behalf of the Prime Minister and his Government. Only four such kris were presented to units during the whole 12-year period of the emergency.

In November 1960, the unit moved to Singapore, leaving only one platoon to continue air-supply to the security forces and jungle forts in Northern Malaya and along the Thai border. To mark the end of this exacting period a Special Order of the Day was published by the Commander, 17th Gurkha Division and Overseas Commonwealth Land Forces: —

'I am indeed sorry to have to say farewell to your Company after long service with this Division. You will still be air-supplying us from Singapore, except for a platoon which will remain in the Divisional area but under new command. I speak for all ranks when I say that you will be missed very much here in Malaya.

Your tour of duty, extending throughout the 12 years of the Emergency,

A despatcher of 55 Company RASC watches as a supply drop parachute floats down into a village in Borneo 1965. (Courtesy Royal Air Force.)

has produced an excellent record and the figures speak for themselves; over 15,000 sorties with 200,000 parachutes used; 650 million leaflets dropped; a total of 29,590 tons despatched with a splendid record in one day of 15 sorties to 75 separate Dropping Zones. At the same time this is a fitting moment to remember the 35 soldiers who lost their lives as a direct result of operations, the highest casualty rate of any unit throughout the Emergency. I am confident that you will continue to maintain your high standard of service in the future.'

The demanding nature of this type of work, the gallantry and sacrifice expected, and frequently demanded, of the air despatch service is more than illustrated by the honours and awards which were bestowed upon the unit during this time. During the Emergency the unit received six Distinguished Flying Medals, five MBEs, one Military Medal, six British Empire Medals, and no fewer than 34 officers and soldiers were Mentioned in Despatches. A truly remarkable record, and one of which both the unit and their Corps may be justly proud.

The unit spent the next two years training interspersed with minor relief operations. The period was not without tragedy: a Hastings aircraft crashed in 1961, with the loss of the crew and nine despatchers, when engaged on a practice supply drop. The unit was not, however, to be long left in the relative calm of peace-time soldiering.

Early on December 8, 1962, an armed rebellion broke out in Brunei and the unit was plunged once more into active operations. Initially, these duties included airfield guards at Brunei, where the unit captured one of the insurgents and uncovered an arms dump, and undertook limited air-supply operations. Large quantities of leaflets were air dropped at this time. Platoons of the Company also undertook the loading and unloading of aircraft at Brunei and Labuan and assisted the reinforcing units moving through the airfields. A few days later an intensive effort was made to drop Christmas fare to the units in the jungle.

In January 1963, in addition to its operational commitments, severe flooding in North Borneo involved the Company in relief supply drops to the populace in the river valley areas on the east coast. One despatcher was lost in these sorties when the Twin Pioneer aircraft in which he was flying crashed, killing all on board.

At the same time, operations were still continuing on the border between Malaya and Thailand. One platoon was kept hard at work with major operations mounted in February and March in which some 80,000 lb of stores were dropped to the security forces.

Meanwhile, a worsening situation in Sarawak led to a detachment of the Company being moved to Kuching to set up a supply drop organization. They found the small civil airport cluttered with tents, temporary buildings and piles of equipment. The situation was further confused by the fact that there was no RAF establishment in existence for operational flying. The RAF supply dropping commitment gradually developed, first with light Auster and Pioneer aircraft, and later with Valetta and Beverley transports. Despite the early chaos, the company was not prevented from undertaking an airdrop of urgently needed diphtheria vaccine to Christmas Island, in the Indian Ocean, on April 13.

On August 31, 1963, Malaysia was formed from Malaya, Singapore, Sarawak and North Borneo, which was now to be called Sabah. The formation of Malaysia was followed immediately by Indonesia's armed 'confrontation'.

The frontier between Malaysian Borneo and Indonesia is over a thousand miles long, and passes through some of the most innaccessible and rugged country in the world. It is badly defined and, to add further confusion, much of it is unmapped. At first incursions from Indonesia took the form of armed raids by small groups, often deep into Malaysian territory. These raids increased

Despatchers of 55 Company RASC at work in Borneo, 1965. The two despatchers are attached to the aircraft by a safety belt and strap whilst the RAF crewman on the intercom gives the signal to release the load. (Courtesy Royal Air Force.)

in size and scope as the campaign progressed, necessitating the deployment of British and Malaysian security forces over wide areas of the country. Forts and defended villages were established which involved the dropping of great quantities of defence stores in addition to routine maintenance needs. Landing strips in the jungle for light aircraft were also constructed, requiring the dropping of considerable amounts of constructional equipment. These permanent bases could not, of course, dominate this vast area and an enormous patrol programme had to be operated, with its consequent demands on the air-supply organization. The great difficulty of movement in this mountainous jungle region increased the importance of the part played by helicopters and light aircraft. To give these aircraft the widest possible range and flexibility, vast quantities of aviation fuel had to be air dropped into forward areas. The fuel was dropped in 44 gallon drums, singly from Hastings or Valettas, or roped together in fours from Beverley or Argosy aircraft.

The majority of the stores dropped were by harness pack, but considerable quantities were dropped in one-ton containers from the larger aircraft. The scale of air dropping was vast. In 1965, the monthly totals from Labuan and Kuching both averaged between 600–900,000 lb. In 1965 this had risen to over a million pounds a month from each detachment.

As in the Malayan Emergency, besides the routine requirements the stores dropped provided many and varied loads, from prefabricated buildings, water pumps and medical supplies from the World Health Organization and civil government, to livestock, Gurkha rum, fresh eggs, a birthday cake and bottled oysters. All this, together with considerable quantities of canned Tiger beer, contributed to making life and work possible for the troops in what must be some of the most inhospitable country in the world.

Throughout the period of the confrontation the Company rotated its platoons and detachments between Malaya, Borneo and the Thai border. Even in Singapore life in the unit was not to be always 'rest and relaxation'. There were internal security duties to be performed during periods of civil unrest and at one stage, during a threat of Indonesian air attacks, the company had to build and man the airfield defences at RAF Seletar. In November 1964, 26 despatchers from Singapore took part in an unusual sortie when four RAF aircraft dropped two-and-a-half million leaflets, bearing a message from a captured Indonesian officer, over Indonesian bases stretching in a wide area from the Rhio Islands, south of Singapore, to Pulua Rupat in the Malacca Straits—an operation which the Malaysian Prime Minister, Tungku Abdul Rahman, described as 'a great success'.

The Future

Throughout history military commanders have sought means of freeing themselves from the strategic and tactical limitations imposed by inflexible lines of communications. Some sought a solution in living off the land, but a modern sophisticated army must rely on regular sustenance. Though not yet a com-

A Land Rover and trailer crated and rigged for parachuting on its platform is loaded into a 3 ton vehicle to be taken to the aircraft. Cyprus, May 1968. (Courtesy Airborne Forces Museum.)

plete means in itself, air-supply as demonstrated in this story has introduced a means, or at least a measure, of flexibility into the attainment of this long sought goal. This was quickly appreciated in World War II and exploited fully and very successfully—especially in the Far East.

Since the war the steady improvement in the performance of transport aircraft and in the techniques of supply by air has continually widened the scope of what can be carried, or dropped, over ever increasing distances. The advent of rear-door loading and despatch ejection in modern aircraft has been, in itself, a tremendous stride forward.

It follows that air-supply will continue to provide a commander with an essential element of flexibility in his logistical planning, which in turn permits maximum tactical freedom of manoeuvre. Indeed, it is difficult to imagine any type of future conflict, or even phase of war, in which air-supply could not play a vital role. Though the future may be uncertain there is no doubt that the men of the air-supply organization will continue to be called upon to play the part that they have so ably undertaken in both peace and war.

APPENDIX D

ESTIMATED CASUALTIES—AIRBORNE FORCES
1941-45 (from official reports)

SERIAL NO.	FORMATION, ETC.	MONTH OR PERIOD	OPERATION	CASUALTIES				REMARKS
				Killed	Wounded	Missing	Total	
1	11 Special Air Service Bn.	Feb. 1941	Tragino—S. Italy	1	1	36	38	The Italian interpreter Fortunato Picchi was shot by Fascist Militia as a spy. Others captured after raid.
2	'C' Coy 2 Para	Feb. 1942	Bruneval	3	7	2	12	—
3	9th Field and 261st Field Park Coys (Airborne) RE.	Nov. 1942	'Operation Freshman'—Norway	34	—	—	34	Majority executed by Gestapo, some killed in glider crashes.
4	1 Parachute Bde.	Nov. 42—Apr. 43	North Africa	380	1200	120	1700	—
5	1 Airborne Div.	Jul. 1943	Sicily	454	240	102	796	—
6	2 Ind. Para. Bde	Sep. 43—Jan. 45	Italy, S. France and Greece	150	229	175	554	—
7	6 Airborne Div.	6 Jun.—3 Sep. 44	Normandy	820	2709	902	4431	Approx. 450 of missing returned, some in 1945 from PoW camps.
8	1 Airborne Div.	Sep. 44	Arnhem	550	250 (returned across river)	6584	7384	Approx. 5,000 of missing returned: some escaping, majority PoW. Some 3000 of the PoW were wounded.
9	6 Airborne Div.	Mar.—May 1945	Rhine Crossing to Baltic	700	750	400	1850	The 'missing' figure is final after all returned PoW etc. had been accounted for.
			TOTALS:	3092	5386	8321	16799	(incl. 5,450 who returned)

APPENDIX E

The Museum of Airborne Forces

The museum was established by a meeting of the Committee of the Parachute Regiment Association under the chairmanship of Brigadier S. J. L. Hill, DSO, MC, on October 29, 1946.

Brigadier C. H. V. Pritchard (now Vaughan), DSO, then Commander Airborne Establishments, undertook the task of supervising the establishment of the museum as a physical reality, collecting exhibits, documents, and producing a display. The museum was first established in the Second Officers' Mess of the Depot, (the Corunna Barracks Officers' Mess) Aldershot until mid 1949 when the Mess was required for accommodation. A Barrack Block in the Depot at Maida Barracks was then taken over; the museum closing for some months in preparation for the presentation of Colours to the Parachute Battalions by his late Majesty, King George VI on July 19, 1950. The King and Queen visited the museum on this occasion.

Official War Office permission to convert the Barrack Block in the Depot at Maida Barracks was obtained in 1950 but the conversion was not completed until February, 1952 when the museum was properly housed for the first time.

The museum remained at Maida Barracks until 1968 when it moved, with the Depot, to the new Browning Barracks. Here it was given a modern architect-designed setting. The museum was closed from February 1968 whilst the exhibits and records were refurbished to produce a permanent public exhibition of Airborne History. During 1968 a number of new exhibits were received, particularly aircraft models and many individuals, civilian firms and military establishments contributed to the work of improvement and repair. On display are the original briefing models for the airborne operations of World War II, (Bruneval, Normandy, Arnhem and the Rhine Crossing); vehicles, guns and parachutes of the early and modern airborne soldiers; displays of World War II German and US Airborne equipment and weapons; sections of gliders; captured weapons; a comprehensive display of photographic material from 1940 to the present day; aircraft models; dioramas of actions and displays of Parachute Regiment and Airborne Forces historical relics. The museum also possesses its own internal cinema seating thirty-five or forty people in which films may be shown to parties and to young recruits.

The museum was opened officially, in its new setting, by Field Marshal The Viscount Montgomery of Alamein, K.G., G.C.B., D.S.O., D.L., on March 23, 1969, the twenty-fourth anniversary of the Rhine Crossing in 1945 (the airborne part of the operation took place on March 24) and is now permanently open to the general public.

APPENDIX F

Important Dates in British Airborne History

Jun 22, 1940	The Prime Minister, Mr Winston Churchill writes a minute to the Chiefs of Staff demanding the formation of a Corps of Parachute soldiers.
Jul 8, 1940	No 2 Commando commences parachute training at Ringway.
Jul 13, 1940	First parachute descents by army pupils.
Feb 10/11, 1941	Tragino Aqueduct Raid (Op 'Colossus'). First British airborne operation.
Aug 1941	Formation of 'L' Detachment Special Air Service (SAS) under Capt David Stirling in the Middle East.
Sep 15, 1941	Authorisation for the formation of 1st Parachute Brigade under Brigadier R. N. Gale.
Oct 10, 1941	31 Independent Brigade Group is reformed as 1st Air-landing Brigade.
Oct 29, 1941	Brigadier F. A. M. Browning appointed to command Airborne Forces with rank of Major-General.
Nov 1, 1941	HQ 1 AB Division formed (in London).
Dec 21, 1941	Formation of The Army Air Corps and The Glider Pilot Regiment.
Jan 15, 1942	Formation of No 38 Wing RAF.
Feb 27/28, 1942	The Bruneval Raid (Op 'Biting'). First Battle Honour of The Parachute Regiment.
Aug 1, 1942	Formation within the Army Air Corps of The Parachute Regiment.
Nov 19, 1942	Ill-fated raid on the German heavy water plant at Vermork in Norway (Op 'Freshman').
Nov 12, 1942	3 PARA capture Bône Airfield, Tunisia. The first battalion strength operation by British parachutists.
Dec 23, 1942	Approval for an Air Directorate at War Office headed by Brigadier R. N. Gale.
Dec 1942 – Apr 1943	1st Parachute Brigade employed in infantry role in Tunisia and were given the title of "The Red Devils" by their German opponents.
Mar 27, 1943	1st Parachute Brigade capture Tamera (Battle Honour awarded).

May 3, 1943	HQ 6th AB Division formed at Syrencote House, Nr. Netheravon, Wilts under Major-General R. N. Gale.
Jul 9, 1943	1st Air-landing Brigade capture Ponte Grande bridge at Syracuse Sicily.
Jul 13, 1943	1st Parachute Brigade operation at Primosole Bridge near Catania Sicily.
Oct 11, 1943	No 38 Wing RAF reforms as a Group under Air Vice-Marshal Hollinghurst.
Jun 6, 1944	6th AB Division secure the left flank of the Allied invasion beach-head on 'D' DAY (including Pegasus Bridge and Merville Battery operations).
Jun 12, 1944	12 PARA captures Breville (awarded as Battle Honour).
Aug 15, 1944	2 Independent Parachute Brigade drop into Southern France (Op 'Dragoon').
Sep 17–25, 1944	1st AB Division at Arnhem (Op 'Market-Garden').
Oct 12, 1944	Seizure of Megara airfield for operation in Greece by 4 PARA (Op 'Manna').
Dec 24, 1944	6th AB Division rushed to the Ardennes.
Jan 3, 1945	13th Battalion The Parachute Regiment capture Bures in the Ardennes. (A Regimental Battle Honour).
Mar 24, 1945	6th AB Division land over the Rhine (Op 'Varsity').
Nov 15, 1945	1st AB Division disbanded.
Apr 1948	6th AB Division returns to UK and is disbanded.
Jun/Jul 1948	2 Parachute Brigade reforms in BAOR to become 16 Independent Parachute Brigade. Its Battalions are reformed to become 1st, 2nd and 3rd Battalions of the Parachute Regiment.
Jul 19, 1950	HM King George VI presents their first Colours to the three Parachute Battalions in Aldershot.
Jan – Dec 1956	16 Parachute Brigade in Cyprus (EOKA campaign).
Nov 5, 1956	3 PARA captures El Gamil airfield Port Said (Op 'Musketeer').
Sep 1, 1957	Disbandment of The Glider Pilot Regiment and formation of the new Army Air Corps.
May 1964	3 PARA operations in the Radfan.
Mar – Jun 1965	2 PARA operations in Borneo.
Apr 24, 1967	Visit of HM The Queen and HRH The Duke of Edinburgh to the Parachute Brigade in Aldershot.
May 5– Nov 29, 1967	1 PARA in Aden – the last Army unit to leave the Colony.
Mar 23, 1969	Field-Marshal Montgomery opens the new Airborne Forces Museum in Browning Barracks.

REGIMENTAL MARCH PAST

THE PARACHUTE REGIMENT

"The Ride of the Valkyries"

1st B♭ CORNET

Published by Authority

Arr. by DONALD KEELING
and E. F. RIPPON

Index

258